A **FLESH** & **BLOOD**

REYNOLDS
A FAMILY MEMOIR

WITH JIMMY GEOGHEGAN

HEROBOOKS

The Reynolds family are donating royalties from the sale of this book
to the Meath Football Development Fund

HEROBOOKS

PUBLISHED BY HERO BOOKS
1 WOODVILLE GREEN
LUCAN
CO. DUBLIN
IRELAND

Hero Books is an imprint of Umbrella Publishing
First Published 2023
Copyright © Pat and Paddy Reynolds, & Jimmy Geoghegan
All rights reserved

ISBN 9781910827628

Cover design and formatting: jessica@viitaladesign.com
Photographs: Sportsfile, the Peter McDermott collection (Navan Library)
and the Reynolds family collection

DEDICATION

To all those who have passed and have worn the famous
green and gold with pride

CONTENTS

PROLOGUE

PHOTO SECTION 1: Pat Reynolds 1967 All-Ireland Winner, 1971 All Star 21

PART I 29

PART II 41

PART III 49

PART IV 57

PART V 63

PART VI 71

PART VII 87

PART VIII 103

PART IX 119

PART X 129

PART XI 139

PART XII 151

PART XIII 165

PART XIV 177

PART XV 187

PART XVI 197

PART XVII 209

PART XVIII 223

PHOTO SECTION 2: Paddy Reynolds 1996 and '99 All-Ireland Winner, 1999 All Star 249

EPILOGUE

ACKNOWLEDGEMENTS

LOCATED CLOSE TO the entrance to the Reynolds' farmyard, not very far from the home of Walterstown Gaelic Football Club, is an office which forms part of the administrative hub of the family business – and it was there that I met Pat and Paddy Reynolds to talk about their lives.

At various times over the course of 10 months or so we sat in that little office and they talked about their lives and careers. They had much to tell. Firstly, I met Pat and together we embarked on a journey from his childhood all the way to the present day.

He outlined how his father and mother set up home in Walterstown, how they had raised a large family. How they worked ferociously hard to build up the family farm, acre by acre, until it became a substantial holding. We talked about Pat's career on the playing fields of Ireland.

He spoke about the steps he took to ensure he became an established county footballer, going on to win an All-Ireland with Meath in 1967 and an All Star four years later. How he helped Walterstown win their first Meath SFC crown in 1978.

As he retraced his steps, he revealed intriguing insights into how he had grappled with various issues on the playing fields of Ireland; how he sought to become the best footballer he could be. He spoke of the formidable task he took on of building up a farming enterprise that has become something of an empire.

It was the same with his son Paddy. He won two All-Irelands with Meath and an All Star, but it was far from easy for him either at times during his football career. He too had his obstacles to overcome.

Over the years, I have watched Meath when first Pat and later Paddy sought to help the county achieve ultimate success. I watched them as a supporter and sports journalist, ensuring a certain familiarity with their respective careers – at least from the outside. Writing this book, however, provided me with further insights into their struggles and triumphs.

The end product of those intriguing hours of discussion - in that office in Walterstown – is this book. I earnestly hope all who read it find it interesting and perhaps enlightening. Working with both Pat and Paddy on this project has certainly been enlightening for me.

It wasn't just the exploits of Pat and Paddy as footballers, it was their respective quests to build up the farming business that also made their individual adventures so captivating. Thanks to them for their co-operation and revealing their memories and thoughts. Thanks also to Gerry Reynolds, Pat's brother, for his insights.

I also wish to extend my thanks to Liam Hayes, publisher of this book, for asking me to embark on this fascinating journey with Pat and Paddy. Thanks also to all the staff in the *Meath Chronicle* where I have worked for the past 21 years.

I would also like to gratefully thank my wife Margot and our daughter Megan for their unstinting encouragement and support.

Jimmy Geoghegan
March 2023

PROLOGUE

IT'S AMAZING HOW they fly past, the years that is. Pat had his career as a footballer, won an All-Ireland in 1967... glorious '67, followed by Paddy, who won two in 1996 and '99. Both of them All Stars too.

They made their mark as players, but the years passed and their careers ended. Time... it's a funny old thing all right.

Yet they made their mark and that's something they should be proud of. All of us have reason to be proud of what they did.

Pat was the oldest in our family. There was seven of us in the clan altogether– Pat, Eilish, Ray, Paul, myself, Christopher and Julie. We grew up in Gilltown in Walterstown. A small farm my parents built up. Bought a little holding. Added to it. They started out with that small holding... acre by acre, year by year. Hard graft was a way of life.

The farm, the work was first. Always, but the football wasn't far behind. There was the football with Walterstown, and football with Meath. Farming and football, the two cornerstones of our lives.

WE ALWAYS SEEMED to have footballers call to our house – and they weren't just from the locality. Down had a great team in the 1960s and a few of their players, three or four of them, would end up staying in our house maybe the night before they had a big game in Croke Park. Maybe they were playing Kerry or Galway or, as happened a few times at the time, Meath.

We were youngsters, but they would heroes of ours. We would have heard their names called out on the radio as we listened to games. Michael O'Hehir's voice echoing down through the ages. The connection between us and them was, I guess, the fact that we all, the boys anyway, went to Gormanston College. Joe Lennon, who won All-Irelands with Down, was a teacher there.

My mother Breda would feed them well. They would go up to Croke Park. They would play the game, stop off on the way back. Another feed. They would stay that night as well and maybe we'd be joined by some of the Meath players. Pat would be there. Great fun, the craic would be ninety. A few hours earlier they might have spent the game kicking lumps out of each other. Once the game ended, it was all forgotten. Friends again.

My father Christy had played for Louth, and he was a big football man. Very little drew him away from the land. Football did. He was the spitting image of Pat in many ways, in appearance and his dedication to farming. We grew up in an environment that could not be imagined by youngsters today. There was, for starters, no TV. No phone to make a call or to tap into and get the latest, up-to-date news. Instead, we got our news from radio mainly – or simply word of mouth, or the papers. The world has changed so much in that regard.

As a youngster, I recall walking home from our local national school. We walked across the fields and I had heard how a nearby farm was for sale. I told my father although he probably knew anyway. He was always on the watch out for more land that might come up. He bought the field, no doubt borrowed the money. That was great in one respect, not so great in other ways. My father had bought the land in the lead up to Christmas and there wasn't much from Santa Claus that year. The man in the red suit wasn't in a very generous mood. Any spare cash that year went towards the land, the house, the farm.

That was the way.

When the time came, I struck out on my own. Like Pat before me. I took the opportunity. Bought a farm, 27 acres near Kilmessan in 1990. Built it up, added on to it, and have nearly 200 acres there now. Again, that ethos was bred into us. Work hard and you'll get what you want. Bridie and myself have a family of three.

Proud of them all… Peter, who runs the farm now, Breda and Lisa.

AS WE GREW up, as teenagers, then young men, we started playing for Walterstown. We won some, lost some, did the best we could in each game but the club was getting stronger all the time. They emerged from the junior ranks in the 1960s and moved up to intermediate, then senior, before winning their first Senior Championship in 1978. The Blacks had arrived.

My father didn't mind us losing too much, but if we lost to our neighbours Skryne he most certainly wouldn't be impressed. That was the worst outcome. That provoked a reaction.

Instead of having to get up at six in the morning to work on the farm, we'd have to get up at five. We slept in the room above the kitchen and very early in the morning after losing a game, especially to Skryne, he would start banging the ceiling from the kitchen with a brush to tell us to get up.

'Get out of that bed!' he would say. If we had won you could lie on until eight o'clock, he would be in a far more benevolent mood. We made an extra special effort not to lose to Skryne. Local rivalries, it's what keeps the GAA's wheels turning.

Football was the main topic of conversation when we were around the farm. During our meals too. Football, football… *football*. Each week, especially after a big championship game, we would be waiting in the house anxiously for the someone to bring home the *Meath Chronicle* to see what was written about the match.

There were five of us on the Walterstown team at one stage, before Pat retired. My mother played a major role too. She did all the washing of the jerseys, the togs, the socks. The boots would be polished, ready for use the next day. In that way she encouraged us to play. She was a nurse, she was dynamite, she ran the show in every respect. She was organised. Kept things in order.

She kept everything and everyone together, working towards the same goal. My father would be going mad at this or that, and she would step in and settle everything with all the skill of a UN diplomat. She was extremely capable, practical. Could tackle any issue that needed to be tackled and find a solution. Sort it out. Extremely capable. Like so many Irish mothers she played a huge role in bringing up the family. These women played crucial roles in rearing children, shaping their childrens' outlook; shaping society itself.

She gave her children the benefit of her wisdom. She showed us values. She gave us a guide as to how to live our lives. Strong values. Work hard but be fair to people too. Honest. On Sundays we went to Mass, couldn't miss that. Mother would say how things could, should be done around the house and farm beyond. She would say it quietly, without fuss, but it would be law. There was no question of going against the mother's wishes or her pronouncements. Her words were written in stone.

OUR FATHER WAS a worker. He would work day and night. On one occasion in the 1970s I remember we were combining in Bellewstown. Pat was driving the combine, I was driving the Ford tractor, after baling all day. The tractor had no cab or safety measures in place that would be demanded today. I was starving with the hunger when, late in the evening, I headed for home. I met the mother coming down the lane from the house to the yard. It was a summer's evening, getting dark.

She came down to tell me the father was away working in one of the fields, and I had to milk the cows. So, after baling all day, I had to then set to the task of milking at 10 at night. I hungrily consumed the sandwiches she had brought me and started the milking. That was the way. It just had to be done. You could grumble all you liked but it had to be done… and it was done.

We were all lucky, we got a good education. We, the boys, went to Gormanston, and the girls were well educated too. You had to have a very good reason to miss school. The only one who had to stay at home was Pat. He had spent a year or two in Gormanston but then he had to work on the farm. The bank insisted he had to stay at home and work with his father. Pure madness. To have a youngster's education undermined like that was shocking. He was only a teenager, 15, but the bank insisted. He had to stay at home. He worked too, got his own place and built it up again through sheer hard graft.

We watched Pat as he made his progress through to the county front with Meath. We were interested, surely, to see how he would fare out against some of the biggest names in the country that were on opposition teams. Household names.

He did fine in that environment.

AT ONE STAGE at home in our family home there was a room where we would put all the trophies and it was full of glittering pieces of silverware we had won over the years... medals, shields, cups. Then as the years passed, they seemed to vanish, I don't know what happened to them all.

The work ethic that was bred into us at home transferred onto the football pitch, without a doubt. When the game started, we gave it everything... don't leave anything behind, don't have any regrets coming off the pitch, that was the mantra. That was the approach. It was one of the reasons why we won the medals over the years.

Sometimes you might be in bad form going out for a game on a Sunday afternoon. Tired maybe after a long week, maybe a late night, but when the ball was thrown in you would tap into a reservoir of energy that you would find from somewhere. The adrenaline would flow. Football was our only outlet; a game and a few pints afterwards. A dance maybe in Beechmount ballroom... Big Tom, The Mighty Avons, some of the showbands. It was the showband era.

I got onto the Meath minor team in the 1970s but it was difficult to get away from the farm, especially in the summer. On this particular day, I recall James Whyte, or Scubs as everyone called him, arriving into a field we were working in Skryne. Scubs would be described today as a member of the backroom team. He used to collect players to go to Meath training sessions and matches, at minor and senior levels. What he did for Meath over the years was immense.

He would pick up Pat and bring him to games. Sometimes, Jack Quinn and Gerry Quinn would be with him. Scubs had responsibility for a specific area. His job was the collect the players within that area. It was an important role. Not everybody had a car and there was no bus to collect the players and take them to a game. No luxury, air-conditioned coach to ferry us to games.

I'm 10 years younger than Pat and I had grown up watching him play for Meath – and that inspired me. I too wanted to play for the county, to wear the green and gold. I watched him in all sorts of games. I watched him lose to Galway in the 1966 All-Ireland final. We travelled to Croke Park that day, our father included. He wouldn't miss that. It was a few hours break from the farm. Galway were a fine team, on their way to a three in-row.

My father was raging as he sat up in the Hogan Stand because Meath didn't perform that day. They didn't play as well as they could have – and lost. Afterwards, we headed back to the car and my father was still annoyed that Meath had lost. We had to be home to do the milking. There was no holding back there, win or lose. The next year Meath beat Cork to win the Sam Maguire. No doubt our father was delighted, although he may not have shown it.

When I think about it, it's perhaps not surprising that Meath lost. I'm sure many of the players on the team would have been working the day before. Pat was harvesting, driving a combine in what we called 'The Big Field' all Saturday and Saturday night. That's what I remember. He wouldn't have got much sleep. He got damn all sleep. There he was the night before games threshing away – and there were no cabs on the combine harvesting back then. He would have had his goggles on to protect his eyes, and an old scarf around his mouth, to stop his mouth getting filled with dust.

He would be harvesting away and this massive cloud of dust would be covering the harvester. You would hardly see him with all the dust swirling about. That was the way for all farmers. Health and safety wasn't big on the agenda. Farming has changed but it can be a lonely, hard, demanding life. That hasn't changed.

THERE WERE ALSO benefits from the farming life back then. Working on the farm was part of your fitness regime. There was certainly no need to spend hours in a gym. You would build up stamina and muscle by throwing bales of hay up on a trailer. Heavy auld bales too a lot of the time. The bales would then have to be carried up to a loft in a shed. Hard, physically demanding work, relentless. In a way it was perfect preparation for the physical rigours of a football pitch on a Sunday afternoon – but you wouldn't find it any fitness manual!

I remember Gerry Quinn, who was on the panel, talking to Pat about working the night before a big game. 'Are you f**king mad?' But that's what we did. You didn't think twice about it, that was the way it was. You did the work, then you played football. Pat and Gerry were great friends, they could talk very openly to each other. No holding back. They played football like that too.

Looking at it from today's perspective, working all night before an All-Ireland final would be unimaginable. It wasn't the best preparation but Pat was at an age when he could get away with something like that. He also had something else that was a huge asset to him. He was very strong. He wasn't the tallest of men but he was built like a bull; strong, physically imposing. No-one pushed him off a ball, not within the rules of the game anyway.

Even towards the end of his career Pat could utilise that strength to his benefit, back into speedy players who were giving him problems, slow them down, impose himself in that way. He could adapt to what was needed at the various stages of his career. He managed it.

Another reason Pat could survive without doing too much training, which he didn't like, was the fact the game wasn't as fast as today. The hitting was there but the pace was much slower. The tempo of modern football is breathtaking. Unbelievable. Only extremely fit, supremely conditioned athletes can hope to survive. Our family were very friendly with the Quinns – Jack, Gerry, Martin and Jimmy. They made up the central core of the great Kilbride team of the 1960s and early 70s that won a number of county championships. They played for Meath too. Jack was the best known of them all; he became a legendary full-back. We knew each other very well; we would joke, have the craic, wind each other up. Martin, a tough, commanding full-back himself, bought cattle from us.

Pat was strong, but he took some punishment too. In one game against Offaly, he got hammered under the Cusack Stand. He was in bed for a few days afterwards, passing blood. He was in a bad way.

Pat winning the All-Ireland in 1967, going to Australia with the Meath team the following year, winning an All Star in '71 provided the rest of us in the family with a role model when it came to football – and that includes Paddy, his son.

WE WONDERED ABOUT Paddy and county football because he wasn't like Pat in that he didn't have the same physical strength, although few had. He was a different kind of player. He evolved his own way of playing that was based on his abilities and assets; his ability to win any loose ball and sprint away from his marker once he had got his hands on the ball. That was a big part of his game. He could switch on the after-burners and shoot away from pursuing opponents in a flash. That was an invaluable quality in his game.

I had played minor for Meath. We had a decent side, managed to beat Dublin in a Leinster final in 1972 and make it to an All-Ireland semi-final. Played Tyrone in Croke Park but that game didn't go so well for us, we were beaten, well beaten. Still, for all of us it was a tremendous experience. I pushed on. Got on the Meath senior team in the mid-70s. I was unfortunate in the sense that I was playing at a time when Meath were really under the shadow of an emerging Dublin. Kevin Heffernan's Dublin. They were powering on, we were slowly falling behind, although few seemed to see it at the time.

One of the few victories we had over them was in the National League final of 1975. It was one of Pat's last games for Meath, but I missed it. I was away. It was a pity. I think I would have got on the panel, at least. I was doing a course in agricultural management at the time. It was up in Monaghan. These days it's no distance. At that time, it was a considerable distance, or at least it was looked at like a long trek. It wasn't easy to get back for training or games. As it turned out, I used to get home once a month. The football had to take a backseat.

In the closing years of the 70s, I started to appear on the Meath senior team, in league and championship. I was brought into the panel but my progress, my development as a county footballer was halted when I broke my leg. You need luck in life and in football. Getting a serious injury like that was certainly not what I needed at that stage in my career. Paul also played for Meath and he damaged his knee against Dublin in a bloody tournament game, that set him back. More than that. He never really recovered, not enough to stake a regular place with Meath.

My injury was to cost me a place on the Walterstown team that won the club's first Meath SFC title in 1978. Summerhill were narrowly defeated in the final. I was raging to miss out but what could I do. My brothers Paul, Christy and Pat were on the team. I missed out but it was a wonderful occasion for the family, the community... the club.

Pat took a bad blow to the ribs that day; a Summerhill player banged into him with his knees on the sideline, broke him up. It was a bad blow. Pat didn't retaliate but a few of us were eager to exact some revenge. We did our best to do just that, when the two teams met the next time. That's how justice was dispensed on the field in those days. In some ways it was like the Wild West. If you gave someone a bad blow you had to expect some retribution.

I MADE SURE to be around and fit when Walterstown won their second title in 1980, when Syddan were defeated in the final. We won that easily, 4-9 to 0-6. We were flying that day. A team at the peak of its powers. It was a grand day for us all. Pat was gone as a player by then but Christy played in that final. You can never downplay what it means for club players to win a senior county title. It was special for me in 1980. Memorable.

It got better too. We had some great footballers, all over the field, a great coach in Mick O'Brien. We went on to win three successive Keegan Cup finals – 1982, '83 and '84. The 1984 victory was one of those occasions that was a mixed bag as far as I was concerned. Bitter, sweet. We defeated our close rivals Skryne, but there was a melee in the closing stages. Somehow, myself and a Skryne player were picked out and sent off, although there were a lot of players who could have got gate.

Just how good the Walterstown senior team was in those days could be seen in the way we reached two All-Ireland club finals. A small, rural club making it to an All-Ireland, playing against and beating some of the best club teams in the country. It was real *Roy of the Rovers* stuff. In the spring of 1981, we won the Leinster SFC by defeating well-known Carlow side Eire Og in Newbridge. What a day. They pushed us all the way but we won, 2-9 to 2-8, with Eamonn Barry scoring 2-5. Eamonn was unstoppable as a forward in those years.

We were ambitious, we had great players. We beat St Mary's from Sligo and got to the All-Ireland final, but unfortunately lost to St Finbarr's from Cork. There was a rule change in the lead up to that game. We liked to use the hand-pass, and did very well with it, but suddenly we were not allowed to use the hand-pass the way we liked anymore. We were well drilled in the art. That change in the rule set us back.

They also had this mad system in place where you played the semi-final the day before the final - at least that's the way it was when we reached our second All-Ireland final in 1984. I know it was the same for both sides but it was mad, crazy stuff. No-one could have imagined the club competitions would become as popular as they have become.

Pat was finished playing, of course, but he was a selector with us around that time. He stayed involved that way.

To prove 1981 was no fluke, we won the Leinster title again in December 1983. Another wonderful achievement. We beat Walsh Island in the final, had to withstand some massive late pressure from them – but the character in the team showed itself again. We held out to win by a point, 3-9 to 2-11. Frank O'Sullivan got two goals.

We pushed on, reached another All-Ireland final but again lost to a Cork side, this time Nemo Rangers; well beaten. It was to be our last chance of landing the big prize. We didn't land the All-Ireland in those times but they were great days.

We had some great players, who were willing to train hard, and a very good coach. We wanted to improve.

It was no mystery why we did well.

The panel in those years included six sets of brothers... the Barrys, the Cooneys, the O'Briens, the O'Sullivans, the Reynolds' clan and the McLoughlins. Maybe that had something to do with it?

Maybe that sense of brotherhood powered us on?

Gerry Reynolds
Brother and Uncle,
March 2023

PAT REYNOLDS
1967 ALL-IRELAND WINNER
1971 ALL STAR

Pat Reynolds (bottom right) in 1966 and on his way to winning an All-Ireland title in 1967, and becoming Meath's first All Star four years later in 1971.

The Reynolds family in the 60s with Eilish and Pat at the back, and front
(from left) Paul, Christopher, Julie, Gerry and Ray. Breda And Christy
(below) with their children all grown up in the 70s.

Pat parades behind Meath captain Davy Carty (above) before victory over Down in the 1966 All-Ireland semi-final and (bottom) the Meath team which defeated Cork in the 1967 All-Ireland final.

The Meath team departs for Australia in 1968 (Pat is fourth from the left in the front row) and despite the bigger, stronger Australians (right) the team came home safe and sound after a victorious trip of a lifetime.

The Meath party enjoy themselves at the Sydney Opera House and under the Harbour Bridge (above). The trip also saw the team stop off in Hawaii with Pat (third from right in the front row) and his teammates honoured with Lei Garlands.

The Meath team (top) which defeated Cork in the 1987 All-Ireland final and (below) captain Mick Lyons makes a miraculous block on Jimmy Kerrigan midway through the game to turn the contest the way of the Royals.

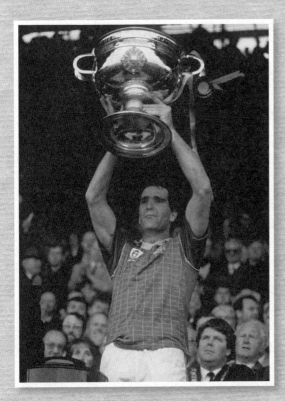

Meath captain Joe Cassells lifts the 'new' Sam Maguire Cup high after defeating Cork in the 1988 All-Ireland final replay and (below) Seán Boylan and the Meath management team go wild on the sideline at the final whistle.

Pat and Attracta (top) with their own family in the 80s (from left) Ivan, Paddy, Niamh, Christopher, Shane and Karl.

Pat and Attracta and family celebrating Niamh's wedding (from left) Shane, Ivan, Karl, Kit and Paddy.

I

1967

Sparky

Croke Park

Cork

Sam Maguire

2022

Covid

Coyler's Point

★★★

PAT

THIS IS A big day… Sunday, September 24, 1967.

A big day for the GAA generally and Meath football specifically. It's also one of the most important days of my life so far, if not the most important, certainly when it comes to football. And I'm up and about early.

I'm scheduled to play in the All-Ireland football final later today. Only the second senior All-Ireland final Meath have reached since 1954. But before all that there is work to be done… work around the farm.

I get dressed, drink a quick cup of tea and head out to bring in the cows. There's milking to be done. Sparky our dog is in the yard when I step out.

I give him a nudge to come with me but he doesn't move. *It's Sunday… leave me alone, I'm going to have a rest* he seems to be saying.

He looks at me but doesn't budge, at least not at first. *Ah to hell with it, I'll go down myself* is what I think and that's what I do. There's no time to waste.

I don't walk down the field… I run.

I'm 21 after all. I'm super fit, full of the joys. Life is good, packed with possibilities. It's not every day you play in an All-Ireland final.

I'm excited, although not over-hyped by the prospect of playing in a final… why wouldn't I be, it's the biggest day in Irish sport. The game against Cork will unfold before the nation on TV. Croke Park will be full… over 70,000 supporters packed into the place. The crowd expectant, buzzing. Not that I get over-excited about it all. When it comes down to it, I tell myself, it's just another football game, 30 lads, two teams out on a pitch trying to out-smart, out-score each other. Nothing more. Nothing less.

I SLEPT LAST night… slept well too. There was no turning and twisting, racked by nerves. That's not for me.

For weeks people have been talking about the game, asking me how I feel. Can we win they ask me? How do you think we'll do? Now I'm glad the waiting is finally over… the big day has arrived, the time for action is near.

I feel I'm ready. Some players never get a chance to play in an All-Ireland final, some great players too. This is my day.

The day is well established when I enter the field where the cows are. It has been bright for some time. My aim is to round them up as quickly as possible, get the milking underway. There's lots to be done. All-Ireland or not, the cows have to be milked… life goes on. There's no time to waste.

It's a pleasant September morning. It looks like it's going to be a dry day, a good day for a football game. A day when players won't be sliding and slipping around the place, the ball like a bar of soap. It will be dry… and it should suit us.

The cows are accompanied by our resident bull. He has been out and about with the cows. He's a nasty, ill-tempered bugger. I know that but I'm eager to get things going and I start to move the cows. There's a cow he's focused on who has moved away from the herd a little. I go to hunt her on, join her up with the rest of the herd.

Then the bull strikes. He turns savage.

He had been following this particular cow and had his own idea of what he wants to do. Now I have disrupted those plans and he's annoyed. He's not accustomed to having his amorous ambitions thwarted.

He surges towards me and hits me with his powerful head on the chest. I'm totally blindsided… BANG. It's like a wrecking ball hitting a building.

I'm sent reeling.

I hit the ground. I'm deeply shocked by the sudden act of violence. The bull has no intention of leaving it there, either. He wants to finish me off.

He wants to punish me for what I have done. He tries to puck me as I'm on the ground. He wants to bash me with that powerful head of his. To do me in for once and for all. He tries to poke me with his hoof too. He's enraged and out for revenge. He wants to inflict as much damage as he can.

I start shouting for help, for someone to hear. Anybody. There is a house nearby, our neighbours, the Kennedys live there. Perhaps they can hear me.

'HELP,' I shout.

'HELP'…louder still, but nobody seems to hear. The bull's anger is in full flow and I'm worried now. Really worried as the sudden, unexpected attack continues.

I'm scrambling… roaring and shouting.

I start to think that this could be it… the end. Frightened. The thought flashes through my mind that this is how the curtain comes down, out here in the field, nobody knowing about the personal trauma I'm facing.

I KNOW I'M lucky that I'm fit and young because I'm able to keep moving, edging away… but he continues to try and gore me on the ground. I keep moving and moving… and moving, rolling this way and that, rolling… trying to get away from him.

I still think I'm done for… I really do. I keep shouting and roaring and trying to get away from him but he continues to paw at me and to try and puck me with his head. If he had made contact with one of his hooves it could have caused me real damage. I start to get tired.

Next thing… Sparky appears. He had come down the field, followed me. He may have heard me shouting. Instinctively, he knows I'm in trouble and what he does next is remarkable. Extraordinary.

Using his mouth, he grabs the bull by the tail. He pulls and drags the tail. Distracted, the bull turns on the dog. Momentarily he forgets about me. Now all his attention is focused on dealing with the dog. I see my chance.

I get up quickly and move away. My legs are weak but I'm powered now by the adrenaline coursing through my veins. It's unbelievable what the dog has just done. He has saved my life.

I get up and move away. I scramble up off the ground and quickly move to a safe distance. I run clear and Sparky then let's the bull's tail go. He has done his job. I'm so lucky.

The blow from the bull has left its mark on my chest. I'm red and sore. My shirt is torn and I'm shaken, but I can't dwell on what has happened. I have to get on with the day… I have to think about a game of football. I have to get ready to play in an All-Ireland final.

When I get to the gate in the field I stop. Look back. The bull hasn't pursued me. I know I'm lucky. *Very lucky.* I take a breath and resolve to continue with my morning's work. I try and shrug off the attack. I get the cows in and manage to complete the milking, but my body is shaking as I get the job done.

Then it's onto Mass.

I RETURN HOME, have my breakfast, put my boots in a bag and I wait until I'm collected by the county board's designated driver who'll bring me to Croke Park.

There's already a few of the players in the car. I tell the boys what had happened. They can't believe it. 'That's mad!' they say.

On the way up to Dublin… and the banter with the boys, the sight of people, many on bicycles… the flags flying, everyone making their way up to the city helps me forget the events of the morning.

We arrive at the hotel.

We get to Croke Park and get ready to play in the biggest game of my life, but I'm still thinking, knowing full well I'm fortunate to be still alive, never mind able to play a football game.

The crowds are rapidly piling into the stadium. We get into the dressing-room. I don't have a pre-match routine that I slavishly follow match after match, but I do have one thing. I always sit in the same corner of the room. If someone is already there, I'll get them to move.

This is the only thing that's nailed into my pre-match routine. It's not superstition… it's just something I like to do. Something familiar.

I LOOK AROUND in the pre-match parade following the Artane Boys Band, step by step. Friends, neighbours… family. They're all here. The atmosphere is buzzing but I'm struggling to rid my mind completely of the morning's events… the attack… and Sparky's heroics.

As I stand there listening to Amhrán na bhFiann…. images of the bull trying to gore me come into my mind. I put the events of the morning to one side on the journey up to Dublin, distracted by other things. Now I start to replay the scenes again, the body and mind still grappling with the shock of it all... and when the game starts, I struggle to get going.

I don't feel right.

I find it hard to get into the zone, to tune into the game... tune into what's going on around me, and that's not like me. I feel lethargic, knocked back, diminished. My legs feel like two tree trunks filled with concrete. My opponent Eric Philpott is a lively, skilful player and I need to close him down more.

He scores an early point.

I have a conversation with myself; my inner voice... *What's wrong Pat you're not playing as well as you can?*

I don't know... I just can't get going. I feel knackered.

We'll fucking get going!!!

This is an All-Ireland final... get focused.

Your man is getting the better of you. He's making a show of you in the biggest game of your life.

GET A GRIP.

I'M NOT THE only one struggling.

We're terrible in that opening half. We can't get going at all. *Is it nerves... or are Cork just too good for us?* It looks for long stretches of the game like we might not even get a point. Imagine... the mortification, the humiliation of not scoring a point in an All-Ireland final.

We don't manage to muster even a score until almost half-time, when Paddy Mulvany sweeps the ball over the bar. At least we're on the scoreboard now. At least we're underway. Not that Cork are flying either, but they are better than us.

Half-time. We trail 0-4 to 0-1.

We need to reorganise. *Reset.* We know that unless we get our act together it will be the end of our All-Ireland dreams.

I know that unless I forget about what happened this morning I will continue to struggle to get to the pitch of the game.

'Are you alright?'

It's our coach Peter McDermott talking to me, as I sit here trying to get my head right. 'Go on more of those runs up-field,' he tells me.

'Make them worry about you!'

I focus harder. I tell myself I must tune in and as I run back out onto the pitch for the second-half I know… the team knows… a HUGE improvement will be needed.

I run back out onto the pitch, back into the light, fully aware that our destiny hangs by a thread. It's time to shit… or get off the pot.

As the second-half gets underway I start to feel the old power return to my legs. I start to play better, find my form. I go on one of my surging runs. The team as a whole starts to play better. *Are we on our way?*

I put the events of the morning out of my mind. I forget about the bull. I forget how close I went to the edge. I get another ball and fire it downfield. The crowd roars. I know I'm on the way now… that I'm *back*!

Terry Kearns, suddenly, scores an extraordinary goal, punching the ball to the net even though he has his back to the goals. The ball sails over the head of Cork goalkeeper Billy Morgan who is stranded in no-man's land. The crowd roars again.

YESSSS… we're on *our way*. At last.

The Sam Maguire Cup is in reach. I can almost touch it.

★★★

PADDY

WE STAND IN the tunnel. It's All-Ireland football final day, the biggest day in the Irish sporting calendar. We stand and wait until we're told to step onto the pitch… onto the hallowed ground of Croke Park.

The stadium is rapidly filling up; the atmosphere, the tension of the big day gradually building, the music pumping out of the sound system. It's a red-letter day in the GAA year, especially for those counties involved, of course. It's particularly special for the players. Not many get a chance to play in an All-Ireland final.

I was one of the lucky ones, I know that now. And as the years pass, I appreciate more and more just how fortunate I was.

WE WAIT IN line.

Then we are told to walk on; to make our way onto the beautifully manicured pitch. It's all well planned. The stadium announcer has already explained to the crowd what the ceremony is all about and there's a bit of a fanfare as we walk the short distance from the tunnel entrance onto the pitch. Then we turn and stand in line looking up at the faces of spectators in the Hogan Stand.

It's a long time since I was on the pitch taking in a view like this.

It's the 2022 All-Ireland senior football final between Kerry and Galway, and we are part of the warm-up act. As is the tradition in the GAA, the All-Ireland winners from 25 years previously are paraded before each final… and this year it is our turn. Twenty-five years. Well, it's 26 actually. Because of Covid we couldn't go to Croke Park in 2021, the exact anniversary. Twenty-six years… they have skipped by, haven't they.

A lot has happened since then. A lot, but how they have passed so quickly.

Twenty-six years since 1996 when we won one of the most controversial finals in the history of the GAA. So as part of the anniversary, the GAA have asked us up to Croker for the day out – and here we are in our grey suits, no tie thankfully. It's too warm for all that. Heavy.

All the lads I had served in the trenches with back in the day are correct and present, most of them anyway. Our job today is a simple one. We stand in line out on the pitch, guys now in their forties and fifties. Our names are called out and we step out of line and wave to the crowd. We are told what to do beforehand, but I've seen it so many times down the years – other teams in previous years feted on the 25th anniversary of their All-Ireland triumph. We all know how it works.

It's a great idea, a nice touch by the GAA and the crowd politely applaud as each of our names are called out and that player steps forward, turning 180 degrees to wave at the four corners of the vast stadium… Tommy Dowd, Brendan Reilly… Colm Coyle, Enda McManus, Conor Martin… Graham Geraghty… and Paddy Reynolds!

It goes on.

It's grand to be back involved on All-Ireland final day, however marginal the role; you get a sense of the day again. The big day, the Sam Maguire up for grabs and what it all means for the players. As I wait to go on the pitch, the Galway players are around, tooing and froing from their dressing-room, nervously.

You know what they are going through. You understood how they are in a different zone now, their minds already turned, like warriors, towards the battle. You feel that tension and think *Jaysus, wouldn't it be great to be back*. You think of how the build-up, that 15 or 20 minutes before a big game is crucial; how important it is to be mentally right. If you lose concentration at that stage, start wandering, you are in trouble. You have to keep focused. I look at the Galway players and see the concentration etched on their faces. They're ready.

There is pressure too on All-Ireland final day. The pressure to win, but if there was some way to reverse the effects of time you'd love to go back again; of course you would because playing in an All-Ireland final is special. It takes a lot to get there, a big commitment, but when you win you can savour that sweet scent of success. It's something you never forget. Never. There's so much that you forget from a career, especially the nitty, gritty aspect of games, moves, scores – but other things are indelibly etched on the consciousness.

EVERY PLAYER WHO was part of the Meath set-up in 1996 had his own individual way of preparing for a big game like an All-Ireland final. Going up for games, the bus easing its way through the Dublin traffic, escorted by Garda motorcyclists. Graham Geraghty might be having the craic with some of the other lads. Joking, laughing.

That's how Graham relaxed. Darren Fay on the other hand would be sitting there with his head in his hands, not talking. In the dressing-room, Darren would have a towel over his head sitting there. It was his way of staying focused. It worked for him because invariably he would come out then and produce a brilliant performance. That's the way he did it. Different people, different ways. Some talked and laughed, some stayed silent.

My approach was a middle-ground strategy between having the craic like Graham and seeking to step away from it all and focus like Darren. I would talk to others, but I didn't want to be too distracted either. I knew I had a job to do and I wanted to keep that task to the forefront of my mind. Focused.

I wouldn't be in the best of form coming up to a big game, I would be on edge and nervous, of course you would be nervous. They would be good nerves, if there was such a thing. Edgy but not burdened down or knocked off track by nerves. Certainly not. You'd be looking forward to it but slightly apprehensive too. You didn't want to make mistakes, give away anything. You had to perform.

Not that I would be doubting myself either. I'd be looking forward to it, running through in my head what I had done well in the last number of games. I would never focus on anything negative. Sometimes, a voice in your head would try to introduce something negative but I wouldn't allow that to happen. That was a big lesson I had learned over the years. It would be positive, positive… positive. Before I would go out, I would envisage what could happen in the first 10 minutes. I would think up scenarios based on what happened in previous games and imagine how I would deal with challenges, how I would confront them and, of course, there were always challenges.

All sorts of things occupied you, in and out of your head in the lead up to a match. *Who would I be marking? What kind of a player was he? What were his strengths? How would I contain him; lessen his influence?* I would think of what I was supposed to do in terms of getting forward, helping the team in any way. It was about getting the mind right. I would go back to a previous game I did something well in, focus on things like that, the good things I did.

Not that I read books on psychology, but I took bits and pieces from what I had picked up myself along the way, from what other players said or from what I might have heard… little nuggets about preparation, ways of preparing for games, things like that.

We had Brian Smyth, the uncle of former Meath player Liam Hayes, working with us at the time on the psychology side of things, preparing us mentally. By the mid-90s the game was changing, science was taking over and we had to respond to that change. Brian was qualified in that area. He was very good at it and he helped us a lot. A lovely man who knew what he was talking about. Brian would instil in us from the start the importance of being absolutely positive going out onto the field; to focus in the days leading up to the game on things we had done well in previous matches. Repetition. He would emphasise to us the importance of filling our minds with positivity and the good things we had done.

Sports psychology was relatively new then, at least in terms of it being employed and utilised by teams in the GAA but Seán Boylan, who was always open to new ideas, had brought Brian on board. Brian worked with us and helped to ensure that when we went out into the arena, we were ready.

When the team of 1996 met up again to be introduced to the crowd at Croker it was just like old times. It was quickly back to the banter, the craic. It's like we were family back then, when we played together and were looking for All-Ireland glory under Seán Boylan. Then it all stopped, time passed.

I haven't thought too much about the 1996 All-Ireland final down the years; I wouldn't be obsessed by it, the win over Mayo after a replay, but every now and again I'm reminded of it. Maybe I'll see a snippet from those games on TV or someone will want to talk about it; mention something about it. That will bring me back.

When that happens, I'm reminded of how Colm Coyle rescued a draw for us in unlikely circumstances in the first game. The score broke Mayo hearts because they led by a point with literally seconds remaining. It looked like they would win their first All-Ireland since 1951.

Coyler won the ball in midfield, and lashed it hopefully towards Hill 16 and the Mayo posts with time almost up. We watched as the ball landed in front of the Mayo goals and bounced up and over the bar. Seconds later the referee blew the final whistle and we had to meet again in the replay a few weeks later. We had played poorly in that drawn game and were fortunate to get a second chance.

From time to time, I'm still reminded of that replay and particularly the vicious, if brief row that broke out early in the game. Everybody, it seems, who was around then remembers that. The row. The most famous, should that be infamous, row in GAA history and I was there stuck in the middle of it.

For a few madcap seconds it seemed like the whole world had gone mad. That anarchy reigned. Players from both sides were engaged in a spontaneous battle, arms and legs flying; punches thrown, bodies falling to the ground, some getting up, some staying where they were, the sound of spectators shouting and roaring providing a noisy backdrop as anarchy reigned.

There were other days too.

In 1999, there were no major bust ups but we still won another All-Ireland. Happy days when we won something major and got to savour the kind of pure joy that was matched only by big life events, such as the birth of a child, a new member of the family. There were less happy days also when we suffered gut-crushing defeats that left their marks on the soul.

Ah yes, the good old days.

II

Pioneers

Termonfeckin

Walterstown

Christy

Breda Flynn

14-Acres

Gormanston College

★★★

PAT

EVERY SO OFTEN I think about my father Christy and mother Breda. I think about their lives, the kind of people they were, their outlook on life. I think too of their courageous decision in the 1940s to leave their home in Termonfeckin and move to Walterstown. It was brave in all sorts of ways.

It's not far between the two places these days, but back then they must have felt like those pioneers making the trek across the Rocky Mountains during the glory days of the Wild West. Pioneers who made the trip into the unknown imbued with little else but a sense of adventure and a dream to make a new home in a new land.

They started with a blank slate. They bought a small farm, about 14 acres, a few cows and set about the formidable task of building it up from there... their new life, their new home.

Christy Reynolds was a Louth man, one hundred percent. He played football for the Wee County. He wanted me to turn out in the red of Louth too, but that was never going to happen.

I was born in Louth, and raised in Termonfeckin for the first couple of years of my life. My father had met and married my mother Breda Flynn who was also from the Termonfeckin area. Her uncle played some football for the local club, so there was football on that side too. When they married, they set up home in the area.

My mother had sat her Leaving Cert which was unusual at the time. Even getting to secondary school was an achievement back in the 1940s and 50s. Most people left primary school at a young age, as they had no way of getting education beyond that point. Local people used to bring her letters they would have received, maybe from relatives in America or England. They'd ask her to read them. They might also have some forms from the government that needed to be filled in. My mother would help them out.

It's difficult to believe now, but a lot of people couldn't read, as educational opportunities beyond primary school were for the few; the privileged few. Few people had cars either, and most got around on bicycles. My father, who was probably in his thirties at the time, had a vision. He had been in the army but he wanted to be farmer. Somehow or other he got wind of how there was 14 acres of land and an old thatched house and old shed available in Walterstown, a few miles outside Navan.

It was very much a rural area. There was a church, a pub, a school... but they were located in different parts of the parish. Farming was the main occupation. And then... there was football.

HE MADE THE trip from Termonfeckin to have a look at this 14-acre farm up for sale. He probably made several trips up – it didn't always turn out to be a smooth journey; he crashed on one expedition, sent tumbling off his motorbike. It didn't put him off his ambition or knock him off course. He continued on. He must have liked what he saw too, the piece of land.

He saw the potential, the opportunities it offered to build a little kingdom and make a living. A place they could call their own.

It was an era when Ireland was mired in economic stagnation so it was a brave move to uproot yourself and your family and kickstart a new life elsewhere. Foolhardy some might say, but certainly brave. Moving to Meath was, in my father's view anyway, like going to the other side. There was a fierce rivalry between Louth and Meath in those day, at least on the football front, and going from one county to the other was seen as a betrayal almost.

He and my mother gathered whatever money they had and decided to make a go of it. To buy the land and make the move. They set about the formidable challenge of eking out a living from the handful of acres. They started to milk cows, they grew their own vegetables; they were basically self-sufficient. And the family expanded.

My father built a house to provide shelter for his growing brood. There was a lot of movement from Termonfeckin to Walterstown at first it seems but, of course, Walterstown became home… even for my father.

I was the eldest, I was born in Termonfeckin. The world was in a state of flux when I arrived into it on September 6, 1945. The Second World War was ending but Ireland was far from a rich country, you had to work hard for anything you had. So, I arrived into an unsettled, turbulent world although all was quiet where we lived in Termonfeckin.

I was the first born, but I was soon followed by Eilish, Ray, Paul, Gerry, Christopher and Juliette.

I was only a youngster when we moved to Meath so I don't remember much about the actual switch. I just got on with the business of growing up in an ever-extending family. We played around the fields as youngsters but we worked too.

While my mother was busy raising her growing family, my father spent long days in the fields. He had a vision, but he was also fiercely determined. Nothing would stand in his way. From an early age we were imbued with a strong work ethic. Driven. It was work, work… work. I didn't mind, it was simply the way it was. There was no such thing as sitting back. It was about getting out, doing what you had to do. Every day.

From an early age you did your jobs around the house and farm. No questions asked. No moaning about it… just get on with it. If you wanted to get on in this world, then you worked… that was the message and we absorbed it early. As soon as you could walk almost, you were expected to help out in some way. That's very important I think for young people to learn.

You also learned to deal with people in an honest way. No double-dealing; be straight even if it might cost you from time to time. It was a tough world but that didn't stop us from trying to be decent. That's the kind of philosophy my parents taught us, that's the way we were brought up.

MY FATHER MAY have moved to Meath, but he wanted me to play for Louth. He was good enough to play for Louth himself. No doubt. For him it was all about the Wee County and their wondrous deeds on the football fields of Ireland.

It wasn't about Meath… Louth people at the time dreaded Meath. There was more than a rivalry between the two counties. There was a bitterness.

In 1949, Meath and Louth had played a three-game saga in the championship. Sunday after Sunday they were locked like two gladiators in mortal combat until Meath won out in the end – and went on to win the Sam Maguire for the first time too. The rivalry was intense.

The first time I was in Croke Park was for the 1957 All-Ireland final. Louth, the smallest county… versus Cork, the largest county in the country. I went with my father. We found a perch on Hill 16. Because of a clash of colours, Louth played in the green of Leinster. It was the first time the Wee County had reached an All-Ireland final for decades. It was a big deal indeed for my father.

He greatly enjoyed seeing his native county win the biggest prize in gaelic football, the Holy Grail. His mighty chest expanded with pride as the Louth captain Dermot O'Brien accepted the Sam Maguire Cup that day. He headed back down to Walterstown that evening with his spirits lifted, delighted, although there were no wild celebrations. The cows had to be milked.

It was a real shock that Louth should defeat Cork in the All-Ireland final… mighty Cork, and we laughed at the good of it all, the smallest county on the island of Ireland getting the better of the biggest. It was a very big deal for the Wee County, of course it was. The huge crowd, the drama of it all, the atmosphere left a deep impression on me. I left Croke Park that day carried along by the press of the crowd, little knowing I would be back a decade later to play in an All-Ireland final myself.

I wasn't obsessed with football as a young lad. I loved running. I had speed in my legs, a burst of pace. I loved sports days that were held around the countryside in villages during the summer months. Sports days were very common and they provided me with an opportunity to shine in races. My natural speed helped me when it came to jobs such as chasing errant cattle but it also helped me make a name for myself too.

Primary school for me was in Lismullen. It was located at Dillon's Bridge, where there was an old RIC barracks that was raided by the Old IRA during the War of Independence. The school had no toilets, just basic facilities. There was a river at the back of the school and the boys would drink water out of that. Further upstream it was common for cattle to step into the river to drink. We knew we could get a disease. Still, we would drink out of the river. Somehow nobody died.

In time, we moved to a new school in Lismullen, which had all the facilities, a world away from our old alma mater. It was an indication of how the country generally was getting a little bit richer... a *little*. During breaks we would go out and play football. *Always the football.*

I was fortunate. Many left primary school and that was the end of their education. I got the chance to go on to Gormanston College as a boarder. It was a secondary school run by the Franciscans. They put a big emphasis on developing their students' sporting talents, and gaelic football featured highly on the curriculum. One of the teachers there was Joe Lennon. He was part of the innovative, swashbuckling Down team that won their first All-Ireland final in 1960, defeating Kerry in the final before 90,000 people, a great team that retained the title the next year against Offaly.

Lennon thought a lot about the game, and later wrote a book about it. He would dispense little nuggets of knowledge to us young footballers. 'Keep your eye on the ball... focus on what you have to do on the field of play whatever your position.'

The fact my parents could afford to send me to a college like that was a sign that they were able to put some money aside; their hard work and foresight, their own determination, was paying off. Yet my parents' ambitions also conspired to bring an end to my school days.

In Gormanston, I wasn't the worst student, but I wasn't the best either. I didn't get the top grades but I also did enough to get by. I was more a doer than academic.

We did our studies but there was plenty of opportunity to play sport, especially football. I was put in as a corner-forward initially on college teams but one of the brothers who was involved in looking after the teams spotted that maybe I wasn't a forward at all. He reckoned I couldn't shoot straight. So, he moved me back down field, back to the half-back line where he saw how I could use my pace to turn defence into attack. Perceptive.

From very early on I was a half-back. I had found my position. I played on the junior and senior college teams. Loved it. On the field, at least, I was getting top marks. I was one of the first students who was still in first year who went on to play senior football for the college. It was a tough environment, but it gave me confidence too.

My closest friend in Gormanston was Joe Nally, we used to pal around a lot. He used to point to the students who were getting the high grades and say, 'See all those boys in the A and the B classes… they'll never make it big'. I also remember him saying once, 'I bet we'll be better off than those boys!'

There turned out to be a lot of truth in what Joe said. He went on to own a number of supermarkets, became a big businessman, very successful. We influenced each other. We were tight friends. Still are. We learned from each other. We might not have been academics but we were driven to succeed, drove each other on. Competitive.

I SPENT TWO years in Gormanston. Happy years yes, but my time there was to prove short. My parents continued to show ambition. My father wanted to develop the farm further. Move on. He and my mother decided to buy more land. A local farm of about 120 acres came up for sale. My parents decided to go for it, add it to the land they already had. There was one problem, however.

They couldn't get the money anywhere. At first the banks wouldn't give it. Eventually, the ACC bank said they would provide them with the money. It was another sign of my parents' willingness to take a risk.

The bank said they would grant the loan but as part of the conditions I, as the oldest in the family, would have to come home from Gormanston College to work full time on the farm. Imagine that happening today? The bank wanted me to stay at home, help to ensure the farm, and the land, would be worked. I suppose they wanted to ensure they would get their investment back.

There were no phones around at the time. My mother wrote to the college to tell the authorities there I wasn't coming back.

I was about 15 or so but I couldn't go back to do my Inter Cert as it was called then. The bank wouldn't give them the money otherwise… and it was only £9,000 for the land. Might not seem much in today's terms but back then an enormous sum of money. Massive.

The nearest phone to us was at Joe Curran's garage a few miles away. Gormanston College phoned up and left a message which we got when we called in there for petrol. The message was… Gormanston were prepared to waive my annual fee if I returned. They wanted me to continue playing football for the college. It was an early lesson that this football lark could bring considerable perks.

I didn't mind too much returning to the land; becoming a young, full-time farmer. My destiny was now mapped out for me. I was going to be a farmer.

Fortunately, I was interested in farming. I liked the way it presented a different set of challenges. Every new day there was a different challenge. I liked that. There was always some issue to be sorted out but once you were determined to take it on full time and get around the problem, then you would be fine.

My father had taught me, more by example than anything else, that life was about overcoming the obstacles you found in your path. Life was about grappling with the difficulties… and there was tremendous satisfaction in overcoming the many daily difficulties you encountered. Rewarding, and no matter what issue you came up against there was always some solution to be found.

The qualities required to be a farmer were also useful, I discovered, on the football pitch… determination, resilience, a refusal to bow down.

A refusal to let anything or anyone get the better of you.

III

1950s
Paddy O'Brien
The Salles
Martin Quinn
The Mascot
Homecomings

★★★
PAT

FOOTBALL HAD BEEN played in the area since the late 19th century at least. In 1902, there was the first mention of a Walterstown team playing in a tournament in Dunshaughlin. They had arrived, although it wasn't all nice and easy from then on. Some years there was no team in the parish, but Walterstown GFC eventually re-established itself as a going concern and became a permanent fixture on the local GAA landscape. Because of our jerseys we became known as simply 'The Blacks' and things started to really happen for us from the early 1960s onwards. We became a new force in Meath football.

When I started playing at adult level, Walterstown was a junior club. We would play in fields borrowed from local farmers or landowners who were kind enough to lend us part of their holdings. Facilities were pretty much non-existent in the late 1950s and on into the 60s and 70s. It was simply a matter of putting up posts, nets if you had them, and marking the field as best you could. Basic. Most clubs didn't have dressing-rooms and showers. A shower, well, that was something that you got when the sky darkened overhead and the rain fell!

The 'pitches' were not manicured surfaces; you often had to move cows or cattle off first before play could begin. You moved some of the cow pats out of the way too; you 'togged out' beside your car or under the shelter of a nearby hedge. There was no glamour involved but that's what you *knew*.

Most clubs were like that.

THE FIRST PITCH I recall used by Walterstown was beside what is now Johnstown village. Then a local farmer gave us a field. That's how clubs managed. Local landowners loaning out fields to GAA clubs was common but, of course, that all changed. Yet farmers or landowners who did lease an acre or two to the parish team are among the unsung heroes of the GAA, because throughout the country that's what people did and only for them some clubs may not have survived; thankfully, there was always somebody willing to give a field or part of a field. Eventually Walterstown bought its own piece of land and developed it.

There were no underage teams in the area when I was growing up. No way for young players to develop as footballers. I played for a time with the De La Salle team in Navan and won minor championships with them in 1962 and '63. There were a number of Walterstown players with me.

In every young player's life, there are usually influential people who can have a big say in what direction a career takes. Paddy O'Brien from Navan was one of those figures who had a big influence on me, pointing me in the right direction. He would cycle out from Navan to make sure I made it to games and played for the Salles. He was great for coaching and giving me encouragement, telling me I had what it took to be a player and always look to improve. I might be milking cows or feeding calves or something and Paddy would ride the bike the few miles out from Navan and say to me, 'Come on Pat, we have a match'. He would cycle back into Navan with me. He wanted me to play at all costs.

I started playing for the Walterstown seniors. I was moving up, a boy among men but I was able for the physicality of it all. I took the hits but I didn't mind that, I enjoyed it all. In the early 1960s, a powerful sign that Walterstown was moving up in the world could be seen in the way we won the JFC in 1961, the club's first ever championship. That was a very significant achievement, a real indication we were well on our way; that our stock was rising. We were a young team, the average age was only around 21, and I was among the youngest. We beat Ratoath 0-10 to 0-1 in the final. Won well. There were great celebrations. A victory dance was held in the old school in Johnstown.

At that time we played a lot of tournament games, they were a feature of the GAA landscape back then. Sometimes we travelled to games, sometimes teams made their way to Walterstown. On one occasion a team from Louth arrived for a match. We were using at the time a local farmer's field. The Louth players arrived on the back of a cattle lorry! There was no luxury bus involved. The 'dressing-room' was a patch of land close to a river nearby.

There was always that intense rivalry between teams from Meath and Louth. It proved to be no different on this occasion. The game got underway and it turned out to be a rough, hard-tackling affair. Nasty. A row erupted.

Things got out of hand and the game degenerated into a farce. We were disgusted with the Louth players and how they had approached the game. The atmosphere was toxic and the Louth players had some of their clothes thrown in the nearby river. They weren't happy, of course.

I started to be selected for Meath at minor level, made my debut against Kildare in June 1962. Won too. I played at minor grade for a few years for the county, learning, all the time; learning about the demands of inter-county football. It was a kind of apprenticeship. I continued to learn. In 1963, I played minor, junior and senior for Meath. The junior side was effectively the second team and we played Wicklow in my first championship debut for them. *His determination was fierce and he could catch and kick with the best of them* the *Meath Chronicle* wrote about me. They were right that I was fiercely determined.

There was one game in those early years with Meath that stands out for me. It was a National League game against Mayo in Castlebar, I recall. Martin Quinn was playing and I was half afraid of him. He was shouting at me, telling me what to do with my marker. 'Don't let him into the square… NAIL HIM!' he would shout at me.

'Ah Jaysus Martin, I can't be doing that!'

Martin was a tough man, a warrior. He had been on the team for a few years, an established county footballer. A good player, 'teak tough' they used to call his kind back then. A full-back. It must have been daunting to be a forward and Martin on your shoulder, ready to pounce. He didn't take prisoners.

His opponent that day against Mayo was another big man, and they were like two gladiators. Neither would give an inch. At one point a row erupted and after it was over and the dust had settled, we had to be locked into the dressing-rooms for our own protection. Outside there was a crowd… an angry mob really and they wanted to get their hands on us.

It was mayhem. There was a madness abroad. They felt aggrieved. Martin had hit one of their players and they clearly felt justice had not been dispensed, at least the way they felt it should have been.

We travelled to the game in a Volkswagen van and there was a canvas on top of the van and on the way out of the ground supporters jumped in on top of us… went through the canvas. Fists flew. We had to defend ourselves. We launched a counter-offensive and pushed them back out of the van. When we got a chance, we took off down the road. It was bedlam. We were lucky to get out of the place alive!

I admired Martin Quinn, for his ruggedness, his strength of character, but for something else too. He didn't like losing – and I was like that. When I went out to play a game, I went out to win. Every game, no matter what level, club or county, challenge or All-Ireland final. There were no half measures. I had to win and if we didn't, it really bugged me. Really annoyed me.

That competitive spirit that was there drove me on to win every ball. 'Don't be bowed down' was my mantra. Don't allow yourself to be dominated. I couldn't bear to be bested by my marker. Fired up I was, it was just the way I was.

By the summer of 1964 it was really starting to happen for me in footballing terms. I got called up to the Meath junior team and we were doing well, winning games in the Leinster Junior Championship. It wasn't high profile stuff but I was delighted to be part of it all. During one of their games that summer Fr Tully who was county board chairman and one of the senior teams' selectors ran out onto the field. He was shouting. 'Pat, come off the field'.

'Why?' I asked. 'Am I not playing well enough?'

'No you're playing fine… but come off anyway!' I trooped off, but as it turned out the senior team was playing a championship game in a week or two and the selectors wanted to save me for that game. The big time beckoned.

★★★

PADDY

THERE'S A PHOTOGRAPH of the Walterstown senior football team from 1980 before they played Syddan in the county senior final and there I am in the front row, a youngster delighted with himself. My father is not in the shot as he had already drawn a line under his career; but my uncles, Gerry and Christy are there, ready to go into battle with the Blacks.

I was one of the Walterstown mascots that day. Not that I remember much about that occasion or the game itself. I was after all only a kid, but it was clear I was already big into football and how could it be any other way.

They were exciting times for Walterstown when after many disappointments they started to emerge as a real force in Meath football winning SFC titles in 1978, '80, '82 '83 and '84. All that too would have made a big impression on my youthful mind, the excitement surrounding the county final triumphs. The big games, the build up to these games. The club also did well in the All-Ireland Club championship, got to two All-Ireland finals too during those years. They lost both but it was still some achievement for a small, rural club as it was at the time. Massive.

I was surrounded by the game from day one. Soaked in its culture. It was such an integral part of the environment I grew up in; part of my DNA. Football, football… football. At primary school at Lismullen, at secondary school in Gormanston College, it was the same. Football. I couldn't wait to get out of the classroom for a kickaround. At home it was much the same… football and farming. I'm one of five… four brothers (Ivan, Christopher, Shane and Karl) and our sister, Niamh. I'm the second oldest. We would kick around in the field at home; mess about, have a laugh. There was always a football around. Always a field we could turn into Croke Park by placing two sticks in the ground as goalposts and switching on our youthful imagination.

AS A YOUNGSTER too I was steeped in the culture of that great Meath team of the 1980s. Because my father was a selector, I had a backstage pass to it all. I was on the team bus going to big games… Leinster finals, All-Ireland finals, the bus going through the city to Croke Park, the old stadium steadily looming up ahead in the distance, fans cheering on the streets, waving their flags. I had a ringside seat to it all… the dressing-room after big games, the place jammed with people, well-wishers.

I tried to make a contribution in some way, make myself useful by carrying the water bottles, retrieving the footballs when they were kicked behind the goalposts at Dalgan Park during training sessions.

Among my earliest memories was the treasured victory achieved by Meath in winning the Leinster final in 1986. Even as a youngster I could sense what beating Dublin that wet day meant to the players, the supporters, the county. What it meant to my father who was a selector. It was a game that ended years of dispiriting defeats and disappointment against the auld enemy. It was a reversal of the prevailing trend, a cherished victory achieved with overjoyed Meath supporters immune to the lashing rain as they drank in the moment, beating Dublin. Magic.

Printed indelibly on my mind is an image of that great GAA man Shane McEntee, who later became a TD. He was in the Cusack Stand that day, taking it all in, watching every move as Meath sought to finally throw off the yoke of oppression exerted by their old foes. He was shouting his team on, exposed to the rain, drenched, but it didn't matter to him. Meath did win and he was simply overjoyed… the rain, the drenching didn't matter. That's one powerful memory that will always remain with me. A special memory of a lovely man who was a Meath supporter to his core.

I knew it was a special time for Meath football, so to be involved at all was wonderful. Meeting up with the players at Ashbourne House and getting on the bus to take us up to Croke Park, often under a Garda escort, sirens echoing off the buildings of the city. People stopping on the streets to look and cheer, or maybe jeer, at the bus as it sped through the streets and onto the stadium.

Then, travelling back to Meath twice with the Sam Maguire in the bus; the victors, the Garda escort again, the supporters in places like Ashbourne or Navan, huge crowds of supporters waiting for us no matter where we went. I was there to see that first hand. I have no doubt it engendered in me an ambition to experience something like that as a player too. If you don't want to achieve what the players of that era achieved, to emulate them, then football, sport simply wasn't for you. It certainly sparked an ambition in me.

All the lads were great, joking and messing with me, but they would watch out for me too. I was like a character in a fairytale given access to this wonderful world of warriors and heroes, great footballers, great Meath men. I would see them silent before games, their faces taut and focused ready for battle. In the zone. I watched them leave the dressing-room, play the games, then saw them return to the dressing-room more often than not as conquerors, sometimes carrying with them a coveted piece of silverware; booty hard won on the field of battle. A few hours later I saw them on TV as RTÉ showed the highlights of the game; ordinary men I knew well elevated to the status of cult heroes, household names. Everything about the Meath set-up in the 80s and early 90s was just great. Inspiring.

There is one story that remained firmly etched in my mind from that era. Colm O'Rourke was coming to the end of his playing days. I was playing in a schools Leinster final at Páirc Tailteann in Navan. I was playing for Gormanston College and we were facing a team from Trim who had Alan Nestor and Barry Sheridan, players like that. O'Rourke, who was teaching in St Patrick's Classical School across the road, came over to have a look at the game. At one stage I won the ball, went surging up the field as I tended to do and got a terrible blow at the back of the head. Concussed. In those days there wasn't much talk about concussion, so you tried to shake it off and get back out onto the pitch. These days I wouldn't have been allowed to go back on. A week or so after that I was with the Meath footballers when they met up at Ashbourne House on a Sunday morning before going up to Croke Park, there was some big game on. Again, I was just there as a helper.

There was a bit of banter going on and O'Rourke turned to me and said, 'You know what, it would be far easier for you to try and go around lads, rather than try and go through them'.

He was taking the mick, of course, engaging in a bit of banter, I know that now but I was a youngster and I didn't know what way to take it. It got me thinking. *Did he mean what he said literally, or do I need to change my style?* It got me thinking about my game. How I could change it to be better, be more effective as a player.

My default approach, my instinctive style, was to try and break the tackle every time but it didn't always need to be like that. There were other ways. Better ways. That's what O'Rourke was trying to tell me.

That was all part of my connection with the Meath team back then, part of my apprenticeship in football. It wasn't any official, defined role. It only involved me carrying the bag of footballs or the bottles of water – yet it still provided me with a football education. A grounding that was to prove very useful to me later on. I got a wonderful insight into how it all worked at that level and it made me want to be a part of it all – as a player not just a helper.

And the day came when I was.

IV

Fr Tully
Louth
The Red
Bertie
Pat
The Dubs!

★★★

PAT

FR PATRICK, OR 'Packie' Tully, was a very influential figure in Meath football back then. He represented a certain type that was common in the GAA at that time – a cleric, but also somebody very closely involved in running the GAA.

He had first emerged as chairman of the county board in the 1940s. He served in a number of parishes before he came to work in Moynalty and later he became the parish priest in Duleek, but combined his parish duties with filling in as chairman of the county board for many years. He was elected chairman in 1949 and served in that role for 20 years. He was a very formidable figure in the GAA.

He was also the Meath team trainer. He had trained the teams that won the Sam Maguire Cup in 1949 and '54 and he was to go on to do the same in '67. It shouldn't be forgotten either that Meath won a National League title with him in charge in 1951.

When he ran onto the field on that summer's day in 1964 to tell me I had to come off I wondered what was going on, but when I learned it was a precaution to allow me to play for the seniors, I couldn't have been more delighted. This was it and to make it all the more intriguing the game was against my father's team… the Wee County.

IT WAS IRONIC that I should make my Leinster Senior Championship debut against Louth, of all counties. I don't know what my father thought of it all. I don't know if he wanted to laugh or cry. He was torn, I suppose, between supporting his son and his native county.

He knew what it was like to play for Louth and clearly had ability but he never burdened me with words of wisdom before a game. He wouldn't say anything really. He just let me get on with it; let me make my own mistakes… learn from those mistakes. That was his way and it was a brilliant approach. The last thing I needed, or at least felt I needed then, was so called words of advice from my father on what I should be doing or not doing during a game. He just left me to my own devices.

It was something I sought to do as a parent myself. Leave them to it. The lessons learned the hard way are the lessons you will never forget.

Meath had started the 1964 championship by defeating Kildare. I was on the bench. For the next game against Louth, I was in. This was it. This was the big one. The notice from the county board would have arrived at the house.

You are requested to be at… it would begin.

It was your county calling you. A clarion call.

The board would give you a jersey for the game, which would have to be returned, but we'd have to bring our socks and shorts. A jersey back then was a treasured item. The concept of swapping them at the end of a game was completely alien, a 'no no'. You would get a blast from some board official or other if you did.

Then the day of the Louth game arrived. Late June, a pleasant summer's day. A big day for me and the family. I wasn't nervous. Nerves didn't bother me like some players. Some players would be very agitated before going onto the pitch, vomiting in some cases. I didn't have an issue like that. I was eager to do well, eager to impress. Focused. Nervous? A little perhaps, but not much.

It was a rollercoaster championship game. The pace, the tempo of the contest was faster than I had experienced before but I settled in, got my hands on the ball, made a couple of runs up the wing. At the final whistle Meath were in front. I enjoyed it. Didn't feel out of my depth. Felt at home.

The *Meath Chronicle* when it came out later in the week made for some pleasant reading. *Young Pat Reynolds made the most successful of senior championship debuts* it reported.

I WAS MARKING Benny Gaughran. He was a player my father admired and I would hear him talk about this marvellous footballer, Benny Gaughran and how good a footballer he was. I admired Benny for his grit and determination. Kevin Beahan was another great player for the Wee County that my father admired. It was from his sideline kick that Louth got the goal that was so crucial to them winning the All-Ireland title in 1957. So, to get a good review in the newspapers after my debut championship game was satisfying.

Not that I paid attention all that much to what was written about me or the team before or after a game, although I suppose if reviews had been negative I would have been disgusted – but they weren't. They were positive after the Louth game and I held onto my place for the next outing… against Dublin in the Leinster final. The auld enemy.

Another glorious summer's day; another chapter in this on-going, never-ending rivalry between the two counties. Well over 50,000 turned up in Croke Park. Dublin were All-Ireland champions, a fact that added another dimension to the occasion. It also turned out to be another victory for Meath. I was marking Brian McDonald, a brilliant player. If you weren't on the ball, clued in, he could clean you out. Playing against quality players like him I was learning fast. Had to or you could be sunk without trace.

One of the lessons I quickly absorbed was that, especially at county level, you had to be adaptable. You had to think on your feet all the time. If something wasn't working you had to quickly assess the situation, see what could be done to improve matters. If you didn't you could be destroyed. Humiliated.

I had to shut out the noise of the crowd and get down to the task in hand and I could do that. It didn't matter what supporters were shouting at me because I simply didn't hear them. I could shut it all out. Played in a bubble. I was fortunate in that I wasn't the nervous type, I didn't use up an awful lot of energy before games worrying about what might or might not happen. I stayed positive. Some of the players talked about how they could hear the supporters shouting this or that at them, insults. I couldn't hear a thing… wouldn't have bothered me anyway.

I was immune to the roar of the crowd once the ball was thrown in and the battle commenced. I was fixated on what was happening on the pitch. I would switch on. Concentration, concentration… *concentration.* I knew I had to keep focused. I didn't want to be cleaned out by an opponent so I needed to focus.

I didn't visualise like some players have done down the years, especially in more modern times; I didn't imagine myself in certain situations and how I would deal with that situation but I knew what I wanted to do going into games. I knew what I needed to do if I was going to do my job.

The way I saw it, I had two main tasks: to stop my man from scoring and causing damage… and getting forward at every opportunity. Turn defence into attack.

I was one of the first half-backs to do that, if not the first in the country. It didn't always work out the way you hoped or planned, of course; you had to adapt to situations as they evolved, sometimes quickly. I had pace and the inclination to surge forward with the ball if the opportunity presented itself – and that's what I did.

Sometimes it got me in trouble because I would need to leave my man, the half-forward, unmarked while I foraged up field but once somebody, say one of the midfielders, slipped back to keep an eye on 'my man' then it usually worked out fine.

THERE ARE CERTAIN stages of a team's evolution; crucial milestones – and that win over Dublin was vitally important for the Meath team that was evolving in the 1960s. Dublin had won the Sam Maguire in 1963; they had great players including Des Foley and Mickey Whelan. That day Ollie Shanley scored a brilliant goal for us, firing to the net from distance. Paddy Mulvany got a second goal. There was no stopping us. No holding us back. We were the new rising force and we won in style. Brilliant.

At the final whistle there was a feeling of relief and delight as I, and the rest of the players, were submerged in a tsunami of people. Delighted supporters poured onto the pitch like an unstoppable flood. After all, it had been 10 years since Meath had beaten Dublin in a Leinster final. The victory opened the sluicegates of frustration and disappointment that had built up among the county's supporters.

We were cheered off the field. Heroes. Our captain Dinny Donnelly was carried shoulder high by supporters. He held on firmly to the cup, he wasn't going to let that go.

After victories like that the 30 minutes or so after the game were special as you togged out and engaged in a laugh and a joke with your colleagues, your teammates, the men who you had just shared the battle with. It was a private moment of contentment before going back out to the real world. Again, the papers made for happy reading.

The team was brilliant against Dublin... *magnificent* as the *Chronicle* put it.

The half-back line that day was Red Collier, Bertie Cunningham and myself. We were starting to really develop an understanding, to be a formidable unit. Red knew no fear when he was going for the ball, he focused in on winning possession and went for it. He was quick, tenacious, brave, few got the better of him. Bertie was as strong as an ox. Formidable. Tough. Nothing got passed him. Strong, but a good footballer too. He was able to chase down an opponent, close him down, deny him time and space, and get the ball away from the danger zone. No messing.

Bertie was my protector. I wasn't the tallest player on the pitch and when I got the ball opponents would rush in to try and dispossess me. Bertie would deal with the fellow who was rushing in. That allowed me the freedom to embark on one of my forward surges. He would help to ensure I could go on one of my runs up the field. It all worked well. We had an understanding.

Yet even on such days the chores that go with the farming life could not be ignored. Cows still needed to be milked. I can't remember exactly what I did after that Dublin game but the normal practice was to go home after games invariably on fine summer evenings. I would have something to eat, then go out and milk the cows. It was only then you would go for a few pints in a local pub, enjoy the banter, relive the game, savour the victory or discuss what went wrong if we lost.

Then up early again next morning. Getting the milking done. Get another week underway. That was the pattern of my summer days.

The rivalry between Dublin and Meath was intense on the field of play. There could be the odd dig thrown, harsh words exchanged as the heat of battle intensified. Yet when it was over that was it, it was over. Whenever we'd meet Dublin players, or those players from any other county, we might have a drink and a laugh about what went on during the battle. Hits would have been delivered and taken, but then forgotten about.

Yet that Dublin-Meath game of '64 did have a far more sinister side to it.

The *Chronicle* reported how two Meath supporters were stabbed leaving Hill 16 after that game. It was so unusual to hear of something like that at a GAA game, especially in those relatively innocent times. The supporters didn't die but they were badly injured, the reports indicated.

It was a dark part of what otherwise was a great day for me and Meath football.

V

Attracta Lynch
Fr Jim
Under-21s
Chelmsford
1996

PADDY

IT WAS AT under-16 level I took the first steps towards fulfilling my own destiny as a county footballer. It was at that level, that modest starting point, I began to embark on the journey. My father, of course, had played for the county, an All Star and all that. That knowledge, the family's heritage and history was always there in the background, something we were aware of, part of the family culture.

My mother too, Attracta, she has always loved football. She played a huge role in making sure we got plenty of it as youngsters if that's what we wanted to do – and I did. Couldn't get enough football.

As a youngster I remember being in Wexford one summer on a family holiday. We were all there, my brothers and sister. I was playing under-12 or under-14 at the time, and we had a tournament game on in Walterstown. It wasn't an All-Ireland final! It just was a tournament game yet my mother loaded the whole lot of us into the family car, the entire gang and drove us back up home. Didn't hesitate. She was more enthusiastic about the games than the rest of us.

Those were the days before the motorway was there; the trip from the bottom of Wexford to Meath was not to be taken lightly yet she didn't hesitate to embark on the arduous journey back home. I'm not sure my father would have done that for a tournament football game; in fact, I know he wouldn't. He would be busy, probably had enough of football anyway at that stage. Every game, my mother would be there… Meath games, Walterstown matches, especially the matches we were in. She would get us to the ground, make sure our gear was washed and ready, that we had our boots.

She came from a family steeped in the GAA, the Lynch family in Carlanstown outside Kells. Her brother Jim Lynch, later Fr Jim Lynch, was a good footballer. He had, I've since learned, an ability as a player, he was quick. He too was blessed with pace, a family trait. My mother had a great passion for the game, still has. She goes now to watch her grandchildren play, never misses a match.

One of the abiding, powerful memories I have as a youngster is the voice of my mother cheering us on from the sideline. So many different sidelines, at so many different grounds. Her voice echoes down the years. Encouraging. A typical mother. Everyone would be wrong except her sons! You'd get used to hearing her voice after a while and, as a youngster it was a comfort, it would give you confidence. Encouraged, not criticised or put down in any way, not pressurised. It would help you enjoy the game more knowing that support was there.

MY FATHER WOULD attend some of our games at underage level. He would look at the games and you would sense him looking at you, watching how you were playing. The following day he might make a comment on what you did during the game, but in fairness to him he would never do a running commentary during the game as some parents did or do. He would never open his mouth during the game, say a word, but then when the dust was settled he'd mention one or two things I could have done, to make myself a better player.

It was the right way to do it. The last thing a youngster wants is to hear a parent shouting in at him or her during a game saying 'do this'… 'go there'… 'do that.' It's embarrassing for the youngster and undermines his or her confidence.

I didn't have all that to grapple with yet there was pressure of another kind. My father had done it all in his career, won the All-Ireland with Meath in 1967, won an All Star in 1971. He had toured the world with Meath. Was a selector in the 1980s, during the golden years. He was known far and wide in the GAA world. Now I was looking to carve out my own career and, of course, the question was asked by sceptical supporters. 'Ah, but is he as good as his father?' and all that.

When you were playing under-16, minor or even under-21 it was fine. There was no real expectations, no real pressure – and I had experienced a lot of county football before I got to the senior ranks. The demands.

I had played on the Meath minor team that reached the All-Ireland final in 1993 where we were well beaten by Cork. That team had some good players. Darren Fay was good the day of the final. Very good. He showed the qualities that were to make him a great full-back. Knew when to tackle, when to get out in front of his man. We were going well in the final before a big crowd at Croke Park, our match the curtain-raiser for the SFC showdown between Cork and Derry. We were motoring nicely then… BANG, we gave away two soft goals. Gift wrapped them, the ball allowed to sail over the goalkeeper's head and into the net. Twice. That killed us. One goal was bad enough, to concede two left us like a stricken ship listing aimlessly.

The team manager was Christy Moore and he was a great manager, innovative, and he did something every great coach should do. He gave the players confidence. He would focus on the positive and gently remind you what you had to do to improve aspects of your game. There was no shouting, no putting people down. He put a huge emphasis on fitness and having us in a very good physical condition. That, in turn, gave us more confidence. We knew that when the battle was at its hottest, we wouldn't be found wanting. Knowing that deep down is a huge factor for any player. Knowing you had put in the hard yards for the hard road. That too was one of the cornerstones of Seán Boylan's management structure.

Christy created this environment for us to thrive in and prosper, and so did the people who worked with him, people like Johnny Sullivan. Losing an All-Ireland final was a big blow, a bitter disappointment, but I was young. I could recover quickly. You always feel, at 18 or 19, there will be another day. That's not always the case in a career. Some only get one opportunity, some don't ever get to the big stage. Thankfully for me, I did get back to Croke Park for Leinster and All-Ireland finals. I did get a shot at tasting the big time.

People like Christy Moore and Johnny Sullivan did a lot to bring young Meath players on during the early 1990s. They helped to lay the foundations for future success, put the structures in place for Seán Boylan later on. By the time I and others in my age group reached the senior team we were mentally and physically in a good place in terms of county football. We were ready; the seeds were sown, the groundwork prepared.

That's one of the chief reasons why it's so important for county teams to do well at underage levels. To win titles – or at least get to provincial and or All-

Ireland finals. It gives young players vital experience. It gives them a taste of the big time and invariably players will want more. Even if they lose on the big stage, players will do all they can to get back to that stage. By getting to finals a culture is created; it removes the fear. Sharpens the appetite.

So, I knew, well before I even became established as a senior county footballer, what it was like to lose an All-Ireland final – and it wasn't pretty. Right from the start with me it was about winning, there was no consolation in losing gallantly. There was no room in my world for moral victories. It was victory or nothing. So, I had an eventful underage career, but one without a major honour – and I still had to prove myself at the highest level. I still had to prove to the doubters I could follow in my father's footsteps. Do what he did. Step onto the big stage and be successful. Some doubted I could do that. I knew that to be the case. You just sensed it, so I had my motivation. Ready-made.

IT WAS WHEN I moved on to senior level, which I did in 1996, that I would really hear that voice, the grumblings 'Oh the only reason he's in the team was because his father was there before as a player and selector'. That kind of stuff. I would pick that sense up from what some people would say to me, mutterings I heard here and there – and it would play on my mind, but I certainly wouldn't let it affect me. If anything, I would use it to spur me on.

It's the pressure every son of a well-known player has to confront and face – and I've heard stories of how it has burdened some, young players who were expected to follow in the footsteps of a famous father; how the pressure stopped talented young players from fulfilling their own careers. My father wanted to ease that pressure as much as possible for me so he gave up being a Meath selector in the mid-90s. He knew I was starting to appear as a possible candidate for a place on the Meath panel. He didn't want to compromise my position so he stepped away. He knew if he was involved it would put more pressure on me.

There was a bit of a clearout anyway after Meath lost to Laois in the Leinster Championship in 1992, a number of big-name players stepped away... Mick Lyons, Liam Hayes. The rebuilding phase continued for the next few years but Meath struggled to make a breakthrough. They didn't make much progress in 1993 or '94 in terms of chasing down an All-Ireland title. Then in 1995 they were beaten by 10 points by Dublin. It was time for another re-set.

I WAS LUCKY in a way in that my progress from aspiring young apprentice to a senior player was relatively rapid. After finishing secondary school, I had gone to study agriculture in a college in England, in Chelmsford not too far from London and I didn't return home until the Christmas of 1995 – yet the following summer I was on the Meath senior team. Just like that. Not only that,I was on a Meath team that won the All-Ireland, the Sam Maguire itself.

I wasn't hanging around on the periphery of the Meath team long enough for any outside grumblings about my presence on the team to start in earnest. I played a few league games in February and March of 1996, so by the time people could have a rattle at me, say 'I wasn't as good as my father', or anything like that, I was already progressing. I was on my way, becoming accustomed to the rigours and the demands of county football in relatively low-profile games; moving along, gaining experience, almost unnoticed.

And because I was in college in England and involved in the county set-up from under-16 on, I wasn't involved much at club level either except perhaps for championship games. Even when it came to the senior club side, I was rarely there. That's the way Boylan had it set up. When you were part of the county set up you trained with the county and not the club, until their championship campaign ended.

In that summer of 1996 when the Leinster Championship got underway, I was thrown on the senior team straightaway, one of a gang of youngsters Seán Boylan put his faith in. I was on the team and thankfully was able to make an impact immediately; to hold onto my position which, of course, was the same position my father played… left-half-back.

There is a connection between the position you play in and the mentality, the make-up of the player. As a wing-back you have to have a certain temperament. It helps if you are somebody who enjoys a certain freedom, where you are not tied down, as I did. If you are a corner-back you have to be extremely fast, extremely focused as a player, concentration has to be intense, unrelenting, but you must watch 'your man', whatever attacker you are on all the time. As a wing back I could afford to be a bit more adventurous, to roam up field.

I didn't need to focus so much on the man beside me. I could be a bit more flamboyant as in taking a chance on pushing forward, moving into midfield to win loose ball. I didn't need the same type of concentration as a corner-back. For me getting my hands on loose ball and bombing forward was where the juice, the buzz was. I didn't want to be constrained, charged with watching my man all the time. Half-back was a position that suited me, physically and mentally.

The whole secret of the half-back role is to change the mindset of the opponent you are marking. If you can get him to believe that HE has to mark YOU, rather than you marking him, a half-forward, then you can help put your team on the front-foot. Your team is now in attack mode. If you can turn the tables and have him chasing you, that's him gone out of the game as an attacking threat. You now have a free hand... that word freedom, to do what you like, to become an attacking threat yourself instead of spending your time in a negative, restricted defensive mode. Constrained.

I've never looked back at say the 1967 All-Ireland final my father played in, but my kids have – and they are fascinated by how my father played. 'Grandad was a strong player... nothing stopped him going for the ball', they say. 'Other players were bouncing off him!' I smile, because that's the way he played, I know that from what others have said. If his mind was on the ball, he was going to get it no matter what. I was a bit like that too.

I looked to forage around midfield, seeking out loose ball, breaking ball. It's a different game now because you don't get as much breaking ball in the middle of the field, but whatever was there I did my best to get it. The way I saw it, that was one of my primary roles.

So inevitably there was going to be comparisons between my father and I. No doubt there was some, those who could rewind back to the 60s and 70s, who compared both of us and felt I wasn't as good as my father – but I was never going to allow negativity to win the day anyway. I was never going to allow negative thoughts undermine what I was seeking to achieve in my own career.

If you allow negativity to seep into your life and your way of thinking, you would do nothing; achieve nothing, say nothing. It's about getting on with it, believing in yourself and your own capabilities. Even as a young player, I knew that, I felt that. It's the way you have to be in life. Look at a challenge, tackle it head on.

There's always a way. Get on with it. If you're not able for a challenge, well, then you're not. If you are able for it, then you are able for it. If you take it on you have to give yourself the best chance possible by working hard, preparing well and telling yourself you are up for this, you can do this. Bolstering yourself mentally and physically.

To me it was as simple, or as complicated, as that. There was only one way to find out if I could do something; ignore the doubters and have a go at it anyway and see. Give it my best, one hundred percent.

All I could do was my best. I know that's the oldest cliché in town but that, when all is said and done, it is all I can do in life. All anybody can do.

VI

1964
Galway
Cyril Dunne
Wembley
Seán O'Neill
The Soil
1996

★★★

PAT

FOOTBALL CAN ALLOW you to experience some wonderful moments, some great feelings of joy, but it can really bring you back to earth too… with an unmerciful bang.

Take the All-Ireland semi-final of 1964. We went into the game delighted with ourselves. Full of youthful optimism. We had beaten Dublin, the auld enemy.

We were on our way. We then had to play Galway and they ambushed us. They were an evolving team, building momentum. That day they taught us a lesson. They taught us we had to be right on our game physically and mentally if we wanted to win the Sam Maguire – or even get into the final. They were a very skilful side… Enda Colleran, Mattie McDonagh, Bosco McDermott. They had quality players all over the pitch. Powerful. Yet we should have beaten them. Losing was bad enough but to lose knowing you should have won. A sickener.

That engaging contest reinforced the concept that you often need luck too to win big, close games. A crowd of 52,547 showed up but it was 5,000 less than the Leinster final, showing the box office attraction of Meath-Dublin games.

We played well for long spells against Galway and Jack Quinn scored a brilliant goal, although it didn't count. Early in the second-half he took the ball from a ruck of players, and gained a yard or two of space. He looked up and let loose.

He fired the ball to the net from distance but the referee didn't allow it. Instead, he brought play back and give us a free in. It was a terrible decision. Jimmy Walsh took the free but he spooned it wide so we were doubly punished. For what? The whistle apparently had blown for a free before Jack had kicked the ball. Nobody knew, except the referee, what the free was for. A goal at that stage would have put us comfortably in front. Granted a reprieve, Galway bounced back and won.

I was sick. Disgusted. Something like that would have bothered me for days. I would play back a game in my head. Wonder where we had gone wrong. What we could have done to stop the rot. I wasn't interested in moral victories, saying… 'Ah well, we won Leinster.' I wanted to know what we needed to do to push on and get to an All-Ireland final. *Could I have done more?* I asked myself. I was marking Cyril Dunne, a fine player and I felt I did well, didn't give him many opportunities. *So how did our wheels fall off?*

It would have bugged me for days trying to decipher what went wrong; episodes from the game running through my mind as I milked the cows or was on some assignment or other out on the fields. That's the way I was and it was something that stayed with me throughout my career. Defeat provoked a search for answers. I was always looking for ways to improve; looking for ways to avoid defeat, something I hated. Knowing you did your best was all very good, I would be pleased to get praise for my personal performance, but it didn't soften the nasty sting that accompanied a defeat.

When the *Chronicle* came out a few days later it referenced our *gallant* effort against a very good Galway side. *Gallant* was a euphemism for failure. I was praised for my efforts in containing Dunne and the reporter asked some searching, very relevant questions. *Why, for instance, did the losers continue to send in lobbing balls to (Galway full-back) Noel Tierney who was in his element clearing them? Why was Ollie Shanley's blistering speed not brought into action by sending long, low punts to his wing?* They were relevant questions. Questions worth trying to answer but the bottom line was that we were out. All we could do was learn from the lessons and push on.

It showed we needed to learn more; to be cuter to beat a quality team like Galway. We had plenty of possession that day but just couldn't translate that to scores and any team that does that will always struggle to win. We only lost 1-8 to 0-9, but we still lost. We were developing into a decent team but we still had our faults.

We tended to miss frees; crucial kicks that went wide or fell short, that undermined us time and again. We were killing ourselves in that way. That was one issue.

WE RETURNED HOME chastened but wiser, not that we benefitted immediately from the experience we were gaining on the big stage. We were now one of the best teams in the country, we had proved that but that didn't mean we were fulfilling our true potential. Far from it.

There was a sweet consolation for me that year in the way Walterstown won the Intermediate Football Championship. The club was going places. In 1964, the club was on an upward curve and the victory over Kilmainhamwood in the intermediate showdown was a sign of that. We had earned our place in the senior ranks which was some feat considering that just a few years before that we were operating at junior B level.

Meath too had shown real signs of improving. The Leinster final success in 1964 was a clear indication we were moving in the right direction. We were full of optimism as we went into the summer of 1965; full of ourselves too unfortunately, and that's not a good place to be if you want to achieve anything because we received a right kick in the guts; another reminder we could take nothing for granted. Longford beat us in the Leinster Championship. A shock, yes. We were rightly caught out. Suckered. On an unforgettable day we were floored by an uppercut we never saw coming. Longford were building a very good team. We found out that day just how good they were.

Yet 1965 did have its memorable moments. Whit weekend, we had headed for London, to Wembley to play Galway in the annual tournament that was hosted at the famous ground by the London GAA Board featuring teams that had appeared in All-Ireland semi-finals the year before.

Wembley, the home of English soccer... the famous ground with its twin towers and carpet-like surface where so many famous games were staged over the years. *The pitch itself just had to be seen to be believed with its billiard table smoothness* wrote Denis Smyth in the *Chronicle*, although he added the turf had virtually no spring – and he was right.

Seeing the facilities of one of the finest sports stadiums in the world was fascinating; an eye-opener. Large crowds showed up for those games, people who had emigrated from Ireland and wanted a taste of the old country. People who wanted to connect with gaelic games again even if it was just for an afternoon. It was a festival of Irishness and somewhat ironic that while the GAA's infamous, ridiculous 'Ban' stopped people in Ireland from participating in sports except gaelic games, we were invited with open arms to the home of English soccer.

I didn't follow English soccer at the time, didn't know much about it, but on one of our trips to Wembley we met Peter Osgood the Chelsea and English striker. He was a very engaging, pleasant chap who asked us about gaelic football. He seemed impressed by the game and the fact that we were amateurs, playing for the enjoyment the game offered. Risking life and limb for the pride of the parish and county. I'm not sure if he got that concept. I didn't know at the time who Peter was or what he was. It was only later I found out. Of course, he went on to help Chelsea win the FA Cup in 1970 and played for England.

A lasting memory I have of that trip to Wembley was our full-back Martin Quinn walking around the goalmouth prior to the start of the game. Like a gladiator marking out his territory. I was marking Cyril Dunne, a very good player, and he could be difficult to contain, you had to be on full alert all the time with a player like that. At one stage during the game, he got in behind me. He was driving towards the Meath goals but as he did so I gave him a shoulder. He stumbled against the goalpost and was lying on the ground, one of his feet tied up in the nets. Big Martin came, shoved him with his foot and shouted at him, 'You're not supposed to be in here… GET THE HELL OUT!" he roared. Cyril wasn't able to get out of the goals, he was caught up in the net. I had to stop myself from laughing.

It was also an incident that highlighted how Martin regarded the square as his own personal domain, his kingdom, and he wasn't going to let anybody undermine his rule. Nobody was going to be allowed any leeway in that area. It's partly what made him a fearsome, respected full-back. He taught me that in county football you had to be tough to survive. Mentally and physically. I learned a lot from Martin.

Wembley was a fascinating experience in many respects but wasn't suitable for gaelic football and certainly not hurling. It was too short, too tight. We defeated Galway before a crowd of about 35,000 but weekends like we spent in London playing in the magnificent stadium that was Wembley was about far more than winning or losing a game. It was about building the kind of team spirit that would

FLESH & BLOOD SERIES

help us through the storms of later years. Those trips were vital in that regard – and it was our formidable team spirit that was to ensure we had success in subsequent years, I'm sure of that. Success yes, but we had plenty of setbacks too.

IN 1966, THE World Cup finals were staged in England, with the host country defeating Germany in the final at Wembley where we played the previous year. By the time the tournament concluded in July with England winning the Jules Rimet Trophy, Meath had already set out in search of another Leinster Championship.

The quality of the players in our team, the determination to succeed and the momentum that had been carefully built up over the previous two years meant that now we were one of the main contenders for an All-Ireland – even if we had been unceremoniously knocked out of the championship in 1965.

As the summer of 1966 unfolded, however, we built up a head of steam with victories over Westmeath and Wexford. In the Leinster final, we defeated Kildare, setting us up for an All-Ireland semi-final clash with Down – a game I had reason to remember although not always for positive reasons.

Meath supporters were excited at the prospect of another big day out at Croke Park. I was looking forward to it too but in the days leading up to the game I picked up a bug that brought me low. Very low. Whatever kind of a bug it was, it caused havoc in my system. I was as sick as dog, as weak as a kitten. I could hardly walk.

THE DAY BEFORE the game I felt so sick I just didn't think I could play, so I asked the selectors if they would leave me off the field. I didn't feel I was strong enough to start. I wanted them to leave me off and that certainly wouldn't have been my form. If I could play, I wanted to play.

I just didn't feel I could do myself or the team justice the way I was feeling. They talked about it and decided they would put me on anyway and see how I fared out, so I agreed to that, although I wasn't so sure about the decision. I felt bad. One of the Down players was the great Seán O'Neill. He was Down's star man, a brilliant forward capable of shooting down any team he faced – if you let him. I summoned up strength from somewhere, driven by adrenaline.

I think I did okay against O'Neill that day. I had the 'flu sure, and that was bad enough, but to make matters worse another one of Down's great players, Dan McCartan ran into me as I was making one of my forward runs and I picked up a nasty leg injury. Very nasty. Very painful.

My leg swelled up and they had to get the doctor to come into the dressing-room at half-time and have a look at me. A blood vessel had burst in my leg. I could hardly walk but they insisted I should play on, so they put me back out again. So, I struggled on, did my best to help the team win the game but it was a very good overall team display. Memorable.

I didn't get too many injuries in my career, at least in my early years, thankfully, but that was one. Another I picked up was a dislocated shoulder I sustained in a club game early in my career. Walterstown were playing Oldcastle and this player hit me fair and square. He was stronger than me. Normally I would be able to take the hits, it was just part of the game, something that was taken for granted. I could withstand what was thrown at me, give as good as I got, if needed. Not this time. Fr Tully was at the game and he was raging. He ran on to the field and started to berate the player who had hit me. Gave out to him good. 'What do you think you are doing?' he said to him. It was very funny in one respect.

It was just one of those occasions when an opponent got me, maybe a little off guard. It was a heavy hit all right. I would be affected by dislocated shoulders at other times in my career; that day against Oldcastle was probably the source of those problems. I have met that player from time to time in subsequent years and we'd laugh about it.

'I got you that time,' he would say, like he had notched up some notable achievement. 'You certainly did,' I'd say back to him.

There was always the sense that if you were a 'county' man you would be a target. A club man could make a name for himself by taking down the county man a notch or two, especially if he was a big-name player. It was a badge of honour. Considerable kudos could be gained by claiming that you had subdued or man-marked the county man. That you had knocked him out of the equation. That day against Oldcastle I certainly shipped a hefty hit and felt it for a long time after.

THERE ARE DAYS when teams blossom and bloom like a carefully cultivated flower. That All-Ireland semi-final against Down on a fine August was one of those days for us. I might not have felt very well but, we the team, were on fire. Unstoppable. We played reasonably well in the first-half but after the break we really started to find our best form, firing over points from all sorts of distances and angles. The game finished with us winning 2-16 to 1-9. The papers had glowing reports about our performance, no more so than John D Hickey in the *Irish Independent. Never have I found myself so rapt in admiration of a football match* he wrote. *And it was all because of the sheer brilliance of the Meath men whose classical performance after the change of ends must rank with anything else seen, even with magnificent displays of long ago, which old-timers varnish with each passing year.* Praise indeed.

The team looked like it was really starting to become a force. Before a crowd of 44, 462 we really hit the heights against Down – although I certainly found myself in the wars that day. It was another step forward for the team. Another game when the half-back line of Pat Collier, Bertie Cunningham and myself really started to gel and play as a unit. Steady. We were building up an understanding as the first line of defence; a bulwark against the hordes that sought to break through our battlements.

We set about preparing for another big day in Croke Park, the All-Ireland final itself. Fr Tully and Peter McDermott began to focus our minds on our opponents Galway who were going for a three-in-row. At least this time I wasn't affected by illness or undermined by injury.

I felt it could be our day.

You had to believe, always. Fr Tully had some old-world ideas about training and getting a team ready for a big game. He was fond of employing one concept that went way back. In the lead up to the game, maybe a week or two beforehand, he would take the balls off us at training, and put them in his car boot. The idea was we would be 'ball hungry' on big match day.

It's easy to laugh at something like that now, to make fun of it, but that was how other trainers and coaches approached things too. It was a concept that was common in gaelic football, maybe even in other games like soccer. It was probably something that was done on a widespread basis in the 1940s and 50s and continued on. Looking back, we would have been better, of course, working with the ball. Keeping sharp. The world was changing, so was gaelic football and how teams prepared.

FR TULLY WAS old school in other ways. When I played, I liked to bomb forward at every opportunity. I had the pace, the energy. Fr Tully didn't like me going forward and there were others who shared that view. One of the selectors Kevin McConnell, who had played for Meath, used to say to me, 'Stop running forward Reynolds... you're leaving gaps at the back'. Fr Tully shared that view.

He felt I should be staying back, making sure my man didn't cause any problems. It was all about sticking with your man and curtailing his influence, especially if you were a half-back. Football came down to winning the battle with your direct opponent. That was basically what you were expected to do when you took your place on the pitch. Win your personal dual and take it from there. Simple as that.

It was a fundamental law of the game. I had a style that was opposite to that way of thinking. I was always inclined to push up field, explore and exploit the opportunities such forays presented. I didn't like being confined, and that extended to many aspects of my life.

I would push forward on those forays and earn frees. I earned more frees than I think people realised – and that could be a rich source of scores.

Training wasn't arduous with the Meath team, certainly not like it was to become later. What we did would hardly be considered a warm-up in modern football. It consisted of a few laps of Páirc Tailteann, no short work at all. Laps of the park. That's the way it was for many teams but new ideas were changing the game all the time and you had to change with them, otherwise you would be left behind.

It was a pity we didn't do much short, sharp work which of course we needed to make us better. The fact that some of us, probably most of us, worked in jobs that were physically demanding helped to keep us in shape. Terry Kearns, for instance, worked on a farm just like me. We were moving all the time. Lifting, walking... moving. There was no need for a few hours in the gym, not that we had one available to us or that we would want one after a day on the land, chasing cattle or milking or ploughing or saving hay or taking in the harvest.

Then some nights after training we'd have a few pints, unless there was a big game approaching. A few of us would meet up in a local pub, have the craic, the banter. Again, it wouldn't be accepted by any modern county manager but there was no issue with it then, we weren't breaking any rules. Then playing at county level was a lot less intense than it is today – and maybe that wasn't a bad thing.

Smoking too was common among players, although I don't think many players on that Meath team of the 60s smoked. I did and one or two others. I smoked since I was 14. We, as a group of players, were probably unusual in that respect, as just everybody seemed to smoke in those days.

Fr Tully had his own views on how players should prepare and play, but Peter McDermott had his too, different ideas. He was an *ideas* man. He looked at things in a different way. More modern. He had been there, done that. He had played his first game for the Meath seniors in 1940 against Wexford. He had helped Leinster win the Railway Cup in 1945. He then won an All-Ireland with Meath in 1949 and a National League medal when we defeated New York in the Polo Grounds a few years later. He was part of the Meath team that lost to Cavan in the 1952 All-Ireland final after a replay.

Peter became a referee and took charge of the 1953 All-Ireland final. Returned as a player and won an All-Ireland again in '54. Refereed another All-Ireland in 1956. Remarkable. He was someone who had picked up a huge amount of experience and he knew how to impart it to the players. He had worked with the Down team that became such a strong force in gaelic football in the early 60s. That Down team looked at things differently. Took a fresh approach in terms of preparation. They were tremendously fit, and they were innovative in their use of tactics. They played a new brand of football that was very successful.

They sought to use the wings more. They would kick the ball out to the wings to a player out there when most teams would just lob the ball out to midfield and hope for the best. They were doing tactical kicking long before someone like Stephen Cluxton was even born. Imaginative. At that time everyone was focused on *catch and kick* football. That's all you had to do… catch and kick.

Peter could see other ways of doing things. Different. Imaginative. No doubt, He had a big part to play in helping Down become a powerful force in football. He brought that outlook to the Meath camp too from the mid-60s onwards.

Peter told us, in the lead up to the 1966 All-Ireland final, about the dangers Galway posed; he told us about the great players they had. He warned us we needed to be on our game just as we were against Down in the semi-final that year.

His approach was the direct opposite to what Fr Tully wanted me to do. Peter encouraged me to go forward, to turn defence into attack in an instant if I could.

He might have been a little reluctant at first about me leaving my half-forward position but he encouraged it later, he knew what it could bring to the team. It was different, a weapon that could help us. He knew a team needed to do something different to win big games; they needed to utilise ALL the forces at their disposal to win an All-Ireland. He knew his football. He gave me great advice. He would point out some aspect of a player's style; some characteristic of the man I was going to mark. What leg he kicked with, what way he liked to turn with the ball. Little things that can make a big difference. He would talk to us about tactics and strategy, put some structure on our game. We needed that. Anything I wasn't told about a player I was marking I sought to learn myself, especially when the game started. Learn about an opponent so that I could deal with him better.

WE FELT WE were ready for Galway in 1966. We were on a mission to make up for the defeat to them in the 1964 semi-final when we felt we were harshly treated, the victims of an injustice. That disallowed Jack Quinn goal still rankled, even two years later. We should have won that game.

Around that time a funny incident occurred in a game against Galway in one of the big games we played against them. A member of their management team – the legendary John 'Tull' Dunne, who was a well-known mentor and team trainer – came out onto the field to shout at one of his players, I think it was his son Cyril, to stop me surging upfield.

'Stop him!' I heard him say. 'Don't let that little fecker from Meath run up field like that.' He was wearing a hat and suit, but while he was running onto the field his hat, a hard hat, fell off and I drew a kick at it.

The crowd roared. It was very funny at the time more than anything. He wasn't too happy, of course, and yes, I suppose it was disrespectful but I was fired up by that stage. The blood was stirred. The battle had commenced.

We had shown how good we could be when we cast aside Down in the 1966 semi-final. We did it by producing – as John D Hickey had pointed out – some brilliant football. The team was on song. We knew it would be difficult against Galway in the final; the ultimate test but we were as ready as we were ever going to be. That's what we thought. I for one was looking forward to it. After all it wasn't easy to get to an All-Ireland final, and *here* we were.

Now we had to take one more step and we were *there*. The Promised Land.

The big occasions never daunted me, they inspired me, drove me on. It was about winning – and if we played, as we did against Down, we had a real chance. A real chance to beat Galway, the reigning champions.

The morning of the game broke… I go out to do the milking. I complete the task as quickly as I can. Farm work on the day of a game wasn't unusual. Later in my career I might be harvesting, driving a combine all morning. I would have often got off the combine harvester or the tractor and I'd be covered in oil and grease, but I would be wanted for a club game. I'd have to leave it and go directly to the game. The other lads on the team would be waiting in somewhere like Páirc Tailteann to play.

They'd be there with my togs and my boots, and I'd have to rush into the dressing-room as quickly as possible and get ready for the game. That was regular. I would be the last man in.

There was no let-up in the work and you didn't think twice about doing it. You could be combining all day before a game, well into the night, maybe the morning of a big game, although maybe not a Leinster final or All-Ireland semi-final or final. For those, you would need to prepare well. Rest up a bit.

For county games, particularly a big match at Croke Park, more detailed, structured preparations would be required. You'd have to focus on getting your preparations right. Give yourself time to get up to Croke Park and settle a little. Usually before games I got up, left time for breakfast, got to Mass to say a few prayers and hope the Man Above is listening… *on our side today.* I would put my boots in the bag, start to think about the challenge ahead. The same the morning of the 1966 All-Ireland. I started to focus on the men from the west and how we can take them down a notch or two. To dethrone the kings.

I had my corner of the dressing-room where I liked to sit. Once I settled myself in there, I was happy. Some of the lads would be very nervous, unsettled. Sick even. It never bothered me. I could never understand why some players got so worked up; racked with nerves.

Compared to modern football our preparations in those years were basic, to say the least. Basic in so many respects. No comparison. The preparations, or lack of preparations, extended to our diet too. Early in my Meath career I'd have toast and scrambled egg before games but, in time, I felt I needed something else. I spoke about it with Jack Quinn, our full-back. I told him how I was getting tired towards the end of games. That I had little or no energy.

'I don't know where I am. I feel my energy is gone. I feel dizzy and I'm getting destroyed in the last 10 minutes of games,' I said to Jack.

I had heard that meat before a game was a good thing, that it provided energy. It made sense to me so I started to have a steak before games... a big steak. That made a huge difference. Suddenly I felt like I could run a marathon, dismantle a mountain. I felt strong in myself right to the end of games. Again, it was about finding out things for yourself. Looking at ways you could be better. There was nobody in the background guiding you. You just had to use your own initiative.

Hydration was another thing we didn't do enough of because not much was known about its value in terms of conditioning. You might have a drink of water during a game if a player was getting treatment – but there was no consumption of vast amounts before games to ensure you performed at your best. The lack of proper hydration didn't thwart us either in terms of fulfilling our potential, or maybe it did, but then it's doubtful many footballers were focused on taking on board vast volumes of water back then. Everyone was the same.

You drank water when you were thirsty, that was basically it.

Some players might have liked to have a couple of pints the night before games – big games, Leinster finals, All-Ireland finals. Just one or two to relax them. That was one thing I wouldn't do. I didn't need a pint to help me sleep before a match. I slept like a baby.

No problem. I would have a few drinks after training regularly but not in the build-up to a Meath championship game, especially a big game.

The science wasn't available to us in terms of telling us how alcohol could undermine our individual performances. I just felt myself I could play better, have that little extra edge, if I didn't have any drink in the build-up to a big game – and finding an extra edge was what it was about. You would just go by what your body told you. Your body is your best doctor. I went with that. Trusted it.

Motivation was never a problem for me. The pursuit of victory was usually enough to get me going. I hated the sickening sense of having missed an opportunity. Before one big game that year, the Leinster final against Kildare, I recall being close to two other guys, supporters of the Lilywhites. They clearly didn't know I was near them, or didn't know me, but they were talking about Meath and I could hear them.

'That Pat Reynolds... he's only a small fella, isn't he?' one said.

That's all I needed to hear. Straightaway.

BANG. That fired me up even more than I already was. I said to myself, *We'll see about that when the game gets underway.* I went out and didn't give my opponent a kick that day. Fired up I was. That's what worked for me.

IT WAS THE same for me in life, in just about everything I did. When it came to farming, I looked on doing a difficult task as a challenge to be met head on. Overcome. It was the same when I was marking a talented player who was hard to pin down, and there were plenty of good players around difficult to contain.

I would think about what needed to be done early in a game. I would change my approach if I felt I needed to in order to curtail my opponent. I would never allow myself to be cowed down or defeated by anyone. I marked players who gave me plenty of problems – I didn't always tie them up as much as I would liked to have – but I never stopped trying. We didn't have DVDs to study opponents before a match.

I would assess the situation in the opening minutes of the game, evaluate what an opponent was like and adapt in whatever way was needed to play him, try to diminish his influence. I learned to do that in order to survive and hopefully prosper at the highest level. It worked for me too.

Those who are good at sport are often very successful whatever business they are involved in. There is a connection between the two – and that's not by accident. In both cases it comes down to determination, tenacity, keeping focused on the job in hand. You have to decide nothing is going to divert you from fulfilling your ambition, your vision. There is an intelligence too demanded when playing football.

A player has to think on his or her feet. It's the same in business. You have to think quickly, adapt to situations as they arise and, of course, every day some issue or other will need to be sorted out, decisions made.

Yet sometimes things didn't go my way, no matter how hard I tried; how much I sought to adapt or how much you might have thought about things. The 1966 All-Ireland final was one of those occasions.

THE BIG WIN over Down in the semi-final was possibly the worst thing that could have happened to us. It created expectations. Maybe created the idea in our minds that we were better than we actually were. We certainly had plenty of reasons not to be complacent. Galway were All-Ireland champions and we knew from the 1964 semi-final how good they were; how they could ransack a team's ambitions in an instant, kill your hopes in the flicker of an eyelash. Yet, we failed to perform. Maybe it was nerves? Maybe we didn't get our approach, our preparations, right? Not that there was much focus on tactics – and our preparations were pretty basic.

The tactics were the usual stuff; put the big man in on the edge of the square and launch the ball towards him. Catch and kick. Stay in your zone. Beat your man and get the ball downfield. Any team that had a player with pace was at a big advantage but all too often that pace wasn't utilised because players were told to stay in their positions.

Mind your zone. Mind the house.

I always tried to move away from that in the sense that when I got the ball, I tried to run forward with it. It put the team on the front foot; we were at least moving in the right direction.

Back closer to home all the talk and press speculation leading up to the final was about Martin Quinn and whether he would play in the final or not. He was one of our strongest performers, a real leader, a regular since the late 1950s. In the 1965 Meath senior county final, he was playing for his club Kilbride against Skryne and he became the central figure in one of the most controversial incidents of the time; an incident that was talked about for years afterwards... still is talked about.

Disgusted at a free given against him in that final, he sat on the ball in protest and refused to get up. The incident escalated and the referee sent Martin off but he continued to sit on the ball, even after he was told to leave the field. He was suspended for 12 months. The suspension ended at midnight the day before the 1966 All-Ireland final. He had been our regular full-back before the suspension, a strong and sturdy presence at the edge of the square.

His brother Jack filled in at full-back and he too was a first-rate defender, superb at fielding high balls that landed in our square like missiles. He was a brilliant midfielder too but had to vacate that position to fill in at full-back.

In terms of preparing for the 1966 All-Ireland I didn't do things any differently to any other game. Nothing special. There would be no such thing as taking the Saturday off, the day before, in order to rest, conserve energy. No way. There was no let-up in the work and you didn't think twice about doing it. That was the priority. The work. The farm. It would have been no different in 1966.

Martin Quinn didn't start the final that day and he came on as a late substitute, but by then Galway were already well on the road to victory, a deserved victory too. Would he have made the difference if he had started? We'll never know. We never got going in the first-half in that final, struggled to deal with Galway's guile and know-how. We performed like we were wearing concrete boots.

Maybe we were distracted by the occasion. The huge crowd, people overflowing onto the sideline, the atmosphere? Maybe we focused more on the occasion rather than the game itself? Got distracted. Ambushed.

Galway ran out winners. They completed the three-in-row. Deserved it too. What an achievement. They were at the height of their powers.

We had a few drinks that night, tried to dampen down the disappointment. It was impossible to do that. I would be replaying aspects of the game in my mind. Analysing, trying to pinpoint how we went wrong. That was always the way when we lost. Searching for answers.

As usual, I would spend days at that. Defeat was the bitterest of pills to swallow.

We returned to Navan the next day. People poured into the town that evening to welcome us back. The expectation, the hope was we would return with the Sam Maguire Cup. It was annoying that we didn't. The crowd cheered us but we could have done without that reception. We felt we'd let the supporters down. Badly.

Red Collier stepped forward and told the people in a little speech he made that we would be back the next year. He knew we hurt badly and he spoke for all of us when he said that we would be back. The grand purpose was already forming in our minds – to get back to the final and this time bring back Sam.

When you have a goal, a purpose, you automatically have the fuel, the momentum to drive you on. We were like that in 1967.

We stored away the hurt and used it to drive us on.

We had a powerful reason to push on and achieve something – and when a group of people have that it can be very hard to derail them.

They're like a force of nature.

VII

1967

Cork
Paddy Mulvany
Kearns' Fist

The Aussies
1995
John McDermott
'King of the Trenches'

★★★

PAT

WE WENT THROUGH the 1966/67 league campaign and reached the semi-final where we lost to Dublin. The Dubs still remained the main obstacle for us in Leinster. They were clearly still the team to beat.

As spring gave way to summer, we cranked up our preparations. With the memories of our defeat in 1966 seared into our consciousness we didn't need much revving up for the championship. Seldom can a team have been as motivated as we were when we kicked-started our Leinster Championship campaign in 1967.

We defeated Louth, and then Westmeath, and beat Offaly in the Leinster final by two points, and Mayo in the All-Ireland semi-final by two clear goals.

There had been a lot of talk about the Mayo player who would be my direct opponent in that semi-final. Talk about how good he was. How he could cause me real problems, run me ragged. Again, that was all I needed to hear. That was enough to provide the spark, stoke up the engine. That was all the motivation I needed to concentrate the mind.

In the opening minutes of the All-Ireland semi-final, I studied my opponent carefully, gauged what his strengths were, what his weaknesses were early in the game. The opening stages of any match are important in that respect. You did your job, but you analysed your opponent too. I didn't give him much ball. I had a good day at the office... and the team had a good day at the office. We sailed home. Another victory.

WE'D BOOKED OUR place in another All-Ireland final. This time, Cork. Another big assignment for us. Not that I was hyped up more than I would be for any other Meath game. I was young and to me an All-Ireland final was the same as any other game. I didn't get any more worked up about it than, say, a Leinster Championship game. Kept things calm. Nothing unusual.

It was like that in 1966, it was the same a year later.

I didn't bother too much with the hype leading up to the game. I didn't become obsessed with thinking about the game… what I had to do! There was still plenty of work on the farm to distract me. There were plenty of things happening in the wider world too in the days leading up to the final. There were fears of a new war in the Middle East. In Rome there were reports of how the Pope asked 40,000 people who attended his Mass in St Peter's Square to pray for peace in Vietnam where the war was raging. Sure, I had an All-Ireland final to play in but I didn't become obsessed about it.

The world kept turning.

Of course, what was unusual about the day of the 1967 final was how I was attacked by the bull that morning. It was my second All-Ireland but I nearly didn't make it. Very nearly, only for Sparky saved me. The trusty old dog saved my life. It was amazing how he diverted the bull's attention by tugging at his tail that day and giving me a chance to get away; to escape the bull's raging, out of control anger.

I was still at the foothills of my county career and had already faced some hardy, gritty, formidable opponents. I had got the better of many of them but I had no answer to the power of the bull that bright September morning. That was one contest that could only end with one result – if the struggle had continued.

Only for Sparky, I was gone.

I have thought of that morning many times down the years. Thought how things could have turned out so different. How fortunate I was. I escaped a brush with death and got up to Croker for the game. The incident with the bull didn't do me any good in terms of preparing for the game. I was still bothered by what had happened as the day wore on, although I tried to make light of it with the lads, to laugh it off. I was still suffering from shock, and wanted to talk about the incident. They, naturally, found it hilarious, but I was certainly shook up a bit. *Shaken and stirred.*

We were a team who often didn't perform all that well in the first-half in games. For some reason it took us an age to get going. It was the case in the 1966 final and we paid a very high price for it. It was also the case in the 1967 showdown against Cork. We were like workhorses trying to get moving.

It was only after half-time we found our form, or at least started to play to somewhere near our best. When the man I was marking Eric Philpott scored the first two scores of the game I knew I had to knuckle down. Focus. He escaped my clutches to fire over an early point and shortly afterwards added another from a free. Cork were better than us. It looked, for a time, like we might be the only team in history not to get a score in an All-Ireland final. We just couldn't convert our chances in that opening half. Yes, we did get to grips with the game, eventually, but the dramatic events of that morning when my life was momentarily threatened couldn't be shaken or forgotten about as easily as I had hoped. I didn't feel right early in the game, couldn't find a foothold until the second-half.

My shaky performance early on mirrored that of the team's, but at least Paddy Mulvany's point late in the first-half gave us something to build on. At the break Cork led 0-4 to 0-1. When, eight minutes into the second-half, Terry Kearns got to the end of Mattie Kerrigan's long punt toward the Cork posts and fisted the ball over the head of the advancing Billy Morgan and into the net, it was a score that underlined how one moment can make a big difference.

We knew then we were on our way. That we had a chance. We hadn't played well but the goal helped us to go in front, and that's where we stayed.

Some people regard Red Collier's tackle on one of Cork's best players, Mick Burke in the second-half, as a turning point but I think we were starting to assert ourselves more by that stage. Burke had to go off injured but he had picked up an injury to his shoulder in the opening half and that diminished his influence too. He was one of Cork's best players and Red's crunching tackle meant he was no longer a threat.

When the Red tackled, you knew all about it. The management had also shown imagination by playing Ollie Shanley as a third midfielder. That was something different and it worked. Ollie had great pace as he showed in that game.

No doubt the memory of the previous year and the deep disappointment of defeat flashed through the Meath players' minds during that game. It did mine. Drove me on. Once in front we were determined to hold onto the lead. When the final whistle sounded, we led 1-9 to 0-9. We were champions!

At last! That final whistle was the signal for an invasion onto the pitch of joyful, delighted Meath supporters. We were submerged in an avalanche of delight. We hadn't won an All-Ireland since 1954 and here we are at the top of the mountain again. In the video of the game, you can see me sitting at the edge of the podium while Peter Darby was accepting the Sam Maguire, that trophy hadn't been back in Meath for so long.

I sit and look back out at the hundreds of Meath supporters that had converged under the stand. The Croke Park pitch was covered in a sea of faces swaying over and back; the guards unable to hold back the surge of joyful supporters. I look like I could do with a drink of water. I already had quite a day.

On the Sunday night there was a reception for the team at the Malahide Grand Hotel. The next day there was a viewing of the game at another reception, something that was part of the All-Ireland weekend. Both teams watched it, painful viewing for Cork, grand for us. Then it was back to the Royal County.

It was estimated something between 20,000 and 30,000 turned out to see us in the various places we passed through on our triumphant return to the county. We were like conquering heroes returning home with the booty. Like Roman soldiers after a famous victory in a foreign land.

Through Clonee, Dunboyne, Dunshaughlin, Drumree and Trim the team passed, this time with the Sam Maguire. We got back to Navan late that night. There waiting for us were several thousand people. Thousands.

There was a party mood. They had waited a long time in every respect. It was wonderful to have Sam with us this time. So different to the previous year. This time around we had made our supporters, our people, our tribe, proud.

Bonfires lit up the landscape in places; the bright flames lapping into the darkness of night – and hopefully the win lit up people's lives too. By the way they cheered us as we made our way back home it certainly appeared that we had brought some joy into their lives; something for them to cherish and talk about. Something to never forget.

We were representing our people and it was very fulfilling to know we had done them proud. That was more fulfilling than just winning a medal. There were pints too consumed, in local pubs, a meal in Navan that Monday night. Lots of back clapping, hand-shaking. The celebrations continued during the week. The cup was brought around to pubs in the traditional manner. Schools too. It was easy to forget we had a game the following Sunday… a World Cup final no less. And after all the euphoria attached to our All-Ireland triumph, I was brought back down to earth with all the ease of a blow from a sledgehammer.

THE 'WORLD CUP' was a competition that was thought up by the GAA, with the winners of the All-Ireland football title taking on a team from New York at Croke Park. It wasn't a competition that was to endure but they tried it that year and a crowd of 10,560 turned up to witness this unique occasion. But it didn't turn out too well for me. I was lucky in my career that I didn't get too many injuries but that day I did feel the full force of an opponent's fist. I was knocked out completely. Cold.

I was at the receiving end of a punch that Joe Frazier would have been proud of… BANG! I didn't see the blow coming, the fist banging into the side of my head like a demolition ball crashing against a building. I was completely concussed. When I went into the dressing-room at half-time I didn't know where I was – and just how bad a condition I was in could be seen in what I did next.

I started to put my clothes on me.

'Where are you going?' Fr Tully said to me.

'I'm going home, the game is over!' I replied.

'No, it's only half-time,' he answered. I can remember that exchange alright. They threw water on me, the old douse of water was the cure for all ills. I shook my head to try and get come clarity.

'Go out… you'll be grand!' somebody said, but I wasn't good at all. I didn't feel good but I thought I might be able to run it off.

Unless you were completely unconscious you were expected back then to make some kind of effort for your team. I was lucky I didn't collapse or suffer long-term effects because I didn't have any recollection of the second-half. Still don't. The rest of the game is wiped from my memory bank. It was shocking.

Instead of going out for the second-half I should have gone to hospital, that's how bad I was. Instead, I struggled on.

It was only some time later I realised we won the game. That it all sunk in. Apparently, the referee John Moloney from Tipperary had to be escorted off the pitch. Meath supporters wanted to confront him about what had happened to me. They were raging about the way I had been struck and nothing much had been done about it. I learned all this later.

I didn't feel right during the next week. Groggy. Sick at times. Again, I probably should have gone to hospital to be checked out. If it was today, no way would I have been allowed to play on against New York.

I rested up a little and I gradually got better. Thankfully, it was the only time something like that happened to me in my career, something as serious as that, but it was some comedown from the high of the previous week when we had won the All-Ireland. A sharp descent from the stars.

Yet we were world champions! We would have joked about that. We might have won the game but my one and only World Cup final certainly turned out to be a forgettable occasion, at least for me.

I don't know if we were even awarded a trophy for all our troubles.

WE CERTAINLY DIDN'T get much chance to sit back and savour what we had achieved. We were in demand. Box office.

Shortly after the World Cup game, we played my father's county Louth in the opening round of the National League and hammered them, 1-13 to 0-3. The red shirts of Louth seemed to inspire me, maybe because it was my father's team. He would have had mixed feelings about that result even if it did go well for me. *Pat Reynolds returned to his best form* reported the *Chronicle*.

I'm not sure what my father would have made of all that. He never really said anything about my performances. I don't think he congratulated me after winning the All-Ireland. He didn't shower me with praise, tell me I was good, bad or brilliant. He wasn't like that, it just didn't happen. I'm sure he was quietly pleased; quietly proud, but he wasn't a man for giving expression to his inner emotions – but then, I suppose he wasn't the only one.

I don't think I ever told *my* son Paddy he was brilliant either, after he won the All-Ireland with Meath. Maybe that's just the way it is between fathers and sons. I would agree that yes, it's good to express those emotions, to tell someone close to you what you think about them and their achievements – it just wasn't my father's way. Did winning an All-Ireland make a difference to my working life? Absolutely it did, a massive difference. People knew you, there were no introductions needed when you were trying to make arrangements with people to, say, supply a consignment of potatoes. When it came to renting land, people knew you. It was a big help to be known, but you have to make use of all that.

As the years went on, it proved to be a massive help.

In the aftermath of our All-Ireland success, we also played Cavan in the Grounds Tournament, a competition that involved the four teams that had reached the All-Ireland semi-finals that year. We played the Breffni boys before 22,680 at Croke Park. Drew with them too in a brilliant, fast-flowing game.

We had other parts on our busy schedule to fulfil – and one of those games would have long-reaching consequences. We were asked to take on this group of Australian footballers in an exhibition game. We were intrigued by the prospect. This was different, a whole new challenge. They were on a world tour and were looking for a game so why not take on the All-Ireland champions seems to have been the thinking.

The game was the idea of an Australian entrepreneur Harry Beitzel, who had seen some Irish people playing gaelic football in his own country. He felt it was very similar to Australian football; he felt there could be some kind of compromise found between the two codes and so this enterprising Aussie set about organising some games. So, in the Autumn of 1967 the Galahs – named after an exotic bird – landed in Ireland. As All-Ireland champions we were due to play them in Croke Park in a kind of exhibition game. We would use some aspects of our game such as the round ball; they would use some features of theirs. They were allowed to pick up the ball straight off the ground.

They had played a warm up game against the Civil Service, and Peter McDermott watched them. He thought they were hopeless. 'Go easy on them!' he told us before we played them the following week in Croke Park.

They destroyed us; they were excellent footballers as it turned out. Maybe they were still jet lagged in the opening game. They certainly weren't when they played us a week later. We underestimated them and got caught. Before 22,000 spectators they defeated us, comfortably. *Australians shatter Meath* ran the headline in the *Chronicle*. That summed things up perfectly.

What that game did do was establish a solid connection between the Australians and ourselves, and soon there was talk of us going to Australia the next year for a tour. We didn't take much notice at first. I wondered if something as radical as that would happen but gradually it became a reality.

Driven by people like Peter McDermott and county board secretary Cyril Creavin, the idea developed legs. Money was an issue but all sorts of projects were set up to generate the finance required. There were dances, Church gate collections. The fact that we were All-Ireland champions was no doubt a help too in encouraging Meath supporters to contribute.

Somehow the money was found. The finishing touches were put on organising the trip and Saturday, March 2, 1968 was pencilled in as the departure date.

THE DAY FINALLY dawned for our departure and we made our way to Dublin airport. The travelling party of 52 included 27 players and officials. Also included were supporters who were paying their own fare. The cost of the fare was about £700 which has been estimated at about €10,000 in modern terms.

It was difficult not to be excited about the whole thing in the days and weeks leading up to our departure. Plenty of Irish people made their way to Australia in the 1960s but they rarely returned home – if at all. They would have had to work hard to make up the fare in an era when there wasn't much spare money around. Here we were about to be brought there, all expenses paid. We knew we were fortunate. Very fortunate.

No gaelic football team had embarked on such a trip before.

We truly were pioneers.

★★★

PADDY

THERE'S NO POINT in thinking about something too much, certainly not in a negative way. Over-thinking. That applies to football – and life.

Throughout my career I knew myself when I wasn't going well as a player. I knew too when I was going well. Nobody knew that better than myself. No player knows that better than him or herself. You have to try and look at the situation, and decide what you are going to do. Make a change if a change needs to be made. Tweak the training regime or adjust some other aspect of your preparation, of your game.

After Meath suffered that heavy defeat to Dublin in 1995 my father had suggested that there was going to be a clear out on the Meath team. That Boylan wanted to reset, build a new team. It was a chance for any young player to stake a claim. I liked the college I was attending in Chelmsford, enjoyed the course. I was learning about the science of farming but I found myself with a choice to make. *Did I want to continue my studies or did I want to play county football, senior football with Meath?*

'Now is your chance. If you go back to England and someone else gets your place, you may not get in again,' my father said. I could see the logic of that argument. It made sense.

During Christmas of 1995 I had to decide. *Would I stay? Would I go?* Boylan rang me around the festive season. 'Will you be going back to England?' he asked. He wanted to know what I was doing because he asked me to join the panel. I thought about it but I knew pretty quickly, in my gut, that I wouldn't go back. The chance was there to get a place on the Meath senior panel. It was a big attraction.

Could I relinquish that opportunity and hope I would get a chance another time? I knew I hadn't done much training, certainly not the kind needed to thrive at county level. I had a hernia operation in '95 but much of that year was spent in England. I hadn't done a great deal of training but Boylan clearly felt I could make up for lost time. I was only 19 after all. *What to do?* I was standing at a crossroads. One of those crossroads we all find ourselves at in life from time to time and the road we take can have a big impact on our lives.

I weighed everything up – and came to a decision. I knew what I was going to do. I rang Boylan back.

'I'm staying Seán, I'm not going back to England!' I said.

'That's fine Paddy, if you're happy with that, I think we can do very well in '96,' he replied.

As people rang in the new year and made ambitious resolutions, I wondered what the months ahead might bring. I was taking a gamble but deep down, in my gut, I felt I was doing the right thing. It was onwards and hopefully upwards with Meath. It was time to step into the unknown.

THERE WAS A lot going on in the early months of 1996 in sport and the broader world. Changes too. Mick McCarthy was appointed to replace Jack

Charlton as manager of the Irish soccer team. It was truly the end of an era. The start of another. The Troubles rumbled with bombs going off in London, including a massive explosion in the Docklands area that certainly grabbed the headlines. In Dublin there were marches demanding peace with thousands taking part. The hope was that all the stakeholders would get together and start talking again – but the prospects of peace didn't look too promising.

I had grown up listening to the radio, watching TV and hearing about bombs, killings, trouble in the North. It was all very dispiriting stuff. It was part of our culture but moves were being made to try and change all that; to bring lasting peace. The prospect of peace was appealing. In music, bands like The Corrs and Oasis were flying. Superstars.

There was a huge controversy too in early 1996 when Irish rugby prop Peter Clohessy was sighted for stamping on a French player Olivier Roumat during a Five Nations game in Paris. Ireland didn't have a good team then but I would watch them play. They had great players, like Simon Geoghegan, but struggled to win any games. It was a time of famine for Irish rugby.

Dublin were All-Ireland champions but playing in Division 2 of the National Football League and they didn't have it all their own way there either over the late months of '95 and on into '96. In one game they lost to Louth. Their emerging star was Jayo... Jason Sherlock. The media loved him and he was a good player for them, quick, difficult to mark. It was cold too in February of 1996. There was a bite in the frosty air as I headed up to Derry for a National League game. Except that this wasn't any old NFL game – at least not as far as I was concerned. I was selected to start. I was about to make my league debut. For a young player like me it was a big deal although I wasn't burdened down by nerves. I knew if I kept focused on what I had to do, I would be all right.

We travelled up to Derry for the game but it nearly didn't take place. A blanket of snow had covered the ground and for a few hours before the game people were out clearing snow off the surface with the help of a tractor. Then there was a further wait as the ground was inspected by the referee, a certain Pat McEnaney from the fair county of Monaghan, who we would encounter later in the year.

I lined out at left-half-back along with Graham Geraghty and John Brady. Behind us was the full-back line of Martin O'Connell, Darren Fay and Cormac Murphy. We had a strong team but we lost, 1-8 to 1-11, our captain Tommy

Dowd getting the goal. I marked Dermot McNicholl, an All Star who had been in Australia. Derry had a certain Joe Brolly playing who scored five points. They were a good team and went on to win the NFL title too.

In the days before the game, the team was picked and I remember looking at the two teams and talking to my father. 'Jaysus, I'll be probably marking this McNicholl fella, he has a big reputation, played in Australia'.

'Ah, sure he's finished!' my father said. 'You'll have no bother marking him, he's well past it!' And to be fair, I kept a very close watch on him that day. He didn't do much. I think my father was using a bit of psychology on me and that kind of thing would have helped. Those words would have been swirling around in my sub-conscious… *You'll have no bother marking him.*

My father knew how important it was going into a game not to be bowed down with this sense that you were somehow taking on this gaelic football colossus who had been in Australia. He was a good player, very good, but he probably was approaching the end of his career anyway but that also meant he was experienced and very physically strong. I had to be alert. It was a solid enough start to my county career up there in the cold and snow of Derry. I was on my way. The same weekend over 10,000 people in Meath went on marches in various places around the county calling for peace in the North. The people hankered after peace. In the league, we pushed on but were defeated in the quarter-final by Mayo, old friends we were to meet later on in the year.

The spring gave way to summer; the summer of 1996. The days got longer, warmer. Suddenly it was time for the championship. Meath were due to play Carlow in the opening round and Seán Boylan created quite a stir by including a raft of young players, new to the senior scene, including myself. This was radical; a bold statement of his belief in the players he was bringing in. Seán was rolling the dice.

THE GAME WAS at Croke Park but I didn't feel daunted in the least. I had already played an All-Ireland minor final there, in the Big House in 1993 as the curtain-raiser to the senior showdown. Okay, we had lost that final, but I had gained valuable experience on that journey; I knew what playing on the big stage was about.

Some people were saying Carlow could beat us in 1996; push aside the callow young Meath lads. That we were innocents abroad. There were a few players from the Meath panel from previous years who said they weren't going up to the game. They said they were going to play golf that day instead because they felt Meath hadn't a chance; they didn't want to witness a massacre. I won't reveal who they were so as not to embarrass them! Yet there was a serious side to it because that attitude represented what many others felt in the county; that was the general mood. A team with a group of inexperienced young lads at the heart of it looked vulnerable. This time, it was felt Boylan had gone too far. What was he thinking putting out a batch of newcomers, as green as hell?

Imprinted on my mind is the image of the ball being thrown in that day to start the game. Our midfielder John McDermott went to tap the ball down. I went ripping in for the break. I got the ball but in the process I collided with a Carlow player. He fell awkwardly and had to be brought off. Unfortunately, it turned out he broke his leg. Pure accident. The ball was there to be won. I was thinking nothing else but *Ball is there, I have to win it*. I didn't even know what had happened at first. It all unfolded so quickly. We moved the ball up the field, scored a point. I looked around. Then I see this Carlow player lying on the ground.

That episode too underlined just how the dice can roll. I could have been the one that shipped a nasty blow, that ended up breaking my leg. I could have been the one to have had my senior championship career terminated before it had got underway in earnest. That day we had started the game with so many doubting us. We ended up winning, 0-24 to 0-6. Even I scored a point and I didn't get too many of those for Meath. We were on our way.

We kept going, building momentum; fostering belief. We defeated Laois in the second round, but the intensity didn't really start to build until we played Dublin in the Leinster final. People began to sit up and believe we could really do something. Before a crowd of just over 55,000 we beat them, 0-10 to 0-8. It was no classic, the day was wet and dreary but the old stadium rocked. It was very like 1986 in so many ways, another wet day with Meath the outsiders looking to take down the big guns. Looking to win a Leinster crown again, our first since 1991.

As in 1986, Dublin were the big target for us, the team to beat, the yardstick. They were All-Ireland champions, had players such as Charlie Redmond, Paul Curran, John O'Leary and, of course, Jayo, the darling of the Hill. There was also on the Dublin half-forward line a certain chap by the name of Jim Gavin who went on to do a few things as a manager! He wasn't the tallest of players but he was driven, strong, fast. You had to be on full alert when players like that were around. Tuned in.

Dublin were a formidable force, so to beat them in that Leinster showdown was a real injection of confidence for us. We knew we were on the right path; making real progress. You talk about luck. We had another large slice of it towards the end of the game. Dublin had a real chance for a goal but the ball rolled across the goal-line. Somehow stayed out. We made it through, by those two points.

THE SUMMER OF 1996 was an eventful time on the broader sporting front. There was the Atlanta Olympics and Michelle Smith winning gold medals for fun in swimming. Sonia O'Sullivan and how it all went wrong for her in the 5,000m, the sad sight of her struggling to finish her race, covered in sweat. That was a high-profile example of how it could all go so wrong in sport; how months, years of preparation could disintegrate on a bad day when the gremlins got to work.

In sport you had to be ready for all eventualities. The important thing was, as a team, to control what we ourselves could control. We were no Olympians but we knew plenty about running ourselves as we had spent many evenings running up and down the Hill of Tara, just like Meath teams of a decade earlier had done. It was gut-wrenching stuff but it helped to fuel our self-belief that we could match anyone; grapple with the most awkward, most difficult opponents. It was the kind of thing that only those who were fully committed to the cause would put themselves through.

Self-belief is much talked about in sporting terms. How teams need it to succeed but where does it come from? How does a team foster that self-belief? Some of it will be generated by the players' own faith in their abilities. Much of it is, I believe, hard earned. Through the slog of training. Knowing you have the work done gives belief.

As he had done previously Boylan was, in 1996, once again using all his experience, his considerable know-how to build a team, create a new project – and sprinting up and down the hills and hollows of Tara did generate a strong camaraderie among the players. It was like being in the great project together. Martin O'Connell and Colm Coyle were two of the older players in the group but they were very good at climbing up the Hill, they had the stamina in them from previous years, they were undaunted by the challenge that faced them... evening after evening.

They showed the way. Set the tone. Leaders. The harder, more demanding it was the better they seemed to like it, especially the short steep part of the Hill. 'Bring it on' they seemed to be saying. 'If we're able for it, you should be too.' Coyler used to call himself the King of the Mountains! Which he was in fairness. There would be plenty of banter about that.

Boylan brought us to a point that we knew we were as fit if not fitter than anybody else out there. In the heat of battle that infuses any group of players with tremendous confidence. Knowing that we had been to hell and back. We were ready for anything that came our way.

The fearsome fitness regime was one aspect of our preparations. We had Brian Smyth working with us, too, as I've said, on the psychology aspects. He focused all the time on the positives and what we can do instead of can't do. Visualisation. That too gave us a very sound platform. He was crucial to the success of the '96 project. Crucial.

Seán was good at that mind-building too, it was one of his biggest strengths, the way he would give a player self-belief. He and Brian would work together. We might do a session for an hour once a week. We would sit down and talk about how we needed to fortify our minds for the battle ahead.

Brian taught us, for instance, how we should react to setbacks by telling ourselves *We can put this right. We can do it by trusting ourselves, trusting the hard work we had done, by trusting our own abilities. Each of us.* We could have crumbled when it all started to go wrong for us, we could have collapsed. We didn't, but then he was working on young minds mainly who were very receptive to all this kind of thing; who knew it was part of a modern game and were willing to buy into all that, especially those lads fresh into the team. Get the body and mind right. Do that and you were onto something big. We knew that was the way to success.

It was amazing too how the thinking of some of the players changed during the championship. Certainly, mine did. My attitude towards preparation. The early rounds of the championship it was about winning but having the craic too. We beat Carlow, then Laois. Suddenly we had to face Dublin. This was serious. After the Laois game and about a week before we faced Dublin a group of friends, including a few players from the Meath set-up, went to a race meeting. We had a good skinful of drink. We let it rip but afterwards the realisation dawned that facing a team like Dublin, our preparations had to be right. This was the real deal now, big time stuff and we had to be serious in how we approached each game, especially a game that involved facing Dublin in a Leinster final.

So there was no more of that, no more days spent at race meetings knocking back the pints. We could still have a laugh but without going too mad. We would, for instance, meet up on the day AFTER a game. Six or seven of us and have a few drinks and reflect back on the events of the day before – but we realised we had to prepare properly for games if we wanted to be serious players. We had to be disciplined, make sacrifices if we wanted to be successful. That was one of the valuable lessons we learned early on.

It was about reaching and sustaining a high level of fitness. Playing to a high level just wasn't compatible with the high life, no matter what age you were; no matter how fit you were. The science had moved on. Sport, including the GAA, was changing fast in the 1990s. Players' preparations were a world away from even a few years previously and a long way away from what it was to become in the 2000s, but it was changing. Rapidly. It was becoming more about diet, hydration. The importance of all that. It was about finding an extra edge.

Diet was an aspect, but not a major aspect of our preparations. You would eat normally. My mother's home-cooking contained a lot of vegetables, good honest-to-goodness country cooking so it was like being on one of those high-powered diets athletes swear by. Good stuff.

VIII

Down Under
'White Midgets'
MCG
Vietnam
GIs
1996
Tyrone's Cries
The Joe Duffy Show

★★★

PAT

THE THUNDER AND lightning storm raged with dramatic effect as we approached landing in Perth. As the plane ploughed through the dark clouds the sky seemed to be consumed by angry flashes of lightning.

The plane rocked and rolled as it made its way through the storm. It was not the place to be for anybody who was squeamish about travelling by plane. No doubt a few rosaries were quietly said. Not that many of us had much experience of flying to draw on.

For some of us, it was the first time to be on a plane.

We knew about some aspects of life in that new world, Australia. We knew about the heat, the kangaroos… but really our knowledge was limited. That reality was forcefully brought home to us as the trip unfolded. Some of the travelling troupe might have read up more about Australia than others, but in an era before travel programmes on TV we had to rely on what we were told – and many of us weren't prepared for some of the sights and sounds that awaited us.

At least I wasn't.

WHEN WE DEPARTED Dublin on an early March morning, we were truly setting out on an adventure into the unknown – in just about every respect.

The trip was for close on two weeks, during which we would play five games against various Australian teams. Rome was our first stop-off point on our trek

Down Under, and I picked up a bug that caused a riot in my system. Food poisoning maybe but whatever it was it really made me sick.

While in Rome we also saw the Pope, albeit from a distance. We continued on our journey with brief stops at Istanbul, Bahrain and Calcutta where we witnessed disabled children begging in what was a very basic airport terminal. Onward we went in the Australian Quantas 707 to Singapore, where we were scheduled to stay for 24 hours.

Before we got off the plane Fr Tully warned us to be careful. He reminded us we were not in Navan now, that we were in a different world – and how right he was.

'On no account do you go out on your own!' he warned us.

'This is one of the most corrupt cities in the world.' That statement ensured we were all going to go out and explore the city as much as we could.

One guy approached us and offered us 'girls'. To a group of young men brought up in Catholic Ireland that certainly was something new. In his book *Australia 1968 Football Immortals* Jim Gammons, who travelled with us reporting on the trip for Irish newspapers, tells the story of how in a department store Fr Tully was approached by a Chinese salesman and asked, 'You like something nice for your wife?'

We would have laughed at that one, but much of what we saw in Singapore was anything but funny.

In fact, it was shocking. Deeply shocking. For years afterwards I regularly recalled the sights, the sounds and the smells we encountered in Singapore. Still do. We had our economic difficulties back in Ireland but there was nothing like the poverty we saw in that part of the world. People literally with nothing, just walking about. Thousands of people.

There was unimaginable poverty that would melt the heart. I just couldn't get my head around the fact that there was such poverty, that people were engaged in such a struggle to survive. Nothing had prepared us for the sights we saw. I couldn't believe it, that was the biggest shock I got.

The images were seared into my memory like furrows in a ploughed field and they have stayed with me throughout my life.

It was all in very sharp contrast to the luxury hotel we stayed in; another reminder of just how fortunate we were. A reminder of the great divide in the world between those who have and those who have not. We departed Singapore carrying in our minds all we had seen. It was onwards to Australia.

The thunder and lightning storm that greeted us as we approached Perth was another experience that was hard to erase from the mind. Some of our travelling party were more than a little shaken and stirred by the whole experience as the plane rolled over and back, but we got through it.

The storm, the nasty turbulence was all in sharp contrast to the warm welcome, in every respect, we got in Perth. It was a beautiful city, a new city. Neat, tidy. At the airport a huge crowd of people were waiting. We couldn't believe it. That was one of the features of the trip. How so many Irish people who emigrated to Australia wanted to talk to us. They would get emotional thinking and talking about the old country. Some travelled hundreds of miles to meet us.

Everywhere we went they were there. They wanted to tell their story.

They were from all over Ireland, not just Meath. We realised we represented a strong, emotionally powerful connection between Ireland and their world… The New World. In the days when communication was limited to written letters, that was a very significant link. We knew many of the people they grew up with; family members. We spoke to them about the folk back home, the last time we met them, the last time we spoke to them. Powerful.

They were people who had made a new life Down Under, like Fr McGearty, a brother of Patsy McGearty who was a goalkeeper on the Meath team that won the All-Ireland in 1954. Some of the people who came to meet us in the various cities were also relatives of the players.

We were constantly reminded by Peter McDermott and Fr Tully that we were representing more than just Meath. We were also representing Ireland. The greeting we got in places like Perth from people all over Ireland was another reminder of that. They spoke to us about Ireland and sometimes the tears would be streaming down their faces. They spoke, emotionally, of parents and other family members they hadn't seen in years and, no doubt, some of them never did see their loved ones again.

We had a hectic schedule. Five games between Saturday, March 9 to Monday, March 17, all against teams made up of Aussie Rules players who were professionals. They were large, bronzed, fit-looking men too who knew how to hit hard when they went into the tackle. Having played the Galahs the previous autumn we knew what to expect.

This time we were prepared for the Aussie onslaught – I'm not sure they were prepared for us.

THERE'S NO DOUBT they underestimated us. We were referred to as the 'white midgets' and 'little leprechauns' in the local media. That really got to me. That feeling that you were being underestimated, dismissed.

That always fired me up, like fuel added to the engine of a steam train. I remember overhearing two Australians talking about us in a less than respectful way, about us as pale little leprechauns. 'They are laughing at us!' I remember saying to Bertie Cunningham. In my own mind I was thinking, *We'll show you if we are little leprechauns or not.*

The heat and humidity was stifling and we only had a few days to get used to it. We had to cut short our first training spin, it was just so hot, but we simply had to deal with it – and we did. Fr Tully may have had old world views when it came to training but he got us in fine shape for that trip. In the intense heat, our fitness proved more than adequate.

Perhaps we were a lot fitter than some of us thought. We quickly accustomed to the heat. We won our first game against Western Victoria 6-6 to 0-3 before an estimated crowd of 13,000. Ollie Shanley got two goals. Tony Brennan, Peter Black and Mick O'Brien, another Walterstown man in the squad, also found the net. So did I, a rare occurrence indeed.

The pitches were rock hard and I had hurt my ankle early on in the tour and that hampered me, but I kept going as best I could.

The rules were basically the same as gaelic football, although the players were allowed to pick the ball up off the ground. Australians were accustomed to robust tackling so they were giving some leeway in that respect. We just had to adapt to that as well. The best thing was to get the ball to a colleague as quickly as possible, especially if he was in a little bit of space. They were big men so we decided to keep the ball low. They found Red Collier impossible to handle with his power.

We approached every game like an All-Ireland final because we were fully aware of the sacrifices people back home had made to get us out there. We wanted to put in a good show.

One of the memorable moments was playing in the Melbourne Cricket Ground. That was a bit special for all of us. We could all remember how Ronnie

Delany had powered his way to a gold medal there in the 1956 Olympic Games. I could remember all the hullabaloo about it at the time and it was a marvellous achievement. Now here we were in the same stadium, the noise of the supporters cascading down from the stands and terraces. The stifling heat making the air heavy and difficult to run in.

There's a photograph from that tour of the Meath team before we played our game there. There we are standing on the edge of the pitch – and there can be seen the marks of the lanes that the athletes used. It was like standing on holy ground. Special.

Like Ronnie, we also enjoyed a victory in the famous MCG, before nearly 30,000 spectators. The atmosphere reminded me of an All-Ireland final. We ran onto the pitch through a paper tunnel and did a lap of the ground before the throw in. That was something we certainly didn't do back home! Among the spectators there were many who were waving the tricolour. That gave us encouragement. The performance that day was one of our best on the tour.

There were heavy hits put in by the big, bronze Australians. One of them in particular, Len Thompson, was a giant of a man. Still, we kept the ball low and won the game 3-9 to 0-7. It was a great display by us. A highlight.

We also played under floodlights in Sydney – and surely, we were the first gaelic football team to do that, although I didn't play in that game. Because of the heat, all the players on the panel got a run out at some stage. Winning all our games was special and hopefully gave the Irish exiles something to be proud of.

Tour operator Joe Walsh had organised the trip and did a good job too. The hotels were first class. We had plenty of early morning flights but things ran smoothly. Joe was someone I liked but he had an unconventional way of paying the bills. In the days before credit cards were widely used, he brought a bag of money with him to pay the bills.

A bag stuffed with money. Once, while he went off somewhere else, he deposited the bag in the hotel room I was in for safe keeping. There it was under the bed, the money in the bag sitting there like a time bomb. I was worried something might happen to it. I felt the weight of responsibility and I was greatly relieved when he came back to collect it. Thankfully, nobody relieved him of the bag as he went around with it. I was afraid one or two of the lads might take the bag as a prank and let me stew in it for a day or so because if that happened, I certainly would have been sweating.

I don't know what would have happened if the bag went 'astray'. Who, or how, would we have paid the bills then?

As well as the games, we had a hectic social schedule, plenty of receptions. Between the heat and the travel, we'd be exhausted by the end of the day.

The time came for us to pack our bags and head back home. On the return journey we stopped off in a few locations including Hawaii and it was there I experienced something that left a deep, *deep* impression on me. Deeper even than what I saw in Singapore or anywhere else on our pioneering tour.

WE WENT FOR a walk on the beach near our hotel.

It was around seven or eight in the evening. I was tired, we'd covered a lot of miles. There was one of those beach bars with people around it. There were loads of women especially around it.

They used to fly in large groups of prostitutes for the American GIs who were based in Hawaii. Some of the GIs were probably coming back from the war in Vietnam, others were going back to that troubled country that was torn asunder by a terrible war that was still raging there.

I came across these four lads. American soldiers. I was 22 but they were maybe a little younger than me, and they were sitting on the beach crying, bitter tears. I got talking to them.

'What's wrong lads?' I asked them.

'We thought we were going home this evening but they won't let us home,' replied one of them. 'We thought we were going home to our parents… but now we can't go,' said another. They were heartbroken. Crestfallen.

They could hardly talk, the tears streaming down their faces. They were all devastated. I'll never forget that day.

It was impossible not to feel desperately sorry for them. Their worlds had collapsed in all around them. Imploded. 'We thought they were flying us home… instead of that, they flew us here to Hawaii before returning back to Vietnam!' another of the soldiers added.

The sadness in the soldiers' eyes as they sat on the beach, forlorn. Young lads who just wanted to go home to see their mothers and fathers. Yet here they were caught up in a terrible war. Instead of the sanctuary of home they were returning to a kind of hell on earth. They were grand lads, decent. They weren't drinking either, it wasn't emotion stirred up by drink.

The picture of what happened that day is seared in my consciousness and hardly a day goes by when I don't think about it. Even still. *What happened to those young boys? Did they return to Vietnam and their deaths?* There is, of course, a strong possibility that is what happened.

How heartless and rotten the American government was to betray them in the way they did. That was my reaction. I still feel like that. They were badly betrayed by their own. They thought they were going home. Instead, they were going back to war.

In Ireland, we had heard regular news reports on the radio of events unfolding in places like Saigon, the Mekong Delta. About the Americans bombing the country and the Viet Cong seeking to take over the place. We were familiar with the names of places in that far-off country but here, up close, in the despair of the young US soldiers, was an example of the trauma of war a long way from the battlefield.

After that I always kept in touch, as much as I could, with what was happening in Vietnam. I tried to learn as much as I could about the war, the country. When I would hear a report from there on the radio or read something about it in the newspapers, I would think about those young soldiers on the beach. The haunted look on their faces would be resurrected in my consciousness if I saw a report on the TV about the war. The whole subject of Vietnam has fascinated me down the years. I have watched films about Vietnam, learned as much as I could about that terrible conflict.

The more I studied the Vietnam War, I realised they didn't want the young soldiers to return home because there was rioting going on in American cities. People protesting against the war, and the authorities didn't want young soldiers going back to their home towns telling people what it was really like. The horrible, terrible reality.

That's my theory anyway.

Those young lads were like so many young men down through the ages. They were caught up in a terrible madness, the madness of war... and here I was returning home from the trip of a lifetime. My only concern was to get rest before continuing on our way back to Ireland. Home. Yet the young soldiers were about

REYNOLDS A FAMILY MEMOIR PART 8

to enter Hell's Kitchen. It just didn't seem fair or right.

It was a perfect example of the unfairness of life. The way fate could be harsh on some and bestow real blessings on others. We were the ones who were blessed.

It made me realise too that you can't believe what governments tell us. Who do you believe… the Russians, the Americans? It made me realise you would need to be on the ground seeing what really goes on to get the full story. The Americans weren't telling the full story about Vietnam. It was a real revelation for me.

From Hawaii we moved on to San Francisco, from there onto New York for a brief stay. It was a tired bunch of people who arrived back in Dublin. Tired and wiser. Yet even then our travels weren't over that year, not by a long way.

IT DIDN'T SEEM long after we came back from Australia that we took to the air once more. This time to England, back to Wembley for another Whit Weekend of action in the famous stadium, this time to play Mayo, a game we won. Wexford played Cork in the hurling game.

One of the consequences of the trips to Australia, and London, was that the squad of players formed a powerful bond. We had known each other beforehand of course but the visits to beautiful places like Perth, Melbourne and Adelaide had provided the opportunity and time to forge strong and lasting friendships. We all got on fine. No issues.

So it was with well-founded optimism that we approached the opening round of the Leinster Championship against Longford in the summer of 1968. That spring, eastern Europe was set alight when there were revolutions in places like Prague and Budapest; there was a revolution on the playing fields of Ireland too.

Longford had caused us problems in the past, but there seemed no reason why we should be too concerned by them. We were, after all, All-Ireland champions… even world champions! Globe-trotting World Cup winners, at that.

On a summer's day we found out just how things could quickly unravel. Because we were All-Ireland champions, we wore a target on our backs and Longford hit the bull's eye. They ambushed us, deservedly winning the game.

We were out of the championship. It was back to the beginning.

★★★

PADDY

IN REBUILDING THE team and bringing in a raft of young players in 1996, Seán Boylan put his faith in us but I think we repaid that faith. That was Seán all over, not afraid to follow his instincts; he felt it important to be faithful to his gut feeling. If he felt you were good enough, had the right stuff, he put you in the team. It wasn't like he was taking a wild punt. He would have studied the personalities of the players, knew what he was getting.

I had known Seán for years before I got near the Meath senior side. My father, after all, was involved picking teams with him so Seán was in and out of our house for 10 years before '96. Seán wouldn't be long about discerning what kind of a character you were. He would soon know what you were about. That was one of his strengths, evaluating somebody and what made them tick – but his greatest asset as a manager was his ability to instil belief in players. That was his secret, if you could call it a secret.

He made you feel you could climb any mountain. Before the game started, he might call us into one of those huddles and remind us we had every right to be there… at a Leinster final, All-Ireland final; to wear the green and gold jersey. We had worked hard to earn that right too, he would add. He was telling us not to feel daunted. We were as good as anybody. When he gathered us together, he wouldn't say we COULD do something, he would give the sense that we WOULD do something.

There was something else that helped us get over the many challenges we faced as young players. We come from a county that had a tradition of success. There is much talk of that in the GAA. Tradition. Some might say tradition never kicked a point, never scored a goal but I am convinced it is a factor in helping one team get the better of another who, say, might NOT have a tradition of success. It is something that can make the difference between victory and defeat on a hot championship day, between relinquishing your hold on a match in the dying seconds or pushing on to win it when the outcome is finely poised. I know that to be the case.

I was aware of how my forefathers had succeeded; of how Meath had won

All-Irelands in 1949 and '54 and, of course, after that. You would have grown up hearing about those heroes of the past. I'm keenly aware of how my father had helped the county win back Sam in '67 even though I obviously wasn't born. As a youngster I had seen, first hand, how they made hay in 1987 and '88, how they became the kings of the country.

Knowing all that, having that awareness embedded deep into our collective consciousness helped us as a team get over the challenges we faced in the 90s and on into the noughties. I am totally convinced about that. Having had a ringside seat in '87 and '88 myself it certainly gave me the belief that I too could be an All-Ireland winner, that I could take up the torch and carry it on. I think I would have felt like that even if I wasn't involved. The other players of my generation would have felt that too. We took up the torch and carried it on into the battles we faced, fully aware of what our predecessors in the green and gold jersey had done.

It's one of the main reasons why teams from Kerry, generation after generation, emerge from the south and go all the way. Sure, they will have times of drought, relative drought anyway but always, always they will find a way back. A new generation, reared on hearing of the feats of their forefathers, will emerge and seek to make their own imprint, create their own history. We were reared in all that, we had seen with our own eyes it could be done, we knew we could do it too.

We are Meath, the ancestors of a rich tradition. That knowledge was a huge factor in carrying us along. It's much the same at club level. A club with a rich tradition will have the edge over another that hasn't, everything else being equal.

BEATING DUBLIN IN 1996 was a real buzz, a real blast, one of those deeply satisfying feats. They were after all All-Ireland champions going into the game and pushing for their fifth consecutive Leinster title. Before getting the better of the Dubs that year there were still lingering doubts about us as a team, about our lack of experience, the fact we had so many young, largely unproven players in the team. Protected by our youth – and that intangible thing called tradition – we didn't share those doubts.

There was also an issue about the fact that two of the players – Graham Geraghty and Brendan Reilly – who had previously played as backs were transformed into forwards. What chance had Meath of getting the scores they needed with two converted backs in their infantry seemed to be the view? That's what some were saying, the doubting Thomas'. The shallowness in such arguments were soon exposed.

Before the Leinster final, I didn't know who I was going to mark. Back in the mid-90s teams were still sticking reasonably close to the old formation of six backs, two midfielders, six forwards. Reasonably close. Teams had yet to adopt the fluid football type of game that is utilised now where players can pop up anywhere. When Dublin named their team they had that old hardy annual 'AN Other' starting as a wing-forward opposite me. I liked to know who was going to play because then you could plan a strategy. Think about how I was going to mark my direct opponent. Look at ways of diminishing his influence. For that Dublin game it was all a mystery until Ciaran Whelan appeared beside me. He, in later years, was to become a very good midfielder but he was at the foothills of his county career back then; just starting out, like myself. He was six foot three; I'm considerably shorter and there we were standing beside each other. Nobody knew who he was, at least not in our camp, or how good he really was.

It was fine when the ball came low towards us. It was different when the ball came in high. He was a good player. Very difficult to manage, to subdue. You had to think hard how to get the better of a player like that. Had to come up with some kind of strategy. I tried to drag him into midfield, get him snarled up in traffic where he couldn't use his height as effectively as he might have liked. It all helped to get us over the line.

Defeating Dublin was a mighty boost for us, no doubt. A vindication of Boylan's throw of the dice. We moved onwards and upwards. Winning Leinster meant we had earned a place in the All-Ireland semi-final and a clash with Ulster champions Tyrone, who Dublin had defeated in the previous year's All-Ireland final. The Ulster side were formidable foes, we knew that. We expected a real hard game – what we never would have expected was all the controversy that was rolled out after the 70 minutes were up.

EXCITEMENT AND EXPECTATION had begun to bubble up around Meath before matches; flags sprouted from the houses in the communities we came from, manifestations of that hope, of that hunger for more success among our supporters... our tribe. Again, just like the Leinster final, we were considered the underdogs. Outsiders. We were going to be consumed by the hard Ulster side made of seasoned campaigners, who knew their way around a pitch.

That perception suited us just fine. We prepared for the game, quietly knowing we could do the business buoyed up by that victory over Dublin; a victory we had dug out the hard way. Chiselled out of hard rock.

People, down the years, have talked of the massive, foundation-shaking, bone-rattling sound that echoed around Croke Park when Tyrone ran onto the field for the All-Ireland semi-final. They talk about it because it really was something else. Ear-piercing, morale-crushing if you let it. Their supporters had travelled in huge numbers – the cheers proved it. We had got a rousing cheer when we ran out but when Tyrone followed us it was something else, up a few more decibels.

'That's for us!' said our midfielder Jimmy McGuinness as we went through our warm-up routine. 'That's for us,' he repeated, using a piece of psychology; turning things around. We knew though it wasn't, the cheering was for them but we were claiming it. Tyrone may have shaded things in the stands. On the field of play we were on song. We produced one of the best performances of any Meath team for years. A display for the history book, especially in the second-half. We excelled. Graham Geraghty was brilliant, scoring 1-4 and making another goal for Barry Callaghan, who also had a serious game.

Imprinted on my memory is Graham coming out to the middle of the field winning a ball. He had a big open space and running, full tilt, for the Tyrone goals. It was a sight to behold. When he was on his game Graham was a special player. Truly special. It was one of those days when the training, the tactics, our youthful eagerness, the experience of the older players, everything combined in a collective force to help us to produce a performance for the ages. We won 2-15 to 0-12.

We can do our calculus before games about pace and strength, about nimble forwards being too foxy for bullish back men. We can draw diagrams, spout statistics. But we can't legislate for what beats within a man wrote Vincent Hogan in the *Irish Independent*. That was getting at the basic facts, the heart of the matter, about the Meath team. That it was Boylan's way to pick personalities, people rather than just footballers who could play a bit. Men of a certain type, a specific character he knew would man the trenches and never give an inch. That team was full of characters like that.

Somebody else put it in a different way.

'You can't show what God didn't put into you!'

That summed it up well too.

ONE OF THE headlines in the press after the Tyrone game simply read *Awesome men of Meath*. It was a headline that underlined just how well we played – and in the immediate aftermath of the game it was all about the force Meath had whipped up in that second-half. Soon however, the spotlight turned away from the quality of our performance to a few controversial incidents that had taken place in the game, particularly the attempts by Martin O'Connell to dispossess Brian Dooher, who was left wearing this huge bandage on his head .

There was an incident too with Ciaran McBride, when he shipped a hefty challenge after a clash with Marty. There was also John McDermott's crunching shoulder that halted Peter Canavan as he sought to get the ball. It was a thundering blow that helped to change the pattern of the game.

People questioned the legitimacy of John's challenge but, as he himself pointed out, Peter had issues with his ankle after the game, not the shoulder. I witnessed the challenge up close and John really rattled the Tyrone player but it was fair enough I thought, it was shoulder to shoulder. It wasn't dirty but some perceived it as such, made mileage out of it. They saw it as another example of Meath stepping over the line in the relentless pursuit of success. Dirty Meath.

Again, there was no pre-conceived plan to target some of Tyrone's marquee players and put them out of the game. Never. It was just part of the ethos of our team to win the ball, to go in hard but stay inside the rules of the game. There was no point in giving away frees. Go out and give it everything. When a ball was there to be won, you gave everything to win it. No holding back, but don't give your opponents an opportunity to undo your good work by giving a free away. That would be counterproductive, madness.

We were well revved up for that Tyrone game; we knew, having beaten Dublin, we were in with a chance of winning. They were beaten All-Ireland finalists, Ulster champions once more. They had emerged from a province notorious for its hard-hitting. They were adamant they were going to beat us that day. Convinced. We sensed that from what we had heard through the grapevine. Maybe they fed off sections of the media who felt they would win. They had power all over the pitch, the pundits said. Meath were callow. Their supporters too believed this. That was shown in the huge numbers who travelled down for the game. That belief echoed around the stadium when that massive sound blasted out from their followers in the stands. It was the kind of roar that champions get. We heard it and took it on board. Used it as another source of motivation. *We'll silence them* – and we did, winning by a comfortable nine points.

Maybe we were even surprised ourselves with the whirlwind we whipped up that day against the men from Tyrone; the ferocity of cyclone we unleashed. We just wanted to win so much. We seemed to be the team more buoyed up by the roar of the crowd when Tyrone ran onto the pitch than they were. Maybe in the end that earth-shattering roar spurred us on more than it did them. There was a great, fulfilling sense of achievement in the dressing-room afterwards. A winning dressing-room is the place to be; one of the most pleasant places in the world. The banter and the craic all adds to a joyous atmosphere that was, as yet, undiminished by any controversy. It was a wonderful performance, one we could be proud of, although we hadn't won anything yet. We had to remind ourselves of that – and if we didn't, Seán Boylan would.

The media storm that was whipped up because of the incident with Marty and Brian Dooher especially was incredible. It was all over the papers and featured prominently on the *Joe Duffy Show* the next day. It became one of the hottest GAA talking points in years. I was standing right beside Marty when it happened down the Hill 16 end. Could hardly be much closer. The two players went for the ball… Dooher fell. Marty wanted to rejoin the play as quickly as he could. He put his hand on Dooher's head and in his rush to get going again he caught the Tyrone player with his foot.

I think Martin was shocked at what happened, how quickly it had happened. The whole world was watching the incident and admittedly it didn't look good for Marty – but he was never the kind of player to leave the boot in. In a split second it happened and helped to fuel the sense that Meath were ruthless. Dirty Meath.

Marty may have been worried that he would get sent off, even if he felt it was an accident. He wasn't, and that says something. I was marking Dooher that day and I was happy enough with how it went. I didn't give him much space or time. I felt content with my performance. I would have studied his style beforehand. He was lightning quick. You had to stay with him, but that suited me.

I could match him in that department. Pace.

IX

Mayo
Post-Mortems
The Row
Boylan's Hand
Pat McEnaney
Dowd

★★★

PADDY

WE HAD PRODUCED a wonderful display against Tyrone and now we were expected to do it again in the All-Ireland final against Mayo. Here was another test for our newly constructed team. How to deal with a soaring level of expectation? It's something many teams have to grapple with – and it can be as difficult to deal with as an awkward opponent. The pressure was piled on by the fact we were made favourites to win the final.

Maybe it all added up, that pressure. Maybe it built up steadily, seeped into our consciousness like daggers in the mind, hampering us, because we didn't produce our best performance in the final, far from it. We were heavy-footed at times. Lethargic. We fell behind, then staged a sustained revival that saved us. We did show tremendous grit in bouncing back from what seemed like a hopeless situation. We looked lost in the helter-skelter of the game. Yet we didn't fold. That showed the deep-rooted, down-to-earth belief in the team that we could be champions.

Even when it looked like Mayo were destined to win the game, we never lost belief. We were six points down at one stage in the second-half. SIX POINTS. There was never any sense of panic because we knew we had done the hard yards in training to stay in the game. We knew if we just kept playing that we could turn it around.

Knowing we had put the work in, we had put the stamina in the legs, was the foundation of that tremendous self-belief that infused the team. It helped to fuel the belief you could face down any challenge; overcome any obstacle. That belief in yourself and your colleagues on the frontline. All the hard graft done on the rowing machines in Gormanston, running up the Hill of Tara had put miles in the legs – but it had fortified our minds also. Provided us with a mental strength that was also crucial, essential.

That sense you had done the hard work allied to a will to win among the players, not to accept second best, were wonderful assets to have in any situation, especially in the white heat of battle… knowing you have the preparation done, the groundwork completed. All that had helped to keep us in a game we should really have lost. Mayo should have won their first All-Ireland since 1951 but they didn't. Instead, the teams finished level, 0-12 to 1-9, with Colm Coyle scoring his last gasp-point to earn us a draw.

I was certainly greatly relieved to get another chance. It was my mistake that had allowed Mayo to work their goal. I knew that. I accepted that.

WE HAD A meeting in the hotel on the Monday morning after the drawn match. Seán Boylan along with selectors Eamonn O'Brien and Frank Foley were with us. It was time for a post mortem. Various players expressed what they thought. I outlined my surprise at how difficult we found it; how good Mayo played. How we, or at least I, had underestimated the Connacht side. 'I didn't think Mayo were going to be that good,' I asserted.

I was a bit wary of my own position and wondering if I would get selected for the replay because Mayo's first goal was my fault. No doubt. I had gone to pick up the ball close to our own posts. Just as I stooped to pick up possession, I got nudged aside accidently by Darren Fay who was also looking to get his hands on the ball. The ball broke, a Mayo player won possession and a pass or two later… the ball was in our net, Ray Dempsey having applied the finishing touch.

I knew at the time when I went to pick up the ball I was in trouble because I was isolated, outnumbered two to one by Mayo players. In that split second the thought flashed through my mind *Bloody hell… I'm outnumbered, I'm in trouble here.*

I went down on the ball, got the accidental nudge from Fay, not a Mayo player, so the referee didn't give the free. I had gambled, but it didn't pay off. The concession of that goal was a real hammer-blow to Meath and to me. I took that personally. I had the ball... I lost it, they scored a goal. I had found myself in a tight corner, I had utilised a strategy to get out but it hadn't worked. Next thing the ball was in the net. That was hard to take. That bugged me for days afterwards. I felt I let myself and the team down. I felt responsible.

I don't know how I would have felt if we had lost; I would have been absolutely gutted. Thankfully, Coyler was able to save the day. I was one of the most relieved men in Croke Park to see the ball land in the Mayo goalmouth and bounce over the bar, although it's only later when you processed all that had gone on, that it really hit you... the relief, how luck plays such a big part in the affairs of men.

Yet the fact we didn't crumble had highlighted the character within the team. Most teams would have been sunk, I believe. Six points behind in an All-Ireland final. It's an awful long way back from that yet we didn't despair, we didn't take the easy way out and simply accept it wasn't going to be our day. In that respect, we had shown the stuff of champions. We had beaten the two teams, Dublin and Tyrone, people didn't expect us to beat and I felt we approached Mayo with a certain complacency. I expressed openly in that post-match meeting what I really felt, that we had played well against Tyrone, but our cause in the drawn final was undermined by complacency. I still feel that.

HOWEVER, I WAS fearful, because of the way the Mayo goal came about, that I might be dropped for the replay so I wanted the management to know that I was aware that I made a mistake and would rectify it in the replay. That, however galling it might be, I was taking responsibility for the breach in our defence. I wanted them to know that while Mayo caught us out the first day, we, or at least I would be ready the next day. Fully focused.

Nobody questioned me or criticised me about what I regarded as the error that led to Mayo's goal. Seán Boylan was great in that way. He knew that I knew I had made a mistake but he wouldn't humiliate you in front of others. What Seán used to do was focus first, and last, on the positives. If you did three good things during a game, he would focus in on those. That was his way. Good management.

There was a time, later in my career, when I was going through a bad patch, not playing well. I had a stinker in this particular league game and Boylan came up to me and outlined how I had made a great tackle here, and a great block there. It was probably the only two positive things I did in the game. So, when I came back into training the following Tuesday night, I was starting at 60 percent, not 40 percent. He would make sure you knew the mistakes you made; certainly, he would. Most lads knew themselves anyway. Gaelic football in the 90s wasn't particularly tactical in the sense that it was very much about marking your opponent, winning the ball if possible and getting it to a colleague. Get it and give it. It was still very much about winning your personal battle with whatever player you were marking.

In 1996, also, we played almost the exact same team in all the games we played; there wasn't much change from one week to the next. We had hardly altered from the 15 players who started each match. There was a positive in that too. There was no chopping and changing, something that is sure to bring with it uncertainty and undermine the overall morale.

Not that we had a lot of experienced players to bring in if we needed to shake things up. We had Donal Curtis, who was so versatile he could cover for almost any position, and players like Colm Brady could fill in at midfield or the forwards. Their versatility may have worked against them in terms of getting a starting place. They were two very talented players we could call on if needed, but we didn't have an unlimited depth of talent on the bench.

As the All-Ireland replay approached, we were focused. We didn't want to perform below our best again and be caught. We knew we might not get away with it a second time. Everything would be different we resolved, but it wasn't all that different as it turned out. What's that saying about lofty plans and ambitions. 'Make a plan and hear God laugh.'

THE REPLAY OF the 1996 All-Ireland final will be remembered by people for all sorts of reasons. The topsy-turvy nature of the game. The balance of playing swinging one way, then the other. Mayo pushing ahead, Meath just hanging onto their coat tails. Then there was… the row!

It was full-on in the weeks leading up to the game, people wanted to talk about the match and who might prevail the second time around. 'What did I think?' I was asked many times. The build-up was intense. There were those who felt Mayo had thrown it away the first day. Couldn't blame them for feeling that. They did let it slip. Any team who goes six points up in the second-half should finish the job. It's a great place to be yet Mayo couldn't finish the job. We knew that would be on their players' minds going into the replay. Had to be.

Yet there were many who believed they would get it right the second time around – and they did start the replay on the front-foot. Then, six minutes in, it all went a bit crazy. The infamous row blew up like a bush fire when both teams were still only getting into the game; only warming up really.

The bust up started under our goalposts down at the Hill 16 end when a Mayo player went in with a tackle on Darren Fay and all hell broke loose. Colm Brady in the book *The Boylan Years* described how one of the funniest incidents he ever saw on a football pitch was the sight of me flying in at the start of the row 'mad to kill' only to slip and go tumbling to the ground. I had been out the field, some distance from where the row started and I tripped over somebody on the way into where the battle was unfolding.

As a younger cohort in the Meath camp, I had never experienced anything like the battle that erupted. Certainly not. After all, I was still only a rookie. Even at club games I hadn't encountered an incident where a group of players put aside any pretence at sticking to the rules and just went at it, fists flying. Some of the other, older lads may have been involved in the odd skirmish here or there over the years. You had prepared yourself for all sorts of occurrences, twists and turns, but not that. When it started, I just tore into it like so many others. It was like somebody blew a whistle as the signal for us all to rush in but there was nothing planned, there was no preconceived plan to pile in if anything happened. Everything happened so quickly.

There is this concept, of being in the moment, in 'the flow' the Americans call it, where you are, especially in sport, so wrapped up in the moment that nothing else exists for you at that moment except what you are at. It was like that for me in games, I would be so engaged at certain moments that all else was blotted out. That doesn't mean you'd remember everything that happens. But that day, as the row started, I recall a blow landing on my head, though there was no real force behind it. There was a lot of pushing and shoving, fists and kicks that missed their targets.

A lot of fury, not much sound and before we knew it was over. I don't think I hit anybody myself. It settled down as quickly as it started. Coyler got his marching orders along with McHale. He was a big loss to Mayo, but so was Coyler to Meath. It was his point that rescued us in the drawn game, his experience was a vital ingredient of that team. To lose him was certainly a major blow to us;

I certainly don't agree with those who say Mayo took a bigger blow by losing McHale. Not for a moment.

One of the strangest aspects of that row actually occurred a week before the game. We were training up in a sports centre beside Dublin airport. Seán Boylan had brought us up there and Pat McEnaney, who had refereed the drawn game, arrived up to talk to us. He wanted to have a chat with the two teams. He had spoken to Mayo at their training base, I'm not sure where that was, and he wanted to talk to us as well. So, he started talking to us and he outlined how the game had evolved. He spoke about how generally, in the modern game, when a row or a skirmish breaks out there is a culture among teams for more than the two players involved to get stuck in. He said something like, how he would expect 'two or three' others to become involved, and he didn't want that to happen.

He warned us that whoever comes in as the 'seconds', the cavalry if you like, are going to be sent off. It was amazing, considering what subsequently happened, that he should mention that. Maybe there was something in the drawn game that he had sensed? An underlying feeling. I don't know, but it was something that stuck in my mind. *Why did he mention that of all things.*

When the row started just about everyone got involved and when the dust settled referee McEnaney acted on his warning. He sent off Coyler and McHale as examples, but the row, the dismissals, did take the tension out of the situation. They were the two players picked out after the dust had settled but McEnaney could have sent off anybody who was involved. He just had to pick somebody to try and restore order. A warning to others. From then on, we concentrated on playing a game of football, not that I remember much about it.

It flashed past in a blur of frantic action. That's the thing about my career. I don't recall much about games. I know other players are the same. The action is just so frantic and everything is done in a micro-second, much of it on instinct. You just don't have the time to think, to process it, store it away and say to yourself *I must remember this or that.* It's all so spontaneous. You work on instinct.

It's one of the reasons why Boylan kept his tactics basic. He emphasised the need to get the ball in early and often to the forwards. It was up to them to win it from there. There is simply no mileage from issuing players with detailed instructions.

AFTER THE ROW everything settled down and the teams concentrated on football. What a game that replay turned out to be. The tooing and froing, the ebb and flow. Mayo looked like they would win at various stages. Trevor Giles converted a penalty for us, Tommy Dowd also finished bravely to the net late on. Yet the teams were level until Brendan Reilly clipped over what proved to be the winning point. We made it across the line 2-9 to 1-11. We were champions. Again. Cue mayhem once more.

All the talk, the media attention, was on the row and it's still shown on TV from time to time. I wasn't in the least resentful that certain people should focus on that rather than what we had achieved or how we had achieved it. It didn't bother me in the least. It did take away from the glow of winning the Sam Maguire in one respect but I didn't lose any sleep over it.

I still feel that sweet sense of achievement that goes with winning the game, climbing to the top of the hill. We still have the medals, solid, tangible proof that we won the thing. Nothing can change that.

There was that feeling that Meath were somehow always embroiled in some controversy or other; that they were a team who went about winning and not very concerned about how they did it. Dirty Meath. That label came from the 80s team, that's where it originated from, especially from the 1988 All-Ireland replay when there was a bust up against Cork and Gerry McEntee got sent off. It stemmed from there, and it was attached to us also. Seán Boylan never told any Meath player to go out and hit anyone deliberately. Never. Yet, at the same time, he picked players who were tenacious in what they were doing. We all had to be tenacious. No holding back, no hesitation.

Go in hard and win the ball, but do so in a fair way. By the rules. A player was of no help to his team sitting on the sideline after getting sent off. That was the ethos in the team. Go in hard but stay disciplined. There is a thin line there but we always sought to do things the 'right' way, within the rules, even if for no other reason than you don't want to be conceding easy frees.

That way is the road to failure.

INTER-COUNTY FOOTBALL is a fiercely competitive arena, that's a given. To survive you have to be totally in tune with what you are doing. Focused. You have to approach your role as a player, as a participant with conviction – same if you perform at any high level in any sport.

When Seán Boylan picked a team, or a panel, he brought in characters he knew had heart. He selected players he could trust and believe in. There were as many good footballers in the county of Meath in 1996 as were on the field for the All-Ireland final that year. Better footballers too in many cases. There was no shortage of skilful, talented players but maybe some of them just didn't have the heart, the desire, that insatiable hunger you need. That drive that can't be taught to any player. It has to be there in someone's DNA.

Seán Boylan went for guys he knew that when it came to the crunch wouldn't let him down. Guys who hated losing with a deep-rooted passion. I was one of those. My attitude was it was no good getting to Leinster or All-Ireland final. You simply had to win them. There is zero consolation in defeat.

When you pick those kind of players, that's what happens when they go out on the field. Victory will be sought and if there is an obstacle to achieving that, well, that has to be faced, full-on. It's much the same in life.

Seán was praised for the way he had constructed another team from the ground up in 1996, and rightfully so. He brought in a group of players and he and his selectors, Eamonn O'Brien and Frank Foley, fused and moulded them into a unit, a formidable unit as it turned out. It was a hell of an achievement.

Not that I had a great year in '96, or should I say I didn't have as good a year as I could have had. Sure, I was part of a team that won the All-Ireland in my debut season. Great. Some players, wonderful talented players, spend their entire careers seeking to get into an All-Ireland final and don't make it. Some don't get near it. I had done it first time out. How fortunate was that.

Yes, it was great to win. To feel and appreciate that deep sense of contentment that comes with setting out to achieve something really difficult and making it happen. To return home with the Sam Maguire, take it back to your county and show it off to the supporters. All that was magic.

That's all great, wonderful, yet there was a lingering, annoying sense I just didn't do myself justice in the championship campaign that year. Yes, I played well for spells in games, but other times when an opponent might get to a ball before me or get a score off me, I felt I wasn't as sharp as I could have been.

I certainly wasn't as fit as I could have been. I knew that. I hadn't done as much training as I needed to do to reach peak fitness, not really. I had been in

England for much of 1995 and I also had that hernia operation but I used to train in England on my own just to keep fit – yet that was far from ideal, so I was left with that nagging feeling bubbling away in my sub-consciousness as we took the congratulations. *You could have played better, you didn't do yourself justice...* the voice in my head told me. Yes, I was familiar with the rough and tumble of inter-county football at minor and u-21 levels but it's a different world at senior. Very different. You're playing against grown men. Men whose job is to get the better of you; to diminish your influence. Blows and tackles came with the kind of power and ferocity I hadn't experienced before.

I shipped a few heavy challenges sure, felt them shaking me to the core but I survived. Didn't ship too many big blows, tended to avoid the big hits. Managed to sidestep many a lunge. I did that because I was quick enough. I was light, I had the pace to escape the clutches of markers, the hit men. I needed to be elusive to survive in the white heat of battle but sometimes you just had to throw yourself into the mix, lunge into the mauls and look to gain possession. If I wasn't quick, I wouldn't have had a chance, my career would have been over before it started. I would never have survived against the physically imposing guys who populated county football. In that world it is literally the survival of the fittest. A jungle.

So, despite the success, I felt the games I played in didn't give a true reflection on me as a player, and that was irritating. Amid all the smiles, the cheers, the bomb-fires, the thousands of fans who greeted us on our glorious passage home, the joyful scenes that everywhere accompanied the All-Ireland success, there was this voice nagging at me.

Yeah, it's great to win an All-Ireland isn't it, but did you do yourself justice?

No, you didn't. Did you?

I told myself 1997 was going to be my year, when I was going to be better, a lot better. When I was going to do myself justice. I had my own motivation. I wanted to show the world what I could really do once I was fully fit. When I was really ready for battle. As it turned out there was no All-Ireland triumph in 1997 but what a year it was. For all sorts of reasons.

X

Farmers' Association
Strike!
A Life in Oz?
The Troubles
Football and Farming
Tayto
Granny Reynolds

★★★

PAT

AS THE SWINGING Sixties drew to a conclusion, Meath could look back and see how they had emerged from obscurity to become one of the top teams in the country. We had progressed, won the All-Ireland but had suffered our share of disappointments too; gut-wrenching defeats in two All-Ireland semi-finals and one final – as well as that defeat to Longford.

In farming too there had been some tumultuous events. If there was the sulphurous whiff of revolution and marching on the streets in some of the communist countries like Czechoslovakia, and also France towards the end of the decade, there were protests too by farmers throughout Ireland. In early 1967 the National Farmers' Association led a strike and I was eager to join in. We were getting poor prices for what we produced, we needed to improve our lot, make our presence felt through protest and I didn't need much encouragement to get involved.

Farming was becoming more difficult to earn a decent wage from, and we had to do something. I was all for taking some dramatic action to highlight our situation. A huge part of the population worked on the land at that time so we knew we could form a powerful lobby to get what we wanted. Politicians couldn't ignore us if we came out in force.

Farmers in our area blocked bridges in and around Navan. Every bridge that crossed the Boyne. It was frustrating for motorists, of course it was, but we had to take drastic action that would put the spotlight on the fact that we weren't getting a fair reward for the work we were putting in. At Kilcarne Bridge there was a brief row between farmers and a few motorists. Blows were struck, blood was spilt but that was an exception to the rule.

Many people supported us. Ireland was still a rural community, many people fully appreciated the difficulties we faced but the Government did everything they could to keep us quiet. I brought my tractor and joined in the blockade, but when my back was turned the tyres of the tractor were slashed at the old bridge at Kilcarne outside Navan. I was annoyed but not surprised. I blamed those who supported the Fianna Fail government at the time because we were protesting against the government.

That really fired me, removed any doubt that I should do all I can to make our protests be heard. I marched to Dublin with other farmers. There's nothing more certain to get somebody to throw their lot behind a cause than to feel you are the victim of an injustice – and we felt the farming community weren't treated right. It was one of the first times farmers tried to do something for themselves, to stand up for themselves, because they were trodden on completely. We had to stand up for our rights.

I loved farming then just as much as when I started – still do. I like the way there's a different issue to be sorted every day. I'll sow a crop of corn and it will be better than last year, hoping the whole time you'll learn more and push on – and you'd never be finished learning in farming, every year there's a different problem. You've a challenge the whole time. It makes you get up in the morning and say I'll do this better today.

AFTER I HAD left Gormanston College I had worked with my father for a few years but I was determined to strike out on my own and that's what I did. We got on well but he was hard enough on me too. He could be a hard taskmaster, but I learned a huge amount from him; the realities of life as a farmer.

The realities of life full stop.

What you had to do to succeed. He worked extremely hard – and he would keep me going the whole time as well; there was no slackening off when it came to work.

When I went to Australia in 1968, I was sorely tempted to stay there. I loved the countryside especially around Perth. It was a beautiful country, good farming country, and I felt I could carve out a new life for myself there. I was tempted.

My father gave me a wage but it wasn't very much in the grand scheme of things. I enjoyed a few pints, or bottles of beer at that time, and I smoked since I was 14. I needed to carve out my own identity, make my own way in the world, and I saw Australia as a way of doing just that.

Life, however, was to turn out a lot differently.

Around the time I went to Australia I had bought a farm of land, 33 acres very close to my father's farm. The cost of the farm was over £7,000, an enormous sum of money at the time. My father finally agreed to go as guarantor for me with the banks, somewhat reluctantly, but he did. It was a big burden for a young man; a lot of responsibility for someone of my age. I didn't allow that to deflect me. I was still in my early twenties but I wanted to carve out my own niche.

In Australia I spoke to one of the people, a great Meath supporter, who had travelled with us Down Under – Michael Regan, a solicitor from Trim.

I had told him how I had just purchased a farm back home in Ireland but that I was also taken in by the idea of making a new life in Australia.

'I'm staying over here, there's some lovely land around Perth,' I said to Michael.

'No, you're not!' he said. 'We want you back home, playing football for Meath!'

'I'm just after buying a farm of land for a big price and I don't know if I have the money to pay for it… but I think there are real opportunities here. I think I'll stay.'

'You're not staying! I'll help you… I'll look after you. Come on home!' he added.

So I did.

I wanted to drive on, be the best I could be. That was in my head all the time. You had to get better because if you stand still you'll only go backwards. I know it's a cliché but it's so true. That's the reality, the bottom line. I wanted to drive on either in Ireland or Australia.

It was about improving yourself – and Michael was true to his word. He did help me to get established with some very valuable assistance and advice on running a business, which, of course, running a farm is. He became my solicitor and always gave great legal advice.

It's the same with any football team or individual who breaks new ground. To be successful you have to be improving, steadily, learning from your mistakes.

Looking at options. You're learning in every match you play. That was my motto, that was my aim especially playing county football.

I never learned much playing club football; the standard was lower, the challenges less formidable. It was only when you went to mark the best players in the country that you knew your strengths, your limitations. Then you realised what you were doing, and what you needed to do. How to counteract them, how to position yourself on the field to diminish their influence. As a defender you would have to try and work out how you could help your team, turn defence into attack.

Like a good football team, members of the farming community in the late 1960s knew they had to be strong and resilient and unified if they wanted to be successful in achieving their ambition. Focused. If you are not like that you will never go anywhere, win anything. I can't understand players who, if something is not working, why they don't adapt, try something else. Why do the same thing if it's not working out? Why get yourself into the same trouble no matter what you are told?

Good players change tactics during a game to ensure it helps their cause. They mould a game the way they want it. They show leadership and adaptability. That's what you have to do. The same in any situation.

I remember we were playing Kildare in a game and Jack Quinn was marking one of their players, Pa Connolly, a big imposing man. He was catching every ball that came into the square. Jack, who was a great footballer, wanted to catch the ball over his head every time but Big Pa was backing into him and knocking the ball down. Another great Kildare player, Pat Dunny fed off those knock-downs and scored two goals, I said to Jack, 'Don't try and catch it… knock it down to me and I'll pick up the loose ball'. That's what eventually happened. We didn't give Pa or the other Kildare forwards a look in. It was about adapting, reacting to a situation.

The summer of 1969 was also full of the sounds of war coming from places like Derry and Belfast as the Troubles in the North escalated. That summer we would break from our work, maybe saving the hay. We would sit down, have something to eat, and turn on the radio.

We would hear of Civil Rights marches, the sound of trouble brewing. The Troubles were really kicking off. It was a strange, disturbing time too in that respect. Some of the Catholics burned out of their homes were brought down to

Gormanston to an army camp there. The camp acted as a temporary refuge.

Talk of war and disturbances and riots reminded me again of those young American soldiers in Hawaii. Their haunted faces; their fear and terrible, disturbing despair.

★★★

PADDY

FARMING, FOOTBALL AND family. They have always been the pillars of my life. Cornerstones. Couldn't imagine life without them.

I grew up on a farm, absorbed the rhythms of the farming year right from the start. As a youngster I got to appreciate what farming meant, how important it was, to keep working at something – like taking in the harvest for instance – until it was done. Get the job done.

The demands of farming didn't put me off wanting to pursue a life on the land. It was what I wanted to do. I knew about the hardships involved, the difficulties, the uncertainties with weather, prices, the vagaries of the market, machinery breakdowns, but I was never diverted from a life on the land. It was something I got a kick out of. It just seemed the most natural thing that I should work in the great outdoors. I suppose we were so steeped in it. It was all we knew. Of course, we could have gone off and done something else; got a qualification and become something very different… marketing, engineering, whatever. That was never going to be the case as far as I was concerned, not really. Even if I went off and did something else there would still have to have been some agricultural element to the course. It was part of my DNA.

There is such variety in farming; the days change, the challenges change, but more important is the fact that it was a life that brought me outside. I could never imagine myself imprisoned in an office, day after working day. That would be hell to me. Paradise lost. There's a physical aspect to it. I enjoy all that.

You have your targets to meet, your sowing or harvesting deadlines. There's a rhythm to the year. The challenge is usually clear; every day you go out, you know what needs to be done although new challenges can arise during the course of a day or a week that you never expected. That can be a frustration. There are many irritants, so many problems that can arise, issues to be sorted out, but it's part of what makes farming so intriguing too. Grappling with the various issues that confront you. It's like everything else in life. What is your attitude towards those issues? Will you allow yourself to be brought low by them or will you conquer them? It's up to you.

MY FATHER HAD started growing potatoes on a commercial basis and developed the business from there. We became known as a potato growing enterprise and I found the whole business fascinating. Yes, we grew other crops, wheat and barley, but potatoes were the mainstay.

Sometimes I would go out in the morning, a fine summer's morning perhaps and I'd look around, take in the countryside and I'd feel we are very privileged to be making a living from the land; to be out and about in the open air in God's own country, breathing in the fresh air. Then, a piece of machinery might break down, frustration would set in, and you are quickly brought back to the practicalities of such a lifestyle. It all went into the mix.

And yes, farming could be deeply frustrating – and dangerous. I had first-hand experience of that. We were young fellas, my brothers and I, growing up around machinery all the time. We learned to drive and utilise those machines early, fascinated by them. But farming can be deadly dangerous. You have to be aware of the threats but no matter how tuned in you are, things can happen.

There was the time when we bought two new forklifts for the farm. Brand new. Myself and my brother Shane were driving around the yard, working with them, delighted with ourselves when... BANG, we crashed into each other. He was reversing, I was going forward. We had been going around a corner, didn't see each other until it was too late. Straight into each other. Both machines were write-offs, even though they were both new. It was a miracle one of us, maybe both of us weren't killed in that incident. We escaped, chastened but unhurt.

We were lucky, but I've come to realise that you need luck in everything you do. It can be your greatest ally. Of course, you can create your own luck but you need the breaks too. You need the breaks in whatever you pursue, in your working life, in football, in relationships, in everything. There is also the fact that by going through experiences like that, setbacks like that, you learn about life and how everything, in an instant, can change. Just like that. Young people can't be over-protected either, they have to get a certain amount of exposure and learn from that or, at least, hopefully learn! Make mistakes, be aware of how things work, how life works. Take the lessons on board and move on.

Luck was on my side in another incident that happened to me when I was only a youngster. We were delivering a consignment of potatoes to Tayto in their plant in Stamullen in a lorry we had. My father was driving and I was in the seat with Shane. I was only about five or six and seated nearest the door – and there's another detail about what happened, I retain. It is that I was wearing a pair of bright yellow Wellingtons.

What happened next is also imprinted indelibly on my mind and will be for the rest of my life. We were travelling along when, suddenly, I went to open the window but instead I tumbled out the door as we were going down a hill towards Stamullen. Panic stations.

My father, for some reason, couldn't stop the old lorry we had at the time. He had to wait until he got to the bottom of the hill before bringing it to a halt. He did that and rushed back up the hill to see what had happened to me. He must have thought he'd find me badly hurt – or worse. Would I be covered in blood when he found me in a terrible condition? Frightened. Terrified by the experience. What would he find? He was dreading going back up that hill. He had asked Shane, 'Where's Paddy gone?'

Shane told him I had fallen out the door.

Remarkably, unbelievable he found me unscathed apart from a few scratches. I had tumbled out of the lorry as it bombed along and landed on a roadside hedge, a big soft bunch of briers! I wasn't hurt. I don't think I was too frightened or traumatised or anything like that. It had all happened so quickly. I simply tumbled out of the cabin and landed on this soft cushion made of bushes. I could have easily fallen under the lorry as it moved along, got crushed by the wheels. Instead, I had tumbled onto a bed of thorns. I was scratched and a little sore probably, a little shocked, but I was alive. I had survived. I'm not sure what my father said to my mother when we got back home – we all laughed about it years later but it could have been the end before I had hardly started.

Farming is full of uncertainties of all kinds, uncertain weather, fluctuating market trends, a sense that as the primary producer you are a long way away from determining what price a product should be and that can be frustrating – and if you were one to worry about things like that well, you'd never sleep. When you are brought up in it then it's second nature, you just deal with problems and challenges as they arise. Then you have the good days, when a crop is saved, when everything goes well, there's a great sense of achievement in that. That's the thing about farming. It has so many lows but it has many highs as well, often in the same day – just like football.

THE FARMING LIFE was always for me, just like my father and his father before him, Christy Reynolds who, of course, also played football for Louth. I remember Christy, but I was very young when he passed away, so we didn't get to form what could be termed a close relationship. The situation regarding my grandmother, his wife Breda was different.

She became an integral part of my routine on match day. Before I'd go to Croke Park for games I would go up to talk to my grandmother in the mornings. Granny Reynolds. Breda Reynolds. She'd make a cup of tea, and we'd have a scone or a bun. We'd sit down and have a chat.

I would have had Mass on Saturday evening in Bellinter with the rest of the players. You weren't compelled to go but I always would want to be part of it, say a few prayers. Help from any quarter was always appreciated! On Sunday mornings I would have free time. The rest of the family would go to Mass at 9.30 in Walterstown, and I would go up to my granny's for an hour. I liked that routine because it helped to calm me down, to take my mind off the game.

Then I would leave her house and get ready to meet up with the rest of the Meath lads in the County Club in Dunshaughlin or wherever, before making our way up to Croke Park. Somehow, I would feel a lot less on edge, ready for the fray. Not that I would be a nervous wreck. I wasn't, but there was always that edge associated with the game. How else could it be. You were going into the lion's den. You were going to perform in front of thousands, maybe on the big days millions of people, watching on TV.

Granny and myself would talk away for the hour or so but we would never mention football. We'd talk about farming, the state of the world, anything happening in the area, the price of potatoes. *Anything.* It would take my mind off the game; for that hour I would completely forget I was about to go out into the white heat of battle. It was a relief not to have the game swirling around in my mind… who I was marking, what I had to do to counteract him, issues like that continuously assailing my thoughts. I would have grappled with such issues for days beforehand – but you can think too much about a game.

So, we would never talk about the game and she would be a nervous wreck herself, she wouldn't be able to watch it on TV. Instead, she would tune into the radio, like back in the old days. I suppose it might have brought her back to her own youth when the radio was all there was and family and neighbours would gather around in a convivial atmosphere, listen to Michael O'Hehir paint vivid pictures of what was happening in Croke Park.

By the time I came on the scene, Micheal O Muircheartaigh was the voice of the GAA. He was the one painting pictures on the radio and granny would make sure to tune in. Her wisdom and advice became a central part of my life – and not just before games. She would advise me on so many aspects of life. It was great to be able to tap into that wisdom.

Granny might say as I left the house, 'Good luck today' but that would be it. There was just that understanding between us. It was great. Looking back now they were golden moments, a grandson and his grandmother chatting. She understood.

XI

1970

Seán McCormack

Offaly

The Comeback

'Snitchie'

Marriage

Spuds

San Fran

★★★

PAT

SUNDAY, JULY 19, 1970. Leinster final day. Our fourth provincial decider since 1964 and this time we played Offaly. They were an up-and-coming team, an emerging force who were defeated by Kerry in the All-Ireland final the year before.

We prepared as usual for the day and any time you get into a Leinster final is a big day. Some of us on the Meath team were nearing the end of our careers, or at least getting on. The years pass quickly, summers fly by – and we knew we needed to make the opportunities count.

Like 1968, the Leinster Championship of 1969 hadn't worked out too well for us. We were dumped out of the championship both years. Deservedly so. We had resolved to have a good crack at it in 1970, and we did.

The arrangement back then was for a driver to pick me up the morning of a match and, at that time, it was our goalkeeper Seán McCormack. There were no luxury coaches to take us up to the venue. Instead, the tradition evolved that one person in the various areas around the county agreed to pick three or four players from their homes and drive them, in his car or van, to the game. It was the custom that had worked without a hitch before.

I WAS READY to go when the car stopped at our gate. Seán pulled up. He was driving a Volkswagen, one of those vehicles that had the engine in the back.

I hopped in and there's the usually banter and chat. There's a certain edge. Of course, there is. We're about to go into battle for one of the biggest prizes in the game, a Leinster title.

But there's a problem too. When I jumped into the back seat it didn't feel right. It didn't sound right.

'The seats are horrid bad Seán, and the noise isn't great... is everything all right with this motor?' I asked him.

As we were driving along, heading up towards the capital, it was clear there was something wrong with the car. The engine certainly didn't sound right.

Next thing smoke starts to pour from the engine. We're going up the road towards Ashbourne at this stage. The noise is terrible; the engine catches fire – and there's nothing for us to do except get out, push the car into the side of the road, smoke billowing out from it.

Obviously, we can't hang about for too long, we had to move on, there was the small matter of a big game in Croke Park to think about. Of course, it didn't take too long before someone stopped.

Imagine the surprise among supporters on the way up to the game. There they were, on their way to Croke Park, and suddenly they see a few of the players standing on the side of the road looking for a lift, smoke coming from a car in the ditch, bags with our boots in our hands. Laughable yes and in time we did derive plenty of humour from it, but we didn't find it all that funny at the time.

That year was different in that the Leinster final was 80 minutes long instead of the usual 60 minutes. A new rule the GAA brought in. We respected Offaly but we didn't fear them. Why should we? As we make our way to Croke Park we have no idea, of course, we are about to play one of the most extraordinary games of our lives – and be part of the most remarkable comebacks in the history of the GAA.

The match started, but Seán is thinking about his car still.

'What about my car?' he says to me at one stage while the match is going on. He was distracted by it all and why wouldn't he be, but I was saying to him, 'We're in Croke Park now Seán let's just concentrate on the game.'

The car going on fire wasn't the best preparation for a game, of course. I wasn't great that day and poor Seán hadn't the best of starts, his kickouts in the first-half weren't going as far as we hoped. But in the circumstances it was entirely understandable. I remember shouting at him.

'AH JAYSUS Seán…
'WILL YOU SORT THOSE KICKOUTS!!'

THERE WASN'T MUCH indication, early in the contest, of what was going to transpire. We started well and went 0-6 to 0-1 up after 15 minutes. Steady. Encouraging. Then, like someone flicking a switch, the world seemed to go mad. Offaly started launching attack after attack. They started scoring point after point… and goals too.

Suddenly we could not do anything right.

They ran at us like a swarm of bees and we seemed powerless to stop them. They surged towards us, sliced thorough us – and that didn't happen very often. Johnny Cooney got the first Offaly goal but there was no need for panic, at least not at first. But it got worse, a lot worse.

Offaly took charge. It was extraordinary. Kieran Claffey sidestepped a few of us and planted the ball in the net. We looked at each other.

What the f**k is going on?

Murt Connor, a young, talented player we didn't know much about at that stage, came on and powered through for two goals. It was like we'd stopped playing. It's like we were in a dream and watching our opponents in their green, white and gold jerseys sail past us on the way to getting another goal or point. We could hardly get the ball down the field. Carnage. We looked at each other again.

What's going on?

At half-time we were trailing 4-7 to 0-9. I was raging. There was plenty of talk afterwards about how lots of people from Meath upped and left Croke Park that day at half-time, understandably believing the game was done and dusted. Many of the them were said to be dairy farmers who decided it was best to go back home to Meath and start getting the milking done instead of sitting or standing in Croke Park and watching their team being humiliated.

I couldn't blame them if they did leave and go back home. We were terrible. *This is a humiliation* I'm thinking as I sit in my corner in the dressing-room. I was annoyed with the team but annoyed with myself too. I wasn't exactly setting the world on fire either.

The anger had been steadily building up in me as the half had progressed. It reached boiling point in the room. We sat down. There was stunned silence at first but then people started talking about what we should and shouldn't be doing. The selectors seemed to be standing around, not doing much.

I had enough. I got up and stood on the table in the middle of the room.

'What the f**k are we at… we're getting roasted alive out there.

'Are we going to allow that to happen in the second-half… or do SOMETHING about it!' I shouted.

Stunned faces looked back at me but we needed to do something. I hate losing but this was beyond that. A roasting. Then the legs go from under the table and it went tumbling over with a mighty crash.

It didn't distract me or stop me. I fell with it and grabbed one of the broken legs of the table and gave it a bang on the floor.

'We f**king need to do something! I repeat.

'WE NEED TO GET OUR ACT TOGETHER.'

IT WAS MAYHEM, but maybe the shouting, the collapse of the table, woke something in us, in our battered collective psyche. We certainly needed to do something dramatic. The team was then selected by seven selectors who looked to me, but they just seemed to be standing around. I wanted some action taken.

How seven selectors – plus trainer Mick Campbell, who was a gentleman – ever made a decision I don't know but, in fairness to them, they made a good move that day that helped us turn things around.

They switched Ollie Shanley from corner-forward to do a man-marking job on Tony McTeague, one of the players who was making Offaly tick. Ollie was able to deal with the famous McTeague sidestep. We had to reduce his influence. Put him out of the equation and Ollie had the ability to do that.

The Meath management also did something else. They brought on Mickey Fay, a lively, enterprising forward from Trim. He started to cause real problems for the Offaly defence when the second-half got underway. He got one goal, skipping in between bemused Offaly defenders to fist the ball to the net. Then he got another, bombing through the defensive cover. The fightback to beat all fightbacks was on.

Unbelievably, we drew level.

The force was with us now. We launched another late attack. Tony Brennan applied the finishing touch by knocking the ball over the bar. The winning point.

Normally I didn't hear the shouts of supporters in the crowd, I shut them out, but I could hear, and feel, the excitement among those Meath supporters who stayed to watch us. An unbelievable end to an amazing match.

An amazing day.

The final whistle. A roar goes up, we hug the nearest colleague we can find. Unbelievable. *We've done it.* The scoreboard has us ahead 2-22 to 5-12. Leinster champions.

Some games, big games, you win and you just have a sense of having done the job you set out to do. You wouldn't be on cloud nine. Instead, you would be just satisfied you've achieved what you set out to achieve. This was different. This was one win to be enjoyed. Truly special. We knew we'd done something out of the ordinary.

As we celebrated the win the journalists up in the Hogan Stand started to try and put some sense on the whole, madcap afternoon.

Leaving the ground I heard a group of youngsters, still in a state of bewildered excitement, agreeing that they had never seen anything like it. Well, I'm probably three times the age of any of them and have seen hundreds more games, and I've never seen anything like it wrote Michael Cogley in the next day's *Irish Independent*.

Denis Smyth's report in the *Meath Chronicle* a few days later made for pleasant reading. *Never before has any team deserved an honour more than Meath merited the Leinster crown they won on Sunday, because never before in the history of Gaelic games, and I feel confident in putting this on record, never before has 15 players displayed such a brand of raw courage, indomitable spirit and unanswerable heart – the ingredients of Sunday's thorough triumph.* Purple prose indeed.

This was one of those rare occasions in big-time sport when spontaneity took over from method to generate a constant flow of unpredictable occurrences that added up to make this one of the truly great games of Gaelic football in the last 30 years wrote Eugene McGee in his book *Classic Football Matches*.

OUR BANDWAGON ROLLED on in 1970 as summer gave way to autumn. We met Galway in the All-Ireland semi-final. The Connacht side had conquered us so often in the past, steamrolled over our dreams and ambitions. This time we were the better team and there was a sweet sense of achievement when we beat them, 0-15 to 0-11. We were back in another final. It looked like our names were going to be written large across the sky again – just like three years previously.

There was the usual hype leading up to the final but I tried to stay away from all that. I didn't let that kind of thing affect me one way or the other. We were facing Kerry, so again we knew we needed to be in the zone. We had to be ready. It was another All-Ireland but to me it was just like another game. That's the way I looked at it. Dampen the hype.

Our team had altered and changed from the last time we were in an All-Ireland final in 1967; it had changed in its make-up, as teams must. Players such as Peter Darby and Red Collier had moved on. Others such as Mickey Fay had come in to make their mark – and we played well in the 1970 final, it wasn't like we failed to ignite.

We were undone by a Din Joe Crowley goal that finished the contest but just before he got the ball and raced up the field and fired to the net, the Kerry selectors were going to take him off. The next thing he got the ball, went on this surging run, and stuck it in the back of the net.

Game over. A deadening blow.

The worst aspect of that defeat is that we were the better team on the day, no question about it. Losing is bad enough; to lose when you know you should have won makes it worse. A lot worse. Sickening.

Another one that got away.

GERRY QUINN WAS one of the players who was part of the Meath set-up in the 1960s, one of the famous brothers who played for Kilbride and Meath that also included Jack, Martin and Jimmy. Gerry was part of the panel that won the All-Ireland in 1967 and travelled to Australia with us also the following year.

In the early 70s, I attended Gerry's wedding and there I met a young lady from Carlanstown, near Kells, Attracta Lynch. She was a friend of the bride's. We started chatting. We got on great. I liked her friendly nature, the way she could laugh easily, get on with people. We began to 'go together' as people said back then about a courting couple.

We decided to take the next step, get married… and we did. The 70s was a time of great change – in all sorts of ways, and I certainly was happy to swap life as a single man for marriage. We started a family and over the years went on to have five boys and one girl… Shane, Paddy, Ivan, Karl, Christopher and Niamh.

AS WELL AS settling down and starting a family, I was also fully engaged in the 'great adventure' running my own farm. I owed the bank money, sure, but that kind of thing, the burden of debt that might have played on the mind of some, didn't bother me. It was a matter of getting on with things, working the problem.

I certainly didn't walk the floors at night fretting about the farm or the money I borrowed to develop the farm. Never. Worrying about something never helped anybody or improved any situation. That was my philosophy.

If you have a problem, an issue that needs to be sorted, will worrying help? Of course not. You work the problem, find solutions; so I didn't worry. I knew my life was better without fretting. There's always a solution.

I always felt things would work out, that we would be fine. It was about action, tackling the problems you come up against, doing the right thing, or at least not doing anything stupid. Most issues can be sorted out with common sense.

Who was it that said common sense is not that common.? Always, it was about ploughing on. Developing things, advancing onwards.

Of course, it was great to get help along the way – and it came from all sorts of sources. At first, I used to use the tractors up in my father's place, and I would use the diesel he had stored up there. Sometimes he didn't mind, sometimes he did, although in fairness he never stopped me. Never. Eventually I got myself sorted, got my own supply and bought my own tractor. Moved on.

Help came from another source, from people like Dessie 'Snitchie' Ferguson. Dessie, the Lord have mercy on him, died in 2021 but back in the 70s he helped me build our house. He was a teacher of woodwork and mechanical drawing. He was an architect too and he designed the house for us. Dessie, of course, was a renowned figure in the GAA. He had played football for St Vincent's and Dublin. He won the Sam Maguire with Dublin in 1958 and '63, and played in an All-Ireland hurling final in 1961 when Dublin lost to Tipperary.

He had moved to Meath with his wife Maire and family, and worked in a local school. He had become involved with Gaeil Colmcille in Kells, and coached the Meath hurling and football teams. He was a great GAA man and helped those involved in the old association whenever he could. He was the father of Terry Ferguson, a great player on the Meath team in the 1980s.

Dessie drew up the plans for our house but when I offered to pay him for it, he wouldn't hear tell of it. I'll never forget him for that. He backed me to the last. Another GAA man. 'I'll look after you,' he said, and he did. It was brilliant, especially at that time when I was finding my feet, working to build up the farm, settling down. I had great time for Dessie.

When I first started farming on my own, I decided I wanted to concentrate on tillage farming, especially grain. I had grown up working on my father's dairy farm and he wanted me to get into cows. He felt that was the sector to be in but I didn't like working with cows. I wanted to move into tillage, the growing of crops... wheat, barley. Since I was the eldest, I felt I needed to start my own enterprise. I could see my other siblings growing up, lining up behind me so I needed to move on.

We built a house on the farm I had bought in Walterstown and that's where Attracta and I lived when we were married. We started to raise our children.

I SHOULD STATE here that it wasn't me who did the rearing. It was Attracta. She was brilliant, looking after the house, the family, bringing the children here, there, everywhere. Wonderful. I was hardly there.

I would get up in the morning at around six or so and be gone. During the summer and autumn especially, I could be gone from six in the morning to 11 at night. Attracta would only see me for meals... if that. She was the homemaker and she did a great job. The family and the way they grew up is a great tribute to her.

I was preoccupied with building up the farm, grappling with the million little things that needed to be done, week in, week out, but I wouldn't be able to do it only for Attracta and her dedication to the family. Every year, it seemed, I would add more land to our holding either through the purchase of farms or by renting land; steadily adding to the 33 acres I had started out with. I was driven to succeed.

Work just wasn't an issue. It didn't matter how much had to be done, it was just a matter of doing it. Ploughing, sowing, harvesting. The seasons moved on. Every day I learned more. I'm still learning after a lifetime in the job. In farming, you can never say you know everything because you don't. There's always something new.

There's always something that's going to hit you the next day and you have to grapple with that; be ready for that. There are plenty of aggravations but there is a great sense of satisfaction too when you sow and nurse a crop through the seasons all the way to harvest time.

Around the mid-70s we moved into potatoes and over the years we have focused more on expanding the production of potatoes. The family name has become synonymous with the humble spud. I was encouraged to go into potatoes by another Meath footballer, Robbie McMahon. I was open to persuasion because I could see other people around the area making money from potatoes. I thought about it, did as much research as I could, took advice – and went for it, and as is my way, I didn't do it in half measures.

It meant taking more risks, paying out big money. It involved investing in machinery. I was the first to buy a de-stoner in Ireland to make our operation more efficient. A big breakthrough for us was getting a contract to supply Tayto. That also was massive, that started me off really. You had good years, bad years, but generally it worked out well for me. We steadily expanded.

THEN, OF COURSE, there was the GAA. There was always the GAA. The decade had started well for me. In 1971, the GAA in their wisdom decided to give the go ahead for the All Stars – the selection of teams made up of players that were deemed to be the best players in football and hurling for that particular year.

The team was selected and announced. Lo and behold, I'm included in it at left-half-back. In there with the likes of Liam Sammon and Seamus Lydon from Galway, Eugene Mulligan and Tony McTeague from Offaly. Exalted company indeed.

For a few years in the 1960s there was an early version of the All Stars which were called the Cú Chulainn Awards. A number of Meath players received them over the years, including Bertie Cunningham, Peter Darby, Pat Collier and others. I got one in 1967.

There were other representative honours. I was selected for Leinster for a couple of years in the Railway Cup. I had also been picked for an Ireland gaelic football team once or twice. That was a selection of players from around the country that played the Defence Forces and the Irish Universities, teams like that – but the All Stars, that was different.

Meath didn't exactly light up the world in 1971. We were knocked out of the Leinster Championship. That wasn't a great outcome considering we had reached the All-Ireland final the previous September. I hadn't lit up the world either with my performances, or so I felt anyway, so when I found out I was an All Star I was surprised to say the least. Surprised and delighted too.

I was in Vaughan's pub in Navan with my father having a few drinks and somebody came up to us and said, 'Pat you've been picked as an All Star'. I thought he was winding me up but they insisted. No, they said, it's true... you're an All Star.

I'm sure my father was proud because the All Stars were a big thing then. To play for Leinster was considered another major honour. The Railway Cup attracted big crowds to Croke Park. Maybe the inter-provincial competition was starting to lose some of its glamour but it was still something worthwhile to get the call up – for yourself, your club, your county. Now I was an All Star.

I ordered another round. It was time to celebrate. A reward for selection was a trip to San Francisco where we were scheduled to play the reigning All-Ireland football champions Offaly. It was all a very big deal indeed.

So, I packed my bags again and headed back across the Atlantic just three years after our trip home from Australia with Meath.

This time, instead of hotels the arrangement was that the All Stars and the Offaly players would stay in different houses owned by Irish people or certainly people with strong Irish connections. I don't know why hotels weren't used as they should have been; maybe it was to save costs?

I was put up in this house. It was owned by a single man. He was a grand fellow. Welcoming. I couldn't have asked for a nicer host. I was extremely tired so I made to go to bed, only for this man to make it known that he wanted to join me. To say I was astonished would be to put it mildly and I made it known to him... with all the firmness I could muster... that I wasn't of that persuasion. It was a startling start to the trip and I felt it would be best not to stay there.

I decided to leave the house the next day, so I sought out some the lads from the Offaly team. They were in another house staying with a family. I told them my story and they said I could stay with them. I knew some of the Offaly lads well. I had played against most of them. The thing was, when I told them my story and what had happened to me they all nearly died laughing. The good of it all. You couldn't help but laugh with them.

San Francisco was an amazing city in the early 70s. The whole 'flower power' philosophy was widespread. It was about expressing who you were. It was about living a life with little or no inhibitions. Free love and all that.

It was a serious culture shock for a group of lads coming from an Ireland that was still firmly in the grip of the Catholic Church. I had been in the city before so I knew something of what to expect – but for some of the other lads on the tour it was all very new; very different.

San Fran… what a city!

XII

Heffo's Army
The Ban
1975
1997
Kildare Marathon
Jody

★★★
PAT

THE EARLY 1970s was a time of transition in gaelic football; philosophies were changing there too in the sense that there were two big Superpowers of the game who were starting to take over – Dublin and Kerry.

Of course, they had been around forever, winning All-Irelands, but they were once more in the vanguard when it came to introducing changes in the early-70s; taking things to a new level in terms of fitness, tactics and preparations for games under two men who were great players in their time and who were to turn into great managers, Kevin Heffernan and Mick O'Dwyer.

They were whipping up a storm of their very own and we were to be blown away by the power they generated. Meath started to fall behind in Leinster, while a team like Dublin started to move up to a new level. It was one of those seismic shifts that have, from time to time, happened during the history of the GAA. It showed us you have to move with the times or you'll be left behind.

Meath learned that the hard way as the 70s unfolded. We were being left behind although we probably didn't realise it until the likes of Dublin and Kerry were disappearing over the horizon. If you are not moving forward, moving with the times, then you are moving backwards. I knew that from farming.

It was the same in football. Always was, always will be.

While football was my game, I did like other sports. I enjoyed rugby and if I wasn't preoccupied with the GAA I think I would have played that. I tried it out, played a few games with Navan rugby team as a full-back. Enjoyed it too, bombing forward, but the fellas I played against wouldn't have had the fitness I had at the time.

The infamous GAA ban was in place at the time so I took a risk by playing rugby, but I wasn't going to let that stop me. Fr Tully heard that I had played for Navan and he was urging me not to continue. He was very worried I might get a ban. I did take a risk but I didn't give a damn to be honest.

The ban was a crazy idea anyway, ridiculous. I never would have agreed with it and I suppose playing rugby was a kind of protest against it. It was a very narrow-minded rule but as it turned out I only played a few games for Navan.

I just wanted to see what it would be like to play rugby. I would have watched rugby and soccer on TV and attended international games – another breach of the infamous ban. I would go to international rugby games with Gordon Davis, a friend of mine, who has sadly passed away. He was into the rugby big time and could get tickets for international matches at Lansdowne Road. I honestly didn't care if I was recognised or not – it was through Gordon I played for Navan. Fr Tully, who could be an abrupt sort of a man, was worried though and did his best to cover for me. He didn't want me to get involved.

Rugby or not, I was soon back on Meath duty again, focusing on the football. Every team needs to take stock from time to time, to rebuild, reset. Just like an individual. The early years of the 70s was certainly a time of transition for Meath.

THE 1970 ALL-IRELAND final had proved to be a disappointment for us and we were unable to generate enough momentum to get back into another final. New players were tried out as a rebuilding process got underway. We fell by the wayside in Leinster, losing to teams like Offaly and Kildare in the early-70s. We were slipping back.

While the search for new talent went on, some of the old guard – such as myself and Jack Quinn – stayed on, eking out a few more years on the big stage, and there was one final, unexpected hooray for us. We reached the 1975 National League final and there waiting for us was Dublin.

The previous September Dublin under Kevin Heffernan had sensationally come from nowhere to win the All-Ireland title defeating Galway in the final. With their colourful, flag-waving supporters – Heffo's Army – they had brought a new swashbuckling freshness to the football scene. Not that it was a fluke. They were a very good team and I particularly admired men like Brian Mullins, a brilliant player who had a terrific work ethic as well. He never stopped bombing up and down the field from his midfield base, and he was very difficult to stop. He typified their approach. They were extremely fit. Focused.

Dublin had reached the 1975 National League final and were expected to walk home with the title – but it didn't turn out like that. We ambushed them. It was one of those occasions in sport when the underdog takes down the hot favourite; when the odds are dramatically overturned.

We had caused something of a sensation ourselves by beating Kerry and Mayo in that league campaign. The way the NFL was structured at the time, a Division 2 team like ourselves could work their way to the overall final – and that's what we managed to do.

A crowd of 40,853 turned up for the final to see another encounter between the two old rivals but Croke Park was packed full of Dublin supporters that day. Meath fans didn't hold out much hope of us winning – or anybody else for that matter. I was selected at centre-back and I was marking Tony Hanahoe, one of Dublin's best players.

I remember Heffernan shouting at Hanahoe to stay out on the wing. That was early on in the match. I had watched Dublin in a game earlier in the year and Hanahoe was going out to the wings, leaving the middle open and leaving the space to allow Mullins to run through and get in on the opposition goals. It was a ploy that worked – so long as Hanahoe's marker went with him, followed him out.

Mullins was a brilliant player. Exceptional. He was hard-working, one of the best I have ever seen. A powerful man who would run straight at you. With him, there would be no turning around and passing the ball back. With him it was about driving on. I liked that. He was a very influential player for Dublin in those years as they started to dominate football, especially in Leinster.

So, when we played Dublin in that league final, I had a plan. I decided to hold the middle. Not to be drawn out to the wings by Hanahoe and leave the gate open for players to push through and get in on our goals. By staying in the middle I was able to stop Mullins breaking through. Next thing, I see Heffernan coming onto to the field and roaring at Hanahoe.

'Will you stay in the centre-forward position!' Heffo shouted.

'But you told me to go out to the wing!' replied Hanahoe. I had to laugh at the two boys and the confusion that was being caused in the Dublin ranks. I knew we had forced them to re-think and maybe they were complacent too. We weren't given much of a chance.

I didn't want to be suckered into leaving a gap open for Mullins to simply run into. It was about having to think and come up with a solution to a problem I felt would have seriously undermined our cause. Every time I went to play football, I sought to do that. When the ball came my way for the first couple of times in a game, I would learn a great deal about my opponent and what I needed to do to counteract him. Either that or I already had a plan in place.

We pushed on to defeat Dublin in that league final – and it was a sweet victory, partly because we were complete outsiders and partly because at one stage in the game we were six points down and looked out of it but refused to accept defeat as our fate. We came back. The *Meath Chronicle* put it well in their match report from the game. *The Giant-Killers!* was the headline over a report on the game by Denis Smyth.

Not that it was the start of something great for Meath. It just proved to be a brief, all too brief, break in Dublin's dominance in the province. A dominance that was to extend well into the 80s – and by then I had taken out the six-inch nail and hung up my boots.

I HAD WANTED to finish with my county career after that league final victory in 1975. I felt it was the perfect time to leave the stage. On a high. Enough.

In the dressing-room after that win over Dublin in the league final, Jack Quinn and myself threw both our boots into a corner. It was a statement of intent. We had enough. Forget it. I said to Jack, 'That's me finished with county football, I'm not playing anymore.' He agreed it was the end for him also.

When he heard about our decision, Colum Cromwell, a lovely man and a Meath official, asked us to reconsider – and like a fool, I did. I said I would play in the championship. Jack did also. Maybe we didn't want to let our county down. I reluctantly said I would play but I wasn't interested. Not really, and I think Jack felt the same. For me the buzz, the enjoyment of taking on the best in county football had gone.

Also, towards the end of my career I kept breaking my ribs. After nearly every game the ribs would be very sore, painful and I just started to feel the pain wasn't worth the pleasure of playing. That too was a good reason to call a halt. Broken ribs and dislocated shoulders became my Achilles heel. It also hampered me in farmwork, held me back in that respect.

So, I got ready for the summer and as fate would have it, we played Louth in the first round of the championship in 1975, just a few weeks after that league final win over Dublin. We were favourites to beat Louth. We were, after all, National League champions. We didn't play well and Louth won. Deservedly too.

I could hardly wait for the game to end. I hadn't trained properly for a championship campaign anyway and we had celebrated in style winning that league crown. The hunger to put in the hard training needed, the interest, just wasn't there anymore. *Gone.*

Before an audience of just over 20,000, the Wee County defeated us 1-9 to 0-15. As I walked off Croke Park that day I knew it was my swansong. It was time. I had played my first Leinster Championship game against Louth, my father's county, and now I had played my last also against the Wee County.

There was a certain symmetry to all that. A neat rounding off. There were newcomers beginning to appear on the Meath team; talented youngsters such as Joe Cassells. It was time to make way for them. Time to let them have a go.

I had been playing for Meath since I was a teenager. I was now in my early thirties, I had a family, a farm to run. I had taken a few knocks over the years, picked up a few injuries, especially the shoulder injuries but it was more the fact that I just didn't have the hunger for it anymore… and you have to have that.

I probably could have continued on for another year or two if I really wanted to but you have to want it.

I didn't.

I could look back on a career when I had played in various parts of the world. I had no regrets. I had an All-Ireland medal, a National League medal. I had an All Star. I felt I had got a great deal from my career.

Travelled thousands of miles, seen sights I could not have dreamed of seeing when I started out. Okay, maybe we could have won at least another All-Ireland, but we had one in the bag.

That was something at least.

★★★

PADDY

A FOOTBALL CAREER, a football game can be like a rollercoaster ride. You try and control what you can control. You let go of the rest. Prepare the best you can, do the right thing as you see it. Be ready for what awaits. If it doesn't work out you have to live with that, pick yourself up and go again. If you do get it right, well then there is the sense of satisfaction that goes with that. It's about being resilient, learning from your mistakes, taking on board the lessons that experience teaches you, storing them away for another day.

Winning the All-Ireland as we did in 1996 did have a significant effect on my life, on all the players' lives. It somehow changed the way people viewed us.

Seán Boylan had told us in the dressing-room after we became All-Ireland champions that nothing would be quite the same again. Not quite. That we would become household names. You didn't realise fully what he meant at the time, only later the truth of that observation hit home. 'Household names'… what does he mean by that we wondered, but as time went on I began to realise that if someone wins an All-Ireland it can bring about subtle changes in your life – and the way people view you.

You are part of a team that has brought great joy to supporters, brought pride to the county, reached the top. You have that sense that you have done the business and can do it again. On a wider front, there are little privileges and positives. Workwise, it also helps to a certain extent. Gives you a certain status, a place in the world. Usually when I went to talk to people about renting land or buying new machinery the chat would invariably turn to football, it helped to break the ice. Still does.

People might have seen me playing live or on TV, so even with somebody who you may not have met before, especially a sports fan, there is that connection. All that was a help, although business is business, you still had to fulfil contracts, get the crops out of the ground. The demands and pressures of farming, of life, remain essentially the same.

Yet time moves on, people move on. A younger generation emerge who don't know you as well. That's bound to happen, of course. Time passes but the memories I have remain precious mementos of golden years – and the older I get the more golden they become!

A footballer's life can also be an insecure one. Insecure from the point of view that you are haunted by the possibility of losing your place on the team either through injury or a fall-off in form. Things can change quickly. Take 1997. I had become a first-choice player in '96; had nailed down a starting place for all the games, yet the following year it was brought home to me how things can change, and change quickly.

THE SPRING AND early summer included a sustained run in the Leinster under-21 FC. We got a run going under manager Gerry Cooney. Got to a Leinster final where we defeated Dublin, a very satisfying win indeed. Got the better of Kerry in the last four, but in the All-Ireland final in Clones we lost to Derry. Just didn't perform on the day. The team contained a number of players who had helped us to win the Sam Maguire the previous year – including Darren Fay, Mark O'Reilly – but in the final we just couldn't perform. It was a reminder of how you could lose traction just when you needed it.

The under-21 showdown was all part of a busy year for us. I turned out also in the NFL over the winter of 1996 and on into the spring of '97. A consequence of the busy schedule was that I picked up a troublesome knee injury. By the time summer arrived and our senior championship campaign got underway, I was laid low by that pesky injury.

It forced me out of the reckoning for our opening game with Dublin in the Leinster Championship at Croke Park – and I hated missing a game like that. Hated having to sit in the stand and watch as another player, Donal Curtis started at left half-back. I hated losing my place almost as much as losing a game. Not that I wished Donal or Meath any misfortune, I didn't, but I hated having to miss out training and games because I knew it could cost me my place and, sure enough, it did.

I watched as Meath hung on to win, surviving a penalty that was awarded to the Dubs in the dying moments. With time almost up, Paul Bealin stepped up to take it. He drove the ball hard against the crossbar, it was caught and cleared. We survived to win 1-13 to 1-10. I trained and trained hard and didn't make the starting team for the next round which was against Kildare. That was a sickener too, but not unexpected. Donal had played well against Dublin. He was a fine player, very versatile, which only served to compound my concern about my place.

I knew how Seán Boylan operated. If he brought in somebody and he played well, he stuck with that player; he would be loyal to him, and so it proved. That's how it had worked for me. I had come in and replaced Cormac Murphy and when I got a chance to nail down a regular place, I did. I wanted to be the man who was handed the jersey, a starting place, but that pesky injury had knocked me off track.

Injury is one of the most sinister of enemies for any player. A bad knock can not only end up with you losing your place on the team; it could even scupper a career. My injury thankfully cleared up and I resumed training with the rest of the players as they prepared for Kildare, who were then managed by Mick O'Dwyer. He had guided Kerry to numerous All-Ireland titles. Micko knew what he was about. He was a mastermind on preparing teams for the big day and he transformed the Lilywhites.

The O'Dwyer factor all added to the lustre of the 1997 championship; an added intriguing aspect to the summer – which was fine, except that I wasn't on the starting team. We drew with Kildare in that first game although Ollie Murphy scored a point that wasn't allowed. That was a bone of contention among Meath supporters – but more importantly from my perspective, I got a chance to get back on the team during the course of the match. I'm sent on at half-time to replace Nigel Nestor.

I had started the afternoon on the subs bench but then, suddenly, unexpectedly, I was asked to go on during the game. I was delighted to get the call. That's what can happen, I knew that too. Somebody might get an injury and you would be back in the fold. Just like that. You just have to be ready. Players are selfish. They want to be on the team first and foremost. The important thing is to be ready when you do get that call because you just never know how things will turn out.

I loved being part of the helter-skelter of it all again. It was a right old contest too, a real cut and thrust championship game. Unable to find a winner that first day, we returned to Croke Park to play Kildare again a week or two later for the replay. This time I start. I had found a foothold in the team again. It was just like 1991 and the protracted saga with Dublin. One game followed another, the series of matches capturing the attention of the nation. That's what it felt like to me.

That second game was a remarkable occasion, unforgettable and at various stages it looked like we might lose out. Not that we thought like that. We didn't. It was about doing what we were there to do. Our jobs. Never give up on a cause. That attitude seeped into the culture of the team and it came from the manager – and from something inside the players themselves. It came from some part of their core; that corner of their minds, their souls, where they believed they could win despite the odds. Had to win. It also came from preparation, the hard graft that had been done in training. We knew the fuel was there to drive the engine on.

As in the previous year's All-Ireland final, we knew we had the stamina in the legs – and sure enough in that second game against Kildare we tapped into that stamina. We came back bit by bit, second by second, point by point. We were greatly helped by four points scored by Jody Devine, who came on as a substitute and fired them over, one after another. Jody wasn't noted as a point-scorer. A tenacious, busy player yes, one you could always rely on to give it everything, totally dependable. That day he was on fire.

What people don't recall is that I gave Jody the passes for those points, at least that's the way I remember it. We can't give Jody all the credit!! For the first of his scores, I'm running forward with the ball. I look up but it's too far out for a shot. There's too much traffic between me and the Kildare posts to carry it forward. I see Jody racing up close to me, so I pass it to him. He's a long way from the posts. He shoots anyway. The ball sails over. The white flag goes up. Brilliant.

I resolve to do whatever I can and I sense Jody is on his game, and so do others, so we try to release Jody at every opportunity. I get the ball to him once more from another pass. Again, he pops it over. A minute or two later he does it again… and again. Unbelievable. We're on our way. So much of a game can be forgotten in the heat and rush of an afternoon; so much you don't remember but I recall that sequence of scores clearly. Magic. The Meath supporters go mad.

We edge in front by a point as the seconds tick down to the final whistle. Now I was taking chances. I was pushing up, chasing the game and leaving space in behind close to our own goals, but we had to gamble. We had to push forward. That's what you have to do during the course of a game… make decisions. A thousand and one little decisions. That's what a football game is made of, many, many little decisions and choices, like billions of molecules that make up an object. During a game you make countless calls, some turn out to be the right ones, some not. Whether to go or not. Stay or attack. Follow your man or cover your ground. Push up or defend. Pass to that player or this player. Off load to somebody or have a go yourself. A lot depends on the circumstances you find yourself in.

The situation we were in that day demanded we move up; advance… go for broke. At least that's what I feel. The trick is to get most of the calls right, particularly if you are a defender. If you leave too many gaps, inevitably you will pay a high price. It's about balance.

I was marking Eddie McCormack, a very dangerous, pacy player, especially if you allowed him any time and space. He could really punish us I knew that, but I still made the decision to push up, to throw the dice. I had a difficulty marking Eddie, but he had a problem marking me as well because he had to decide to follow me or not every time I pushed up the field. We both had a dilemma.

In those Kildare games Eddie McCormack gave me lots of problems. We were very alike in our styles. When I was marking the same type of player it's harder to get the better of him; we cancelled each other out. When I was marking a slower player or a big tall player, it was in a way easier; there was always a way to get around him.

In that second game against the Lilywhites when we had hauled ourselves back from the brink and Jody fired over his flurry of points one of the great days for me in a Meath jersey; one of Meath's greatest ever days. There was one amazing statistic. We only led for six minutes; they were ahead for 82 minutes. We trailed 3-16 to 2-13 in extra-time, yet we finished level… 2-20 to 3-17.

We go to a third game, a second replay and this time there was a winner – us. Another breathless, rollercoaster ride, though maybe the match itself wasn't a classic. It rained and the contest itself was messy, fractious, affair. They had Davy Dalton and Brian Murphy red carded. We had Mark O'Reilly and Darren Fay suffer the same fate but the important thing from our perspective was that we won. We led from start to finish and at the final whistle we're ahead, 1-12 to 1-10. We had made it through. Finally.

I had another good reason to remember that series of matches with the Lilywhites, apart from the fact we ended up as winners. In that second game I shipped a blow to my head, had to get stitches put in just above the eyebrow. All this was happening while the game was still going on. They brought me in under the tunnel.

The whole idea was to get the job done as quickly as possible and it was. Our doctor Jack Finn was brilliant at doing what had to be done. The needle was out, the task completed, just like that. He had said to the management, 'We'll have him back in five minutes', and he did. I didn't want any delay myself just in case someone else was put on.

In the third game, I got rightly shaken and stirred once more. In the wars… again. This time Glenn Ryan's knee bangs into the back of my head. The incident unfolds like this. John McDermott gets the ball. He solos forward. Glenn Ryan and Willie McCreevy chase him down. I'm one side of McDermott. 'Pass it, pass it!' I urge him. He doesn't give the ball until the last minute. When he does throw it out to me, it falls at my feet. I have to go down and get it. I know Ryan is thundering towards me. He's close, very close. Speeding towards me like a steam train. Like me, he has to go for the ball. Has to. I'm a sitting duck. BANG. His knee crashes into the back of my head.

The whole place become a little woozy and fuzzy. I'm like a boxer who receives a haymaker, a sucker punch. My senses are scrambled and I'm trying to put some shape on the world. The sound of the crowd becomes muffled. Distant. I try to get up but I can't, so I grab the nearest thing that would help to lever myself upwards. I see something and reach for it. Turns out to be the referee's leg!! I don't know where I am or what I'm supposed to be doing. I retreat into myself. Maybe I'm about to check out.

They give me smelling salts. It gives me a jolt and I start to come around. Start to become aware of where I am again and what I'm supposed to be doing. I start to feel the pain in the back of my head. I have received a cut there too. I need stitches they tell me and they get to work.

After I get the treatment, I run back onto the pitch to resume my place but it takes me a while to shake off the effects of it all. My hearing is scrambled, the head fuzzy. I'm a little dazed going back out but I want to get back out and resume my place in the battle. Badly.

Again, I don't want to give any hint that I'm not able to continue. The adrenaline is flowing. The battle, the contest now is all that concerns me. I'm totally engaged in the game. The cut and thrust of the thing. In the zone, in the 'flow'. I don't blame Ryan for banging into me. I know he had to go for it. I would have done exactly the same thing as he did. If I had pulled out and tried to save myself, I would have been hurt anyway. I had to go for the ball, to REALLY go for it – and that's what I did.

I was more than happy with my own performances in the second drawn game and the final replay. It was probably the best I ever played for Meath, the peak of my county career although I didn't know it at the time. I was fit, young, I had shaken off the injury that affected me earlier in the summer. I was flying. I was on top of the world. Whatever the challenge I felt I was ready for it.

THEN THE WHEELS fell off. The victory over Kildare was great but it had cost us. It weakened us in the sense we had expended a huge amount of energy and effort, and we didn't have much time to recover. A week after the third Kildare game we were due to play Offaly in the Leinster final. There wasn't enough time to recover. It underlined the importance of recovery, finding time to regroup, mentally and physically, individually and collectively after a titanic struggle. We were shattered.

Another consequence was that we lost players to suspension and injuries, including Mark O'Reilly and Darren Fay, and Graham Geraghty who had been sent off in the first drawn game. They were all suspended for the Leinster final. Huge losses. It got worse too, as if fate was determined to conspire against us. On the morning of the Offaly match Martin O'Connell hurt his back and couldn't play. He picked up the injury as he walked out of the dressing-room. Remarkable.

We lost our momentum in that game. Lost our shape, our way. The disruption to the team and the fact we were still feeling the effects from the third game with Kildare only a week earlier drained us. Roy Malone, a good player, had the game of his life that day, rattling home a few goals. Vinny Claffey ransacked our defence too. We were way off the pace and were well beaten. Within a week our fortunes had nose-dived.

I was sick after the defeat to Offaly. Not just that day. For days afterwards. I would replay scenes from the game. Look at how we did this or that; how I did this or that during the course of the game and what I could have done better. It was eating into me.

We were no longer kings. No longer champions. Our reign was over.

XIII

'The Blacks'

1978

Keegan Cup

A Selector

1985

Downing the Dubs

★★★

PAT

A PLAYER, I think, knows in his or her bones when it is time to draw a line in the sand; to say... *Enough! I'm done now.* After packing it in with Meath I continued playing for another year or two at club level. The demands weren't the same even though Walterstown were a rising force. At club level too, standards of fitness were rising, there were more demands on players and I didn't have the inclination to make the sacrifices involved.

Sometimes, someone would call into the yard and remind me there was a game or training on, but I might have been out in the fields all day. I might be covered in oil. Sometimes I would go, sometimes not.

After winning the Intermediate Football Championship in 1964, Walterstown had steadily improved their status. We followed up with an intermediate title and on into the senior, and we made some inroads there too. Mick O'Brien was an innovative coach who got us fit and worked on our tactics, explored ways of getting better although, as the 1970s drew to a close, I didn't train as diligently as I might have. There were plenty of other demands on my time.

I kept battling as a player and in 1978 we reached the Promised Land. We won the Senior Football Championship... at last! We had been close a few times without managing to close the deal. Summerhill, who had Mattie Kerrigan in their ranks, were a powerful force at the time. They were going for their fifth successive title and were strong favourites.

On a wet day in Pairc Tailteann we defeated them 0-7 to 0-6. The scoreline suggest it wasn't a classic but it was a cracking contest nonetheless. The *Chronicle* described it as a game full of *super football… with a pulsating finish*. We made it across the line. The *Chronicle* also had something else to say about that match.

To Pat Reynolds congratulations are extended on receiving that medal which had escaped him for so long and he put in his usual wholehearted display before running out of steam.

Those last few words *running out of steam* was an indication of the reality that the end of my playing days were imminent. I was, after all, in my mid-thirties but in truth I wasn't putting in the level of training I needed to do to attain full fitness. There was just so much to do on the farm.

We celebrated in style the night of that final. I had won the All-Ireland with Meath but claiming a big prize with your club is something special. Brilliant. We had a big shed on the farm and that's what we used as the place to celebrate the win. A barn dance.

The music, the craic was mighty. The celebrations continued well into the night. The Blacks had arrived in the big time although there was plenty of pain too that accompanied the win.

During the final I cracked one of my ribs. Again. The way I went for every ball left me very open for a hit and I did ship some big hits. Afterwards, I was barely able to move with the ribs. A Summerhill player hit me hard under the stand. He got me good with a kick. I battled on although I shouldn't have really, but at least we won. The injury was very painful and that took something from the celebrations for me. In those days there wasn't too much attention paid to injuries like that. It was a case of getting on with things.

I was very pleased too, of course I was. At last, to help Walterstown to the top of the mountain, but to be honest by that stage I was just going through the motions. Filling in the gaps. I had done my best but it was time to draw a halt. I struggled on for another year but I just couldn't wait to give up playing. The tank was empty, at least football-wise. I was so busy.

I hadn't a minute to spare or at least it felt like that. People from the club would be coming down to the house or the yard looking for me to go training but, more often than not, I wouldn't go.

The last thing I was thinking about was football.

TOO MANY PLAYERS hang on for too long anyway. They struggle to eke out another year or two but for so many of them the genie has gone from the bottle. Many of them play on and are just a shadow of the player they once were, at least that was the way for some great players of the past. Madness. They try to eke out one more big game, one more glory day, and maybe pick up an injury or are roasted by some up-and-coming young player.

To see a once great player struggle to do the basics is a sad sight on the football field. I may have stayed on just that little bit too long as well. By the late-70s it was certainly time for me to step aside.

We were growing more potatoes all the time. Expanding. Taking people on.

Somebody said to me, 'What are you going to do when you give up the football, you'll miss it.' I replied, 'I can't wait to give it up'.

And I couldn't. I didn't miss anything about it. Nothing. Even the big days in Croke Park when the old stadium would be shrouded in summer or autumn sunshine and the crowd whipping up a wall of sound. Even that I didn't miss anymore.

It was never about the glory, the publicity, the adulation when you won a big prize. It was never about chasing the Hollywood moments and basking in what you achieved. It was simply about the football; playing the game, trying to win every game and when I lost my hunger for all that, well, there wasn't anything left.

You would miss the banter and craic you'd have with the lads, being part of a team, but at the same time I doubt there were many footballers as glad to hang up the boots as I was.

The carousel has to stop sometime and I had reached the end of the road as a player. I was happy to step off the stage.

It was over.

AS THE 70s moved into the 1980s, I continued to keep a watch on what was happening on the football front, especially with Walterstown and Meath, but it was mostly from a distance – standing on the banks or terraces at grounds watching games. I was happy enough doing that. I did serve for a time as a selector with Walterstown, made a contribution in that way.

Then, out of the blue, I was brought back into the thick if things. Big time.

Life can take you in unexpected directions and that's what happened me in the mid-80s. I was asked to answer my county's call and this time I did so. I set out on another road – and what an adventure it turned out to be. An adventure of a lifetime.

One day a jeep appeared in the yard and who stepped out of it, but Seán Boylan. He was on a mission. He had a few years earlier taken charge of the Meath football team and he was looking to make changes. One of them was to scrap the old system whereby the team was run by a 'trainer' and team of selectors – and it was a team. Literally.

Each year up to seven selectors would gather to pick the team for matches. When games were on, all these selectors would have to converge, hold a conference on the sideline and make the changes that needed to be introduced. It was ridiculous. Dublin had long abandoned that structure, if they ever had used it. Kevin Heffernan had just two selectors and that's the way Boylan wanted to go.

Start afresh. Clean out the old, bring in the new.

It was the modern, far more sensible approach. Against the face of considerable opposition at official level he got the green light to change the system and bring in just two selectors.

When Seán stepped from his jeep, he said he wanted to talk to me.

'Pat, I want you to become a selector of the Meath team?' I didn't need all that long to think about. He was looking for me and Tony Brennan, my colleague from the Meath 1967 team, to join him on the management side of things. I was intrigued and I said I would. I was extremely busy but this was an opportunity too good to pass. I had my views on what needed to be done in terms of improving the county team. Strong views. I felt I could use my experience as a player, as a football man, to evaluate players, bring something to the table. I had often expressed those views when talking to Seán.

When I told Attracta I was going to become a selector, she couldn't believe it. I still had a young family, and a growing farming business to look after. There was still a huge amount of work to be done around the farm, but I just couldn't let this one pass. This did intrigue me.

It was a much wider, interesting role than merely playing. It was about seeing the overall picture and making the most of the resources you had available to you. It was about turning potential into success. Turning talent into profit if you like, just like a business – and I found all that fascinating. It was about understanding people, evaluating and assessing the various characters and personalities you had available to you. Getting the best out of people.

Seán and myself sat down and discussed what the role would involve, what he wanted from me. For a few years leading up to that, I used to help Seán out in terms of talking to him about the team, about players. He would ask me about this player or that player, his strength and weaknesses. He would want to hear what I thought about things. Seán had great confidence in me and what I told him. I would tell him what I thought. Straight.

I had some experience in the role with Walterstown. At one stage we had as the club's team manager Jack O'Shea, the great Kerry midfielder who was living or working in the area so we asked him to lend a hand and I think it was him who suggested me to Seán. I was strong in my beliefs and in my views about football and everything else. I worked with Jack as a selector and on one occasion I told him we had to take off one of the well-established players, I felt he wasn't playing well.

He said we can't, because there were a few other family members on the team. He was afraid they would all leave the team, the set-up, if I took one of them off, but I insisted. We had to make the move and we did. We took the player off and his brothers stayed with us. It was a risk but sometimes you have to do something like that; to take the hard decisions for the good of the cause. Sometimes you just have to be ruthless.

IN 1983 AND '84, Meath pushed Dublin hard in the Leinster Championship but ultimately fell short. The following year – the first season Tony and myself were on board as selectors – we were defeated by Laois. Not only that, we were hammered by 10 points. It was a big fall back in form from the previous year. Those who felt the change from seven to two selectors was too dramatic, too radical, had their ammunition to use against us, but we persisted.

Nothing that happened to me in my playing days caused me to become as enthusiastic, revved up, about games as when I became a Meath selector. I became deeply engrossed in the project. This was something that fired me up, in a way playing never did. It was more fulfilling.

As a selector you had to use your head a lot more than as a player. You were on your own when you were playing football. It was about getting the better of your man, your direct opponent. You always had your man to mark; to make sure you did your job whether that was attacking or defending.

When you were a selector, it was different. You had 30 lads to look after. It was like in business having a big staff, you had to look after them, manage them in a proper way in order to get the best out of them. You had a responsibility to them, try to ensure they were in the right positions, that you had the right players on the team, that you had the right tactics to counteract opponents.

Being a selector was a much bigger challenge, far broader than a player and I liked that aspect to it. You always had something to think about, some decision or other to come to every time they played a game, no matter what game that was. You would see something that needed to be improved, maybe some aspect of a player's performance, or some way to improve the team generally.

THERE WAS ANOTHER side to the job that wasn't obvious at the start. It was the side that demanded the skills of a UN diplomat.

I might not have been regarded as the most diplomatic of people. I was seen more as a straight talker but gradually I began to take on a role in the Meath management as a kind of liaison officer, a sounding board… an agony uncle. Somehow the players felt they could talk to me, express their feelings, let off their frustrations.

I would get it in the ear from players and supporters, but I didn't take it personally. It wasn't me they were getting at, it was the situation, it was life they were getting at – and that approach helped me take on the job of helping others.

I would get letters from supporters who were giving out about this player or that player being left off the team. Then there would be a line of players who wanted to talk to me about their own situation. I had no problem sitting down with them and talking to them about whatever issues they had.

In his autobiography *The Final Whistle*, Colm O'Rourke outlined how it worked describing me as *the most abused and best-liked person involved in the team!* Then he went on to add how *Players took out their frustrations and anger on him and he never lost his cool or batted an eyelid. Every side needs someone like that, because when players get dropped, taken off, or left out they need someone to vent their feelings on, and there is nobody better than a selector.*

Colm referred to how I would listen to players letting off steam and end up going out having a drink with them and he was right, that's often how it did work out. Seán could be sensitive when it came to criticism, he would take it hard but it didn't bother me in the least. They could say what they wanted, within reason, about me, the team, the way it was selected. I wouldn't be offended. No way.

I knew they were just venting off. I knew also that it was good for the player and the team generally. The players attacked me about everything, they wouldn't go to Tony or Seán, it was me they made a B-line for the whole time, just like O'Rourke outlined.

THERE WAS THE day Gerry McEntee was dropped.

It was I remember in Páirc Tailteann and by that stage I had been a selector for a couple of years. I had said to Seán not to pick the team until later in the week but he decided to name it after training. Seán didn't know trouble was brewing… but I knew it was brewing. Gerry found out he wasn't on the team.

He was enraged and he made a run at me out on the pitch. I ran up into the stand to escape him, it was funny. I didn't want to start an argument with him because he would be asking me *Why was I dropped?* I had to avoid the trouble. Let the steam out of the situation first. Gerry was right in guessing that I didn't want him to start.

I was saying to Seán, 'Leave Gerry on the bench until the last 20 minutes… then bring him on and that will give the crowd and the team a great lift'. This was near the end of Gerry's great career but the episode was an indication of the way players went for me when anything went wrong. It also showed Gerry's great passion for Meath football.

I had seven or eight fellas who worked for me in my own business and I knew you are only as good as the men or women who work for you. In business you have to bring the staff together as a team focusing on achieving the same objective – just like a group of footballers. You are only as good as the people who are working or playing for you. If your team is not happy, if there is growling going on, discontent in the camp, then you have a problem. You have to bring them with you.

If something happened on the farm, someone broke a piece of machinery say, made a mistake, you couldn't be too hard on that person, start shouting, giving out. If you're too hard with them, a Hitler, you've lost that person. If a group of people won't help each other, work as one, then you are in real trouble too. Morale will collapse. Nothing will be achieved. It's the same with the football, exactly the same.

A good worker can make a mistake, just like a good player. It's about learning from it. That's why I think a manager of a football team needs to run a business themselves, or be in charge of people, to fully understand what's required. You can get plenty of people to do the tactics, looking after the fitness, but you need someone at the top able to keep the 30 or 35 players happy. That takes a special temperament, special, specific skills.

Look at the top soccer mangers in English football, they are able to look after the boys in the dressing-room, they never lose the room. Pep Guardiola, the Manchester City manager, might spend millions and millions on the best players in the world but he still has to get them playing together – as a team. It was the same when Alex Ferguson managed Manchester United. A good manager doesn't lose a dressing-room. If you have a squad of 30 players and you have three or four in that group spreading discontent, not happy, it will eat into the morale of the team. Destroy it in time. You might as well forget about it.

Nothing will be achieved in the end.

I learned some valuable, painful lessons that first year as a Meath selector. That heavy defeat to Laois in 1985 was my fault. No doubt. I had insisted on the inclusion of certain players but it didn't work out. They were good footballers but big men, not the quickest and the game had changed. You didn't need big slow men, you needed players with pace. They just weren't able for what county football had become. I misjudged the situation, didn't fully appreciate how gaelic football had changed, but I took it on the chin; stored away the knowledge for another day. Moved on.

So, we readjusted and brought some strong but quick young players into the squad. We readjusted our way of doing things. We also put a huge emphasis on fitness. That too was crucial.

Seán looked after the training and what could be done to improve the conditioning of the players. A herbalist – and somebody who was interested in the body and how it worked – he had a wonderful understanding of what was required to get players into the peak of fitness. He also used fitness methods to save them from compounding their injury problems. He brought them out to my old stomping ground in Gormanston where they could use the pitches to run around; build up stamina in the legs. He brought them to Bettystown where they ran along the sand dunes and in the water, reducing the wear and tear on knees and joints. He brought them canoeing out near Kilcock. He brought them to the Hill of Tara. The players ran up and down and around the Hill and it was tough. Cruel but they stuck with it. They wanted to achieve.

It was revolutionary stuff, very different, and the players, some of them anyway, thought we all had gone a little mad, but far from it. The players were as fit or fitter than any other group of players any Meath team had ever been. They had a positive attitude – and that's always a good starting point. They were prepared to put themselves through the pain barrier in order to improve. That's what you need. You have to have the players with the right attitude, who are prepared to suffer for the cause.

IN 1986, THE new way of thinking, and the hard training, paid off. Beautifully. We made it into the Leinster final where Dublin awaited. They were still the team to beat as far as we were concerned. The team that posed the biggest challenge for us, physically and psychologically. There was a feeling among the players that if we could beat them, we could beat anybody.

We travelled up to Croke Park. We felt we were ready but with Dublin you just never knew. It was early July but the day was cold and dark. During the first half of the game the clouds opened and the rain came pouring down. Torrents. Maybe that helped us. It rained so hard the dug-out we were in started to fill with water.

We had decided to do something radical with our team selection for that game. To select Joe Cassells at right-corner-back knowing that he would be dragged outfield by his opposite number. Joe Cassells was more a midfielder so he ended up in familiar territory and picked up ball around there.

Shortly before half-time, Liam Harnan hit one of Dublin's main marksmen, Barney Rock with a shoulder charge. It was a fair challenge, shoulder to shoulder, but the Dublin player went down injured, eventually he had to go off. Suddenly, they were without one of their best players. That was a turning point in that game, a crushing blow to the Dubs. They still led 0-6 to 0-4 at the interval but in the second-half we edged in front.

They had their chances but this time they weren't going to take control. We held on to win 0-9 to 0-7. It was a brilliant achievement, a landmark moment for that Meath team.

One victory can make a major difference to a group of players – and winning that Leinster final was truly special. It was the first time Meath had claimed the Leinster final in 16 years. More than that, it gave the team great confidence; that they were able at last to defeat Dublin. It showed that the team had the qualities to succeed, as we knew it could if the players performed to their full potential.

I had enjoyed some great days in my playing career but few occasions hope to compare with that day. It was like we had found our way to the bottom of the rainbow. Just the great sense of achievement. The sense that you had worked towards meeting a target and got there in the end. Great, truly great.

The dressing-room was full of people, all kinds of people, supporters who wanted to congratulate the players and reporters who were looking for quotes from the players about how they had done it. That was the way back then. People, supporters, journalists, could just walk into the dressing-room, no problem. It was mayhem. A happy mayhem. If we had won the All-Ireland for the third time in-a-row the atmosphere couldn't have been more celebratory.

Attracta and the kids were in Bettystown. We had booked a house for the summer holidays there and they had already moved out to the location. That evening, after the match was over, I drove to where they were. I will never forget driving up the road from Dublin, the rain falling against the windscreen and just enjoying the feeling of having been part of what was for us a great victory. It was a long time in the wilderness. Now the exile was over. I was, so proud of the players, of Seán and Tony and everybody involved.

You don't experience many days like that in life. Just that warm feeling of having been part of something special. There was that great buzz, sense of pride I suppose at having achieved something really significant or at least of being part of some great victory. The players had worked hard for that win – and they were richly rewarded.

The events of the day were recreated in the reports published in the newspapers the next day. It was easy reading. *This was the day that Meath at last found their footballing soul. The irrational fear of failure – that has haunted their search for dignity over 16 long, lonely years – finally subsided. For once, they held onto their nerve* wrote Vincent Hogan in the *Irish Independent*.

Yet the journalist didn't seem to like some of the confrontations, the physical aspect of the game. *This was a bitter confrontation, bad tempered and often dangerous* Hogan also wrote.

The team had, it seemed finally arrived although we were brought back down to another reality in the All-Ireland semi-final against Kerry. There was great excitement and anticipation in the lead up to the game. Then, they hit us hard, exposed a certain inexperience, a fragility – among the players and the management team. It was a big thing for Meath to take on a great team like Kerry at that stage.

A big test and for much of the game everything was going to plan. Grand. We started Joe Cassells again as a corner-back knowing he would end up going out to midfield. The plan didn't work so well this time.

Then there was the terrible mix-up when Mickey McQuillan, Joe Cassells and Mick Lyons went for the same ball. BANG. Mickey's face was covered in blood, Joe and Mick were shaken up, stirred. It shouldn't have happened but it did, although we came back and led 0-7 to 1-2 before Kerry pushed on. At half-time they were in front 1-9 to 0-8.

At full-time it was 0-12 to 2-13. Afterwards a *Chronicle* reporter, Cathal Dervan asked me about what I thought about the game and I told him straight. I felt we had made mistakes but I also felt the team had the potential, the talent to get better.

'We gave away a lot of possession stupidly but we'll learn from it. The new blood will come good in time,' I added. I got some things wrong as a selector but I was right about that. Things did come good.

Eventually.

XIV

Kevin Foley

Jinksy

1987

Warriors

Marie Louise

1998

Walterstown

★★★

PAT

WE WERE ON a sharp learning curve. I would have spent many hours in subsequent days and weeks thinking, away from the maddening crowd out on the fields, thinking about how it had all gone wrong against Kerry. What we could have done differently. I would have a word with players, one to one mostly, about what they could do tactically, nothing major. We didn't worry too much about tactics, even in the 80s. The main thing I would advise a player going for the ball would be to drop their shoulder. I hated to see a player put his hand in for a breaking ball, that would kill me, there was no benefit from that. You would have to go for it, full on, to make sure and win it.

I would say to the players drop your shoulder as you go in for the breaking ball, that way you're pretty sure of gaining possession although, come to think of it, maybe that's why I dislocated my shoulder so often. The shoulder was my battering ram!

A lot of time and thought went into preparing the team for big days like the Leinster final or All-Ireland semi-final – a lot of time and thought went into selecting the 15 players for each game we played. Full stop. That's the way it had to be. Seán, Tony and myself would meet up, maybe in Seán's house in Dunboyne, and we would spend hours and hours discussing the merits of this player or that player and how he could contribute to the team. We would spend hours at it drinking tea or, in my case, having a cigarette from time to time.

Seán had, in theory at least, the final say, but if we wanted some player or other in the team we might keep talking until about five o'clock in the morning when he would start falling asleep. Maybe at that stage he would relent and allow us have the player we wanted. *Maybe.*

It worked very well. We enjoyed the banter and the chat with each other as well as the serious discussions about this player or that player We respected each other's views and we generally agreed. It all worked out well. Many times, we would sit down some evening and start picking the team. We would often go long into the night although sometimes also we would have to adjourn matters until the next morning if we couldn't agree on something. We would meet somewhere else then and finally settle on the starting 15. That often happened.

Part of our job as selectors was to go around looking at club games to identify new players we felt could make the cut. One of those was Kevin Foley.

KEVIN FOLEY WAS to become a very important player for us. A regular too for a number of years. I remember going over to Trim to watch them play. I didn't go to watch Foley. I wanted to have a look at another player but I couldn't but notice this particular player with a mop of black hair and a great attitude. Foley had a serious game, he cleaned all around him. He hit hard, he could have been put off twice, but he was brilliant too. He could play football but was tough, mentally and physically, hardy, strong. Just the kind of qualities you wanted. I knew he could do a job for the county team. I went into the dressing-room after the game. I said to Kevin that Meath are playing in a tournament game, and I want you to come in and play. He said he would.

Somebody, a well-known referee came up to me and said not to bring Foley into the panel because he'll only cause trouble. 'He'll hit hard maybe too hard and get sent off.' I said to him, 'That's exactly the fella we want'.

I felt Foley would add some steel and that's what you need. I liked Foley straightaway. He was my kind of player.

I was mad on David Beggy as well. There were plenty of stories going around about him. That he had only been in Croke Park once before he helped us defeat Dublin in the 1986 Leinster final and that was to attend a U2 concert. Some might not have looked on him as a typical county footballer but I was one hundred percent for him. I knew he could cause mayhem in opposition defences.

He played for Navan O'Mahony's and someone said to me he's not an out-and-out footballer; that there is 'not all that much football in him'. As a half-back myself I tried to imagine what it would have been like marking him and I could only come to the conclusion that it would be an absolute nightmare. He was so quick, as elusive as an eel. During my own career I played against all sorts of opponents. The taller or the stronger they were the better as far as I was concerned. I could handle them. The opponents that gave me the most trouble were the speed merchants, the fellas who had jet-heels, who could run at the speed of sound. They were a nightmare, even though I was pretty quick myself. For any defender, pace in an attacker is a scourge, a plague. Very difficult to curtail, the stuff of nightmares.

'Would you like to be marking someone like him?' I said to those who expressed doubts about Beggy's football ability. 'I certainly wouldn't,' I would add before outlining what he had to offer and what he could do for the team.

'Wait, and you'll see he will be a good one!' I told them.

I had no doubts about him and I'm very happy to say I was proven right. He scored a point in the All-Ireland final in 1987 that was sensational, bobbing and weaving his way through the Cork defence before popping the ball over the bar. Magic. In picking players, I looked at things rationally but I went with my gut too from time to time. You would look at the personality, the temperament. They were huge factors too. *Did he have the right stuff?* That's the question you would ask yourself about a player and you wouldn't just be looking at football talent.

We first brought Beggy in for a tournament match to mark the opening of Walterstown football pitch. He arrived on a motorbike and brought a free-wheeling kind of flamboyance with him onto the pitch. That was the first time he played for us and he was brilliant. As a selector, and, of course, as a manager, you are constantly required to make judgement calls on players and tactics, but especially players. You have to trust your own judgement. I knew that and that's the way I operated. You didn't always get it right but when it came to players like Foley and Beggy, I'm glad to say I did get it right.

WHEN I WAS assessing a player, I would look at his attitude and position on the field – but not just when he had the ball. I would watch him more when he didn't have the ball. I felt you could learn more about a player in that situation.

You would see a player standing on the wrong side of his man when the ball was up at the other end of the pitch – or in the wrong place on the pitch. That wasn't good.

You would just know after 15 minutes into the game if the player in question had the right attitude or not; had the necessary awareness of what was required. That awareness of what was happening around him. Aware of the possibilities. In my view a lot of players start to lose concentration, start looking around them, when the ball is away from their area but that's the time when their concentration needs to be at its most intense. If the ball is 50 or 60 yards away from you, you have to be looking around, asking where is the open space, where is your man... where is the danger likely to come from, how can you make the most of a situation if the ball suddenly does come back into your area? How can you take full advantage? These are the questions that you have to be asking yourself. Football is as much about when you haven't the ball as when you have it.

If you go to watch a player and he's day-dreaming, looking around him, not focused, then you know that sooner or later he will be caught out and if that happens in club football he's certainly going to be caught out at county level. That player is not going to be much addition to what you are seeking to achieve.

If a player is not aware of the space around him all the time, and aware of the possibilities, then he's not going to be within five yards of the ball when it does eventually arrive back in his area. Space awareness, being open to all possibilities, that's what is required. Concentration from start to finish. Awareness of what is happening not only in your area but around the whole field. Massive. When a player switches off, he's in mortal danger. That's usually when disaster hits.

You also want a player who, once he has decided to go for the ball, goes full on for it. One hundred percent. He has to go with the intent to win the ball and nothing should divert him from that.

Once they had possession, it was about breaking the first tackle. In modern football I see players when they have possession, the first thing they do is look around to give it to somebody. What they should be doing is breaking the tackle get into space and then look for a pass or a colleague who is free.

It was the same back in the 1980s, get past your man because then you and your team are on the front-foot... attacking. Go forwards, not sideways or backwards.

Forward. Always.

★★★

PADDY

SOMETIMES I HAVE wondered what I would have played if I didn't focus on gaelic football – although I tend to come up with the same answer each time I ask myself the question.

Rugby is a game that has always fascinated me. The mechanics of it, the variety of skills and talents required. The physicality. The mentality and fitness required. When I was in England attending the agricultural college in Chelmsford I dabbled in the oval ball game. I trained with a local team just to keep fit. It was a small, rural club, Division 5 or 6 standard, something like that. Strictly for fun until they went out on the field and the game got underway. Then it got more serious, a lot more serious.

'Where do you play?' somebody from the club asked me when I went up there first.

Somehow, I ended up as a forward. Ended up training with these monsters. Giant locks, huge props. I nearly got killed. After that first training session with them I said I needed something more to improve my own fitness. There was no point me doing scrum after scrum, especially as I was never going to be a forward. I quickly realised that unless you have played the game from a very young age, became accustomed to its rhythms and demands it was going to be difficult.

These boys are only pushing and shoving for half an hour or so, that won't do my fitness much good, I better start training on my own, I told myself.

So, when they were all gone to the shower, I just did laps on my own. I didn't get to play a competitive game for them but I think I would have enjoyed rugby maybe at scrum-half, out-half or the wing but it was clear you needed to play it from an early age.

Soccer never gripped my imagination. I never became a passionate follower of Manchester United or Liverpool like some of my friends. I did however come to admire and follow the fortunes of another team who wore red – the Munster rugby team. In the 90s and onto the new millennium, they had a super side made up of a group of players I admired for their dedication to the cause. The cause that involves overcoming all opponents, all kinds of obstacles in order to attain ultimate success.

O'Gara, David Wallace, Paul O'Connell, Flannery, Stringer, Denis Leamy. They were winners. How many times did they come back from impossible situations to prevail. They hated losing. They had the kind of spirit, heart, call it what you will, that ensured that even when a situation appeared hopeless they were never beaten. They were a team with qualities impossible not to admire. Warriors.

I do have a certain personal connection to Munster rugby. My wife Marie Louise is a cousin of the Wallaces… David, Paul and Richie each of whom played for Munster and Ireland. The Lions also. I first met Marie Louse or Marie Louise Conachy as she was then, when we were both in secondary school.

There was this North Leinster Athletic Championships at the famous Santry track and I was running for Gormanston and she was running for Mercy, Navan. Her father Colm was a miner who worked in Tynagh Mines and when Tara Mines opened he moved up to Meath and settled here with his family. He was HR Manager at Tara Mines.

Marie Louise was living in Navan since she was six or seven and she had a great interest in running and sport, not surprising considering her family connections. So this day I was representing Gormanston College in hurdle race at Santry, she was in the 100m sprint. I took part in my race just before her in the hurdles. I wasn't that concerned about my athletics career, I never trained as diligently as I did for the football but I did enjoy it to a certain extent.

After football training I would practice my hurdling technique on the track at Gormanston College. I was just interested in the science of hurdling and what was needed to improve your technique. I was blessed with pace so I felt I could utilise that on the track.

That day in Santry, Marie Louise and I started chatting – and we kept up the connection. Our shared interest in sport certainly helped to bring us together. We went out for a few years before we got married in 2005.

It helped greatly to have a significant other who understood sport. Who appreciated a sports person's mentality and what it took to get to a high level and achieve success at that level. The sacrifices required, the pain and disappointment that goes with falling short of reaching a set target. The pain of losing. We talked about this or that aspect of fitness and how I could improve my own fitness as a footballer. That was all a great help.

Marie Louise was a better athlete than I was; she won a few All-Ireland gold medals as a runner. My claim to athletic fame was achieving third in the 400k hurdles All-Ireland final. I knew I was never going to get to the Olympics. I had some talent as an athlete but football took my full attention. It was on the football pitch where I wanted to make my mark.

NOT THAT I got to make much of a mark in the 1998 football championship. It got underway on a positive note for us. Then we became bogged down; besieged by forces and events that were to overwhelm us.

We had plenty of motivation to do well in the 1998 championship and as luck would have it who did we get drawn in the first round but Offaly, our old nemesis from the previous year. This time we didn't have a spate of injuries to hamper us. This time we were fired up big time to make up for the previous year and won comfortably with 12 points to spare. We needed considerable luck to get past Louth, they made us work for our win. Luck too was needed when we played Kildare in the 1998 Leinster final. We didn't get enough of it or maybe we were just not good enough on the day. They defeated us. They were thirsting for revenge from the previous year and they exacted that revenge.

Another summer ended. Another championship campaign in ruins.

IN MY EARLY years with Meath my uncle Fr Jim Lynch would say the odd Mass for us up in Ballinteer, the players and backroom team. We used to get the priests out of Dalgan Park seminary but if they were preoccupied Fr Jim would step in and I think he loved that. He was a passionate Meath supporter. He would go to games but he couldn't sit still; he would be roaring the team on. Kicking every ball. Meath games and how the team fared out meant a great deal to him, still does. A real fan. He played football for St Finian's, Mullingar. He served as a priest abroad on the missions and back home in places like Tullamore and Kentstown. When he said Mass on a Sunday morning of a big game you could be sure it would be a short mass. No lengthy sermon. He would be gone. Out, his focus already turning to the game that had to be played that afternoon.

That dedication and commitment to the county team wasn't just because I, his nephew, was playing. He had long supported Meath but it did add another dimension to following the green and gold.

I was very aware I was representing people like Fr Jim when I took to the pitch with the green and gold jersey on my back. He wouldn't be trying to give me advice. He wouldn't be telling me that I should be doing this or that. Instead, he would be appreciative of what we had achieved. Very positive and encouraging. It was lovely to have that in your family circle; your support team.

Things were changing in the game as the 90s moved along. Tactics yes, but also the way teams prepared for games and Seán Boylan was very good with all that. It was something that was an integral part of his career as a manager. His awareness and full appreciation of the fact that the game was constantly evolving and that little things could make a big difference.

Seán knew the human body so well so he would work with us on warm up routines, to get us ready. Somebody else might work with us on the training side of things. In 1996, Eamonn O'Brien and Frank Foley did a lot of the ball-work routines. Seán was very good in the sense he introduced these routines that ensured there was an awful lot of one-on-ones. Routines that ensured there was no place to hide. Drills. He would have collective drills followed by one-on-one drills. I, for instance, would be paired with a forward, maybe Ollie Murphy.

The ball would be kicked into us, just us, by Seán or somebody else. We had to go head-to-head and try and win possession. There was no place to hide. You had to step up. Show that you were ready for the next ball, the next challenge, the next game. In a lot of the systems in place today in modern football there are loads of hiding places, where you are not exposed. Seán would have you one-on-one. It was to get you sharp; to ensure you were ready for the game – so you had to ensure you were up for the fight.

He would have been looking at other sports and how they were using science to improve the performances of the players. From 1996 onwards there was more a focus on players' diets and Meath sought to stay in step with the evolving trends. Before a game, in Croke Park, for instance we would meet up, usually in the County Club in Dunshaughlin. I would have chicken but as time went on there was a greater variety of food available. Fish, meat, salads, vegetables.

Changes were undoubtedly occurring on how teams prepared – although there were some things that didn't change. We had more or less the same backroom team, people Seán Boylan trusted every step of the way and he stuck with those people. We stayed a tight unit. They were brilliant people, experts in their field.

For months we stayed closely connected; all part of this community who were involved with the county team; players, physios, backroom team members. We became a kind of family, a sporting family. We met up a couple of times a week, prepared for games, played the games, focused on the next assignment. Then suddenly, as happened in 1998, we were out of the All-Ireland championship and that routine ended. Just like that. The camp broke up, the troops disbanded; the project halted. The campaigning was over for another year.

The players went back to their clubs; the various people in the backroom went back to their jobs. The players focus changed to helping the clubs – O'Mahonys, Seneschalstown, Simonstown, Dunderry, Walterstown – whoever it was to achieve their ambitions and I found it difficult at least initially to change track just like that. One day you are fully focused on helping Meath in the quest for All-Ireland gold. Convinced it was possible. The next that's gone, that dream has died.

One of the changes I had to make as my career moved on was my role in the team. With the county I was wing back and that's all I could play in the early days of my senior career. It was the same at club level also. I was relying on just one or two strengths such as my pace and my ability, a willingness to battle for loose ball, win it and give it to a colleague.

As time moved on, and I became more experienced and developed my game a little more. I continued to play wing back with the county but with the club I started playing as a wing forward or in midfield, even though I wasn't the tallest of players around.

Wing-back to midfield or half-forward; different positions, different demands. The change in role meant I would have to make subtle little changes in how I played. Subtle but significant. With a couple of years of county football behind me I was more street-wise, more clued into a game as it unfolded. I could read it an awful lot better. I understood the game a lot better the older I got, appreciated its little quirks and nuances.

Walterstown didn't make it into a county final in the 90s. We struggled to recreate the kind of success the team had enjoyed in the 80s.

XV

Tony & Pat
Bellinter House
Agony Aunt
Brian Staff
Sam
Fairyhouse

★★★

PAT

WE EVENTUALLY WON the All-Ireland in 1987.

It was certainly one of the great years for Meath football, but before we got to that stage there was a fair amount of turbulence we went through.

In the spring of that year Seán Boylan looked like – however momentarily – that he was going to step down. Resign. He wanted the players to do some extra training on their own but he felt they weren't doing that – so one night at one of those famous meetings we held every now and again he told the players he wasn't going to accept it.

'We might be Leinster champions but that's all we were going to be', he told them. To push on we needed something extra; to go that extra mile. The players' fitness needed to be extremely sharp. He knew that and had asked the players to do some training on their own in addition to the collective work we did. He felt they weren't doing the extra work.

Those meetings could get heated. I remember one of the players saying to Boylan, 'Seán you don't know what you are talking about… because you never won anything'.

I got up and said, 'Look lads, myself and Tony Brennan won an All-Ireland, we know what it's about, we know what it takes… but you fellas haven't won an All-Ireland and the way you are going on you won't win one either!'

I wasn't long about pointing out the reality of the situation. That's the way I believe in dealing with a situation. You have to be straight talking, honest about expressing how you feel, but no bullshit and while they might not always like what I would have said, I know the players appreciated what I said at the same time. I think that was one of the reasons why they came to me when they had an issue to work out.

The players were good footballers but they weren't able to make full use of their talents because they needed to work harder on their fitness. Seán was right. The players needed to work harder to make it to the next level. Some might have thought it was going to just happen, but it doesn't happen like that. You have to keep moving on, working on your game, working hard. You have to keep improving to land the big prizes, otherwise you become static.

Some of the players, including Joe Cassells and Colm O'Rourke, approached Seán a day or two after he had stepped down and persuaded him to come back – and we continued on. There were other aspects of that year that were far from smooth. Colm Coyle left Ireland to go to America, although he did come back later in the year and rejoined the panel.

In the National League quarter-final, we played Galway in Portlaoise and were well beaten by them. That was just a few weeks before the championship started. It didn't augur well but I wasn't too concerned. I knew the potential was there to make an impact. A huge impact.

At Bellinter House, where we went for meals after training, we used to have those by now famous open discussions and they were very effective in allowing everyone their say. It was about giving everyone a platform to express their views rather than players grumbling about this or that, causing discontent among the squad.

Seán felt that everyone should be given a chance to air their views and we agreed with him. It worked very well, and ultimately led to a happier, more productive group of players. If some were still unhappy, they came to me! Vented their fury at me.

On one trip when we were away in the Canaries, Seán asked me to organise a 'men's night' out. No girlfriends or wives, just the players. So I did. I brought all the lads down to the bar. There was plenty of drink and chat. That night turned out to be a real eye-opener. I learned a huge amount about what preoccupied the players; what was on their minds. What they thought about the way we trained or played. What they thought about many things. What they thought about how we could improve going forward.

Not everyone was happy all the time.

Martin O'Connell was one of our best players, a very good footballer but he had a tendency to give the ball away and he had to work on that. He started out in the half-back line but we switched him to the half-forwards, but he wasn't happy there and at one stage he left the panel. He didn't like to get the ball and have to turn. He left the panel but Seán asked him back and he did return. Eventually, we moved him back where he was much happier. He worked on his game and become a fine half-back.

It did take some time for us to find the positions that suited some players. There were mistakes made by us, the management team, but we always sought to learn from them. Learn and move on.

By 1987 the team was pretty settled and even though we had to go through a spell of turbulence in the spring of that year, we started in the championship in good shape. We started to reel off the victories in Leinster. We beat Dublin again, 1-12 to 0-11, in the Leinster final another very significant win.

We got the better of Derry in the All-Ireland semi-final. We learned from the mistakes of the previous year. That was another huge step forward for the team – and the first time a Meath side had made it to the final in 17 years. That represented real progress.

CORK MADE IT out of Munster and into the All-Ireland final also. It was the first-time we played them in the championship since 1967. The build-up to the final in Meath was incredible. Flags *everywhere*. All people wanted to talk about was the final. Unbelievable hype. There was a mad scramble for tickets.

Everyone was looking for a ticket. People came home from the US and England to go to the game. Meath people who had been abroad for years. I knew we had to work on keeping the players' feet on the ground. Stay focused.

It was important that we didn't allow the players get distracted by it all. You have to stay focused on what you are seeking to do. Win a game of football, nothing more, nothing less. It's just a game of football, the rest, all that other stuff, is just noise. There is so much stuff around an occasion like an All-Ireland final. We had to remind players what we were aiming to achieve. Remind them not to

fortunes but it certainly helped us that day. We discussed the issue and came up with a solution that worked. Thankfully. We ended up winning. We got there.

To win an All-Ireland as a player is great but to do it also as a selector is very pleasing too, in a way even better. Not everyone who had achieved both feats will agree I'm sure with that but there is a tremendous satisfaction involved in helping a team make it to the top of the mountain.

THE ALL-IRELAND FINAL unleashed a long spell of celebrating and it was great. Twenty years was a long time for Meath to go without winning an All-Ireland. The famine had ended. The pints would have been flowing for a few days afterwards, great craic in the pubs, but the work on the farm still needed to be done; decisions still needed to be made. In those years I continued to build up the farm, ramp up the growing of potatoes. When the opportunity presented itself, I would buy land. Push on.

It all involved getting loans from the banks, taking a risk. It's what I wanted to do.

'Are you nervous? How do you keep your head?' people would ask me in relation to standing on a sideline and watching maybe a Leinster or All-Ireland final.

'I'm all right!' I'd say, and I was.

I didn't get frustrated or sidetracked when it came to football, or farming for that matter. I didn't allow myself to get flustered. What's the point? Where's the benefit of that?

As a selector I could stand on the sideline and watch a match and even if it was going against us, I wouldn't start panicking. I knew that was vital. If you are part of a management team and start panicking then it extends to the players as well. They will see that, sense that panic, uncertainty. If you start shouting and roaring, you're sure to lose your concentration, you won't be able to decipher what's going on – or what needs to be done to rectify matters if a solution is needed. Stand back.

You'll end up looking at one player and the mistake he's making, but you won't be able to see the wood for the trees; to see the overall picture. You have to keep the proper perspective, assess the overall situation. You have to identify what's working and what's not working for the team. Again, it's about staying focused. Concentration.

We were All-Ireland champions but we simply didn't have much time to bask in that reality. Just a few weeks after Mick Lyons had lifted the Sam Maguire into the air at Croke Park we were back in the same venue for the start of the league.

Normally newly crowned All-Ireland champions were clapped onto the field by the host team who line up outside the dressing-rooms – at least that was what tradition dictated. Dublin decided not to stick with tradition that year. The Meath players ran onto the pitch while Dublin were kicking about in front of Hill 16, before a modest crowd. It might have been 'only' a league game but we wanted to beat Dublin and did so.

Brian Stafford played a crucial role in helping us get through a number of tough games in the league and championship that season. He had announced himself on the county stage big time in 1987. He really became an important member of our team. I could remember from my own playing days how Meath had lost a game they should have won because they didn't have a consistent free-taker. Stafford filled that role for us and filled it brilliantly. He was so consistent, reliable, yet we almost lost him before his career had started in earnest.

BRIAN IS A lovely fella but back then he was very shy. He would keep to himself. I remember him talking to me one day, saying one of the senior players wouldn't talk to him. I said of course he'll talk to you but you have to talk to him too. He felt he was out of his depth at first playing in the same team as players like McEntee and O'Rourke. Brian looked like he might give up coming to training.

I think he felt he wasn't part of it all. We didn't want to lose him so we asked another player from his club Kilmainhamwood to come in with him, travel to training and games – and that's what he did for the first year or so until Brain got used to everybody, until he felt comfortable being part of the squad.

That's the crucial thing in any situation where you have people, different personalities. It's all about managing them in ways to ensure you get the best out of them. Seán Boylan was great at doing that. His greatest strength was that he couldn't see anything wrong with anybody. It didn't matter who you were or what you were, he saw value in people, he didn't see any faults. No matter how average a player was Seán would find something good in him; identify potential.

Players might come in from junior clubs and it would be a huge jump in standard for them to play at county level but Seán would fill them with confidence

– and some of them bridged the great divide. Soon they started to blossom. Some managed to make the transition from a relatively low level in club football to the county stage. Others found the gap just too wide.

Stafford's free-taking was, of course, a big factor in helping us carve out a win – and take home the Sam Maguire in 1987. The temperament you need to take frees in pressure cooker situations and score from them is a very rare thing. The technique too has to be right. Brian had it all, but it had to be coached and coaxed out of him.

There was another twist to the tale that year. In our last game of the season just a week or two away from Christmas, we played Armagh in Kells. It was a cold, frosty day yet still a big crowd turned up. The game ambled on until the referee Mickey Kearins sent Colm O'Rourke off. In those days if a player was sent off he had no chance of winning an All Star, so the sending off ruled O'Rourke out, immediately, and that enraged Meath supporters.

When the final whistle sounded supporters tried to get at Kearins and what they said to him, well, let's just say some strong language was used. Players and stewards ushered Kearins off the field. It was mayhem and it showed what football meant to Meath people.

It was a crazy, mad way to end the year when we had reached the top of the mountain but there was even more fireworks to follow in 1988.

★★★

PADDY

FOOTBALL CAN BE a funny old game alright. You can work hard, prepare the best you can. Get yourself in the right frame of mind, get your body right. Then it all goes wrong. Horribly, hilariously, badly wrong. Hopes melt away like snow in a warm spring. 1998 was like that for Meath and me. 1999 was different. What a year.

There was, as usual, the National League campaign that unfolded over the winter of 1998-99. Routine stuff, but there was one game which we lost that proved to be a catalyst for big change; for a new direction that was to prove crucial to our summer. The defeat underlined how, in some situations, a defeat can be more beneficial than a victory.

We played Cork in the closing stage of the league and lost. Not only that, we lost 0-3 to 0-6. Three miserly points was all we could muster. We only scored two from play, it was ridiculous. A wake-up call wouldn't cover it. I scored one of our meagre total of points from play, Jimmy McGuinness got another and we didn't get many points, either of us. The team was terrible that day and our lack of sharpness, our listlessness precipitated something of a crisis in the camp.

Seán Boylan was disgusted. Disgusted with our performance, the lack of any real spark in our game. He didn't hold back. He told us we needed to really up our game or the summer would be a washout. 'That's it lads, Monday night we're going to Fairyhouse. We need to put some stamina in our legs, we need to get down to work... REALLY get down to work!' he said or something to that effect. The message was clear.

We looked at each other and mumbled something like, 'Ah f**k!' Because we knew what was ahead of us. We knew the pain that awaited – but we still turned up, at least those who REALLY wanted to be part of it all did.

We gathered on the famous racecourse and started to run around it. Hard stamina work. We also did sprints, long runs, long sprints. Unrelenting. Around and around... and around again we went. A relentless, stamina-sapping, soul-searching slog. Hard. We have to do it for two weeks, he said, every evening and I mean... EVERY evening.

So, we gathered and set off around the course where they held the Irish Grand National. The first couple of evenings were the worst because your legs would be sore from the evening before. A reaction from the previous day. Nine furlongs up to the top... and back. At times you would think *I can't do this, I just can't do this.* Then you would delve inside yourself and say *Yes, I can do this. I must do this.* You didn't want to relent or display any sense that you were slacking. There were plenty of players who would be only too willing to take my place; to step into my boots. Others who would sense that you were weakening and you certainly didn't want that, you definitely didn't want Seán sensing you were slacking. We drove each other on.

There was of course plenty of banter but we knew too what faced us each evening. You just had to steel yourself mentally and go for it. You knew the stamina put in the legs would stand to us further down the line – and having that knowledge added to our self-belief. Making it through the torturous training gave us a certain feeling, not of invincibility, but an armour-plated confidence that helped us when we faced a crisis. It was like putting money in the bank so that it would be there when the rainy day arrived – and for a team, any team, there is always a rainy day.

Seán had us where he wanted us. It was about bringing the whole thing back to basics. Right lads, do you want it or not? That's basically what he was asking us. How badly did we want it? Did we really want to try and win the All-Ireland or were we happy to just go through the motions?

It was savage. It was also different to the kind of work we did in Tara but then that was Seán Boylan. He liked to change the environment from time to time. Different location, different pain but basically the same question was asked. Did we want it badly enough?

He had told us that we would be running every evening for two weeks. It didn't turn out like that. After about nine or 10 days he said. 'Right lads, we have enough done here!'

XVI

1988
'Dirty Meath'

90s
'No Bottle'

1999
Ollie Murphy

Holyhead

★★★

PAT

LIFE WAS BUSY on all fronts – and there was no let-up in 1988. Yeah, what a year that turned out to be. There was a trip to the Canaries early on for the team; a holiday, a reward for winning the All-Ireland the previous September. It was great. An opportunity for the players to spend some time together, the entire squad, their wives and partners.

As I knew from the playing days, trips like that can do wonders for team spirit. The players had a chance to relax, everybody could go down a gear or two and reflect. It was on trips like that you really learned about the issues players were facing; their grievances, their worries, concerns. Sitting together in a bar somewhere having a few drinks, a lot of issues would be discussed; ideas put on the table on how we could make things better.

The 1980s was an era when a great many people found it difficult to make ends meet. There weren't many job opportunities about. Some of the players had no jobs, not much money, like a lot of people at the time. Emigration was rife.

We were only back from the holiday a few weeks when we were on our travels again. This time we were heading across the Atlantic, to America as part of the All Stars trip. As All-Ireland champions we were due to play the All Stars in various games in Boston and San Francisco. Again, more craic, a few drinks, and some serious training for the players added into the mix. They trained in local parks, basically wherever we could find an open space.

The trip was in May. With the championship so close Seán was anxious that the players get some training done. Sometimes some players would train after a long night out. The schedule included lots of receptions, that kind of thing, games too in places such as the famous Gaelic Park in the Bronx, and considerable travel as well. Again, it was a chance for the team to bond although Colm O'Rourke and Gerry McEntee, two of our main figures, weren't able to travel.

Before we went to the States, we had to play Dublin in a league final. It ended in a draw. When we returned from America we won the replay. Liam Hayes got a wonder goal, a spectacular effort from distance. The championship went smoothly enough. We didn't play all that well in games but we did enough to get through, defeat Dublin again in a rough and tumble encounter, another great game, although we did just about enough to get over the line. Mayo in the All-Ireland semi-final. Again, didn't play all that well but made it through.

THAT SUMMER OF course, the country was enthralled with Jack Charlton and his team in the European Championships. I followed the games, it was my country taking part in a major competition for the first time. I wasn't obsessed by soccer but I did follow it. You could see how Big Jack got a group of players playing as a team, working together. He had the ability to do that – and he reaped a rich harvest. That's the sign of a good manager.

You could see how Jack got along with players, brought them with him. While Jack was a success in bringing people together, you could see why someone like Roy Keane wasn't particularly successful when he was a manager. The way he fought with players and others in the camp before the 2001 World Cup could have undermined the team's morale. When he became a manager he had some initial success at Sunderland, but then he struggled.

Meath, by 1988, had developed a sturdy self-belief that carried us through games. We got to the All-Ireland final the hard way, but we got there. Again, Cork were our opponents. We thought we were ready but we weren't. Not really. They blew us out of it the first day with their physicality. We were caught by their approach. Surprised.

We didn't often get pushed around but we did that day. Colm O'Rourke took a very heavy blow. He wasn't well afterwards. Others too knew they were in a game.

The replay was a few weeks later. Before that, we went over for a few nights to

Ballymascanlon near Dundalk. Just to get the players out of their usual routine. Changing approach. Seán was great at doing that as he sought to find a new freshness in the team. New horizons gave a fresh perspective, he felt. We played a challenge game among ourselves at the home of Cooley Kickhams and a Louth player at the time I knew, who was also involved in the potato business, watched the game. He was amazed at how hard-hitting the game was, the intensity of it. All the players wanted to lay down a marker before the replay. The players knew there would be changes. They knew… because we told them!

Like anyone in any context when they see an opportunity, they want to lay down a marker, so the players went at each other like it was the All-Ireland itself. They hit hard. The fact the players were so determined to impress showed the hunger that was in the team to succeed. It was a powerful demonstration of just how competitive the players were. They all wanted to ensure they would be in the team for the replay, especially those who might have felt their place was under threat. It was that kind of competitiveness, that kind of hunger that drove the team on.

Finally, it was time for Seán, Tony and myself to sit down to pick the team for the replay and we had indeed decided changes had to be made. We had been very lucky to survive the first day. We only equalised after David Beggy had been awarded a soft free, and it was very *soft*, but overall, we didn't play well.

We were lucky.

Your job as a selector is to look at the reasons why things went wrong and try to make changes that would help our cause the next time around. We were physically out-muscled the first day, sure, but we also looked vulnerable in defence at times. We brought in Colm Coyle, Terry Ferguson and Joe Cassells, and dropped Mattie McCabe, Padraig Lyons and Kevin Foley. They were difficult decisions, hard on the players who were dropped but our job was to make the hard decisions we felt was needed for the good of the team. We felt we had to make sure we didn't give Cork space to operate the way they could in attack. They had players like Larry Tompkins, Don Davis and Dave Barry who could really hurt us. We made our choices and had to live by them.

The selection we decided on caused friction, and there was some discontent to put it mildly. Some players were not happy of course but we knew that. We expected a strong reaction from supporters and in the press. Some wondered what we were thinking about dropping a player like Kevin Foley, who had played as well as anyone all year. I got it in the ear again. I was the one they again approached to voice their displeasure. I was the sounding board.

Mick Lyons understandably was one of those not happy, he didn't want to see his brother miss out – and, of course, I was the one who was tackled the whole time by players over decisions that were made. I tried to smooth things over as best I could, explain our rationale, and I think it worked fairly well. Everybody eventually settled down and focused on winning the replay, which we did. Seán also talked to the players who were dropped, explained our reasons for the decisions we had made.

It was just as well too, because if we had lost no doubt we would have taken a barrage of criticism but the team played much better in the replay. We had Gerry McEntee sent off early on so we had to dig in, adjust, but we did that and made it across the line. Gerry was a huge loss but his sending off didn't knock us off course. If anything, it sparked us into even greater efforts. To win an All-Ireland is one thing, to do it with 14 men for nearly all the game makes it sweeter. Special.

We had to adjust to deal with the new circumstances we found ourselves in and we did. That's what you have to do to win an All-Ireland. Find a way because there will always be difficulties, obstacles and irritations to deal with. We trailed 0-6 to 0-5 at the interval. We kept at it. Martin O'Connell made a couple of inspirational runs. Bernard Flynn, who had swapped positions with David Beggy, won the ball well out and fired it over the bar in the second-half. That seemed to set us on our way, but they came back.

We were four points up with seven minutes left.

They came back and almost equalised but we held out to win, just about. We had to defend well, tackle like tigers. We did enough. We were All-Ireland champions… again. Winning two All-Irelands as we had done in 1987 and '88 requires a huge amount from any team and some felt we had done it all by being too physical; too eager to adopt roughhouse tactics.

SOME JOURNALISTS HAD been writing for years of how over-physical we were. How we engaged in the 'dark arts' in the helter and skelter of games, but football was a hard, physical game in the 1980s and 90s. That's the way it was. I don't think we were any more physical than other teams. We weren't any more dirty than anybody else although to read people in the newspaper or hear people talk on the radio or TV you would think we were after doing something terrible, constantly engaging in the dark arts.

We were painted as demons by some, praised by others for the way we fought back, dealt with the problems we were confronted with. It seemed to go on for ages after we had won our second All-Ireland; the only time Meath had achieved such a feat.

The way we were portrayed in the media and called *Dirty Meath* never bothered me. It did annoy some in the camp. Not me. Seán was brilliant at dealing with all that because after every game, especially the games when some controversy or other sparked into a blazing fire, he would look to play it all down. He would put out the bushfires.

Yes, there were times when we did hit hard – and some of the players took the flak for that. Mick Lyons got a lot of criticism; his certain image as being one of the truly, legendary hard men of football, but there was nothing underhand about him, he wasn't a dirty player. Never. He was only sent off once or twice in his county career. One or two other players were very good at hitting hard but they did it in a way that ensured they wouldn't be caught. Mick was an open book. When he fouled somebody, he was caught every time.

Sure, we had steel in the team. Sure, we were involved in some hard, uncompromising contests but you would have won nothing in the 80s unless you had that element of steel in the team. You would be blown away. We had a team of players and when they went for a ball there would be no holding back. That was part of the players' nature but we would have encouraged that also. Go for the ball. Give it everything. Don't hold back. I'm sure we weren't the only team who took that approach. Every successful team was like that. You had to be. No holding back.

As a selector you have to make decisions and we made some good decisions in 1987 and '88 that helped to ensure we won the All-Irelands in quick succession. We didn't do so well in 1989 and '90, lost our way. We had to freshen up the team, try and bring in new players.

After winning the All-Ireland in 1988 we thought we were too good, I really believed that. When you achieve success it's inevitable players will start to think they are better than they really are. Then they will ease up. People are constantly clapping them on their backs, telling them how marvellous they are. The management can warn against any such complacency as much as they can but it's very difficult to maintain the hunger you need in a team to succeed, year after year. In 1989, we lost our way – and were defeated by Dublin in the Leinster final. The three in-row dream was over.

We kept the team as fresh as we could; won back the Leinster in 1990, beat Dublin 1-14 to 0-14, but we led 1-10 to 0-5 at one stage. Nearly got caught. Comfortably accounted for Donegal in the All-Ireland semi-final. Reaching the 1990 All-Ireland final was a huge achievement but we ran out of steam at the end, lost to Cork 0-11 to 0-9. Cork caught us at last – and I had a role to play in helping Billy Morgan and the Rebels, although it certainly wasn't my intention to do that.

LET ME EXPLAIN. In the late 1980s and early 90s, I generally stayed in the background. I was happy with that. It was never about getting my name in the papers when I was a player and it was the same as a selector. If I was asked to give my opinion, I would do so, but I was happy to stay in the background. Seán was manager after all. I was a member of the backroom team and content to stay there but I found myself in the spotlight big time.

Front page news. We were in Dalgan Park where the team was training. Approaching big games there could be hundreds of supporters there, just watching the players train. It was remarkable and showed the connection between the team and their supporters… the people.

On one of the evenings leading up to that 1990 All-Ireland final, a well-known journalist with a national newspaper met me and we started talking. He said, 'Will we have a pint?' I said fine and we went to a nearby pub. It was all very pleasant and civilised.

A few pints, a nice chat. I could talk about football for hours with anyone and this particular journalist, this highly-respected, renowned journalist talked away. I also said to him that anything I say is off the record. Not to be published. I knew this journalist very well, all down the years. I had no reason whatsoever not to trust him; to be wary of him. I just spoke to him like I might talk to a friend.

Next thing I open up the paper… there's a big story: *Reynolds says Cork have no bottle* or words to that effect.

Later I heard how the Cork manager Billy Morgan, who was a friend of mine, had the newspaper article stuck up on the wall of his team's dressing-room. He could point to it and say, 'Look at what Reynolds is saying about you'. It was the perfect motivation tool; the ideal way to get a team fired up.

I took tremendous flak for that. There it was in black and white. In stark detail… *Reynolds says Cork have no bottle.*

I couldn't believe it when I saw it. Did I feel betrayed? Of course, I did. I had never intended or thought that the line would end up on the front page of the newspapers. If it was on the back page, it wouldn't have been so bad but the front… for all the world to see? Seán Boylan wasn't too happy about it all either. Why should he!

I was giving Cork the ammunition. It was the perfect headline for Billy to put up on the dressing-room wall to drive his players on. No motivation speech would be as good as that. If they had said it about us, we would have done the same. Got great mileage out of it.

Of course, the lads slagged the hell out of me after that. 'You must have a few bob on Cork Pat, helping like that'… all that kind of thing. In one way it was a laugh, but I will never forget it… never. It was a huge factor in helping Cork win the final that year. Of course, it was. You didn't have to be a sports psychologist to imagine the kind of motivation it provided for the Cork players. It was, no doubt in my mind, one of the chief reasons why they beat us.

I did feel, in the 80s, that the Cork side lacked a certain something… composure, confidence, call it what you will because they hadn't beaten us in a long time. We were always able to get the better of them. Even when we didn't play well against them in big games, the games that really mattered, the Meath players were able to tap into something deep inside them and emerge stronger. Winners. I really felt we had something Cork didn't – although they were later to discover the x-factor and become deserving champions.

They learned from their defeats and became genuine champions. That's what you have to do. Learn from mistakes, put things right. That's what they did and it eventually paid off for them.

For ages after my comments were published in the paper, bags of bottles would arrive at my house posted up to me by people in Cork. They made their point that way, rubbed it in. They had to put a special postman on the job, to take all the bottles that arrived at the sorting office that were addressed to me. It was crazy and funny too, in one way.

Letters arrived too, giving me plenty of abuse. I didn't lose any sleep over it and if there was social media at the time, I would have taken terrible abuse. No doubt.

Then 1991 happened, and the four-game saga with Dublin. That too was something else.

★★★

PADDY

THE SUMMER OF 1999 rolled on. We got ready for the championship and kicked off with a game against Wicklow. We had to work hard but we got over the line. Then Offaly, defeated them too.

Surprise, surprise, our opponents in the Leinster final were, wait for it, our old friends, Dublin. This time we were ready for them. Croke Park heaving. The old rivalry resumed. After a few years of losing to them, we prevailed. Cormac Sullivan made a super save from Jason Sherlock. Ollie Murphy snatched our goal. We won 1-14 to 0-12. Each test we overcame, we became stronger.

Armagh awaited us in the All-Ireland semi-final. Those lads thought they were going to come out and steamroll us. I'll never forget it. There was just this demeanour they had. 'We're here now boys, stand aside,' kind of aura. They came out with their chests out. They had a very good team no doubt and sure, they had emerged from Ulster as champions. They were a formidable foe but we felt they looked down on us; felt they could take us. Maybe somebody in our camp just sparked off that rumour that they thought they were better than us. Maybe it was all part of a rouse to motivate us?

We had heard they had done a lot of weight training. We had heard that when we defeated Tyrone in the 1996 All-Ireland semi-final, they blamed it on the fact that we had muscled them out of it; that we had used physical strength to knock them off track and win the game. Which to some extent was rubbish because we had relied on our other assets to win that game – our fitness, hunger, the defensive fortitude of players like Mark O'Reilly, Darren Fay, skill of players like Trevor Giles, Graham Geraghty, the finishing ability of Ollie Murphy. It was a complete team display.

In that game – as in every game we played – it was about winning the ball, moving it up field quickly. It was not complicated. It was our ability to stop scores at one end allied to our ability to chalk up goals and points at the other end. That's what won it for us. It was as simple or as complicated as that. It wasn't our physical strength that was the deciding factor but the perception grew, the idea gained legs.

It was a line of thinking that was off the mark. Way off. We had little or no gym work done in 1996. We had very little of that kind of heavy work done either in '99. Armagh had. They were in serious condition, like sculptured marble gods you might see in an art museum in Rome. I recall looking at Diarmuid Marsden and thinking this man has certainly done his hours in the gym. He is at the peak of fitness. Added to that was the plain fact that Armagh had some first-class players. Marsden was one. They had Kieran McGeeney. They had Enda McNulty, Justin McNulty, Jarlath Burns They had Oisin McConville, who was one of the finest forwards in the country at the time. He could finish a team off on his own if given half a chance.

In the Ulster final Armagh had defeated Down and beat them by something like 11 points. A hammering that showed very clearly they were a serious side. McConville scored 2-7 against the Down men. That too underlined the kind of threat he was. Then there were the McEntee brothers, twin brothers John and Tony. They were strong, hardy. Men of steel. In the '99 semi-final, I tried to break the tackle as the two of them, one on each side, tried to stop me moving forward. I got unceremoniously pinned back on my arse. I still had the ball though and I held on too. I bounced back up and got motoring again but they were physically imposing and you had to deal with that. My way was to try and get around them. You couldn't just plough through these lads – that was for sure, and that incident underlined the point for me.

We did find a way around Armagh. We were able to deal with their physicality although it was a hell of a struggle. We led by 0-3 to 0-1 at one stage early on. Then just to remind us we were in a real battle they fired home two goals. Just like that. BANG… BANG. Suddenly, we're behind, struggling to grapple with their hunger, their desire to win; their power. They were roared on by the big support. Like every northern team who played in Croke Park they brought with them legions of supporters who whipped up a deafening din every time they scored. There were over 60,000 fans at that game.

It is in a match like that a team finds out about itself. It finds out about its character, the collective character. When a crisis strikes, when the opposition asks the serious questions, a team is forced to look inside itself, to find the solutions needed. If there are too many people in the team who, for one reason or another, are not up to the fight, when the threat is at its most intense, then there is trouble on the horizon. Weaknesses will be exposed.

Unless a positive response is found the team, the COLLECTIVE, will struggle and more than likely suffer defeat. We had players in our side who knew about losing and didn't like it, hated it. Men who weren't going to accept defeat that day. Sometimes events will conspire against you – injuries, just sheer bad luck, a deflection, an own goal – and you lose out despite having the qualities you need. Sometimes the bounce just doesn't go your way, but on the law of averages if you put in the work, show the desire, have faith in yourself and your colleagues, trust them, victory will be achieved.

We lost Ollie Murphy to injury against Armagh too although he was replaced by another fine forward Ray Magee. It was an indication of the kind of strength in depth we had. The kind you need to get to the summit. Ray came on and had a great game. Armagh also missed some good chances. We were fortunate they left their scoring boots at home. They also had Ger Reid sent off. That certainly didn't help them. Sometimes a dismissal can spur a team on to greater efforts. It didn't halt our march to victory that day. We won 0-15 to 2-5 in a game when our character, our hunger was tested.

We were through, back in an All-Ireland final. There waiting for us was Cork, who had proved too strong for Mayo in the other semi-final. Another Meath-Cork showdown.

IN THE LEAD-UP to the All-Ireland final he decided to do something right out of left field. A day trip was organised on a Saturday, a week or two beforehand. There was an air of mystery about it. The players were told to be ready to be collected by bus very early that morning. *Where to we wondered?* Turned out we were heading for, not Hollywood, but Holyhead. We were brought to the ferry in Dun Laoghaire. We sailed across the sea, landed in Holyhead. We changed in a hotel there, the footballs were brought out and we had a kick-around on a local soccer pitch. There was plenty of joking and banter. Afterwards, we went back to the hotel, had something to eat. Headed back home.

Seán Boylan firmly believed in the benefits of breaking routines – doing something different to stop us getting mentally stale; and that was one of those sudden twists, unexpected, twists in routine.

The most famous of these routine-changing trips Seán liked had occurred in 1991 during the protracted, never-ending saga between Meath and Dublin. Before the fourth game, the third replay, Boylan had brought the players to Scotland. It was there they had practiced a similar move to the one that led to Meath's dramatic late goal scored by Kevin Foley the following week and that helped win the game – and the four-game series.

That Scottish trip had gained a certain legendary status but it had served to refresh the players after a series of draws with Dublin that had brought their own pressures; the players had no doubt themselves that that trip was a crucial factor in them eventually winning the series. Our skip, hop over to Holyhead eight years later was to be more subdued. It was only a short hop across the sea, but it did have the desired effect. It was a shift from the mundane, the expected, the everyday, from the hype that was building up ahead of the final.

In the days leading up to the final showdown with Cork the flags appeared out of windows and on hedges and telegraph poles all over the county – just like 1996. At Garlow Cross, beside the N3, not far from my home a few friends of mine, got their hands on an old Cadet car and painted my jersey number on the car and changed its colour to green and gold. It was put on display for all to see, sitting up on the bank beside the busy roadway. It was there for days beforehand.

Then, on the day of the final, my friends started the car and began driving it to Dublin, to the game, joining the steady stream of traffic that was heading to the capital from all parts of Meath. Except that they didn't make it – at least not in the car. It was an old car and it broke down in Ratoath, they had to park it up there. This car covered in green and gold with a giant number seven on it, just parked there.

However, there was a big banner that appeared in Croke Park. **WE'VE PLANTED SPUDS ON HILL 16** it read, or words to that effect. That was another source of inspiration, to see that, knowing it was being waved by people who were part of your community, who were right behind you. On your side.

XVII

Mark O'Reilly
Sam Again
Geraghty
Cat & Cage
Another All Star
'The Four'

★★★

PADDY

THE 1999 ALL-IRELAND, for me at least, whizzed by, like a flash. It was like that in most games. It seemed like about 10 minutes had been played when the referee blew for half-time. By then we led 1-5 to 0-5, our goal scored by Ollie Murphy after it was knocked into his path by Graham Geraghty. Murphy showed his classy, goal-poaching instincts steering the ball home, somehow finding a narrow gap to squeeze the ball through, past Cork goalkeeper Kevin O'Dwyer. The tempo of the game really picked up in the second-half as the Rebels came storming back.

Early in the second-half they scored a goal themselves; a brilliant individual effort from Joe Kavanagh who did a jig through our defence. They went in front. The rain continued to lash down. The fans roared their teams on. Both sides missed chances. I even had a pop at the posts. The ball sailed well wide. I didn't mind as long as we got back in front. We gradually regained the initiative, went three in front. We won a penalty. Trevor Giles took it, but O'Dwyer saved it. That could have knocked us off course. It didn't. We still led by three.

I was marking Podsie O'Mahony, a strong, busy player. I had to keep an eye on him but I managed to go on a few forays myself. Give him something to think about. My wide was one of 12 wides we registered that afternoon; it was a lot and could have proved costly indeed, but what greatly helped our cause was that they registered 15 wides.

They missed even more than we did. They spurned some very good opportunities.

In the final minutes Tommy Dowd came on. The captain in 1996, he had played superbly in the opening game of the championship against Offaly, scored four or five points. He had issues with his back, had to have an operation. He missed the rest of the championship, until those final few minutes in the final. It was great to see him coming on. The management might have been keeping him in store, in case we trailed and needed a lift in the closing stages. As it turned out we didn't need that lift, we were the better side in the closing stages, but it was great to see him come on anyway. No way were we going to lose after that.

I FELT I played well that day. Felt I was in the running for Man of the Match but I didn't get it. Mark O'Reilly received it instead and he had produced a big performance but I was pleased with my own display. I felt I got my hands on the ball enough times to cause Cork problems – and Podsie O'Mahony didn't exactly run amok either. It was one of those days when I found the right balance between my defensive duties and my efforts to contribute some way to attack also.

By the time the final whistle ended we led, 1-11 to 1-8. Champions again in the rain. Magic. Your first reaction is to find a colleague to hug and congratulate. Commiserate with your opponents. Unlike the old days when thousands of people would charge onto the playing arena to surround the players, the presentation of the cup was made on the pitch in 1999; the players and members of the backroom team standing in front of a hastily erected podium. Graham Geraghty accepted the trophy for us. One of the most talented footballers ever produced by Meath, it was fitting he got the honour to captain that team.

After games in Croke Park, Colm Coyle and myself used to love going down to the Cat and Cage pub in Drumcondra for a few pints. There would be the usual crew there, Meath supporters yes, but others too, some we knew well, others we came to recognise and know over the years.

The craic would be particularly mighty after Dublin games. Every year, that gang we met up there seemed to get bigger and bigger. Unfortunately, after the All-Ireland final in 1999 I couldn't go back there. I had to go out to the reception in the hotel, the post-match reception that was usually televised.

We had our post-match dinner. Then the homecoming, people, a sea of people waiting for us in places like Dunboyne, Dunderry, Garlow Cross, Kentstown, Navan… waving their flags, proud of their county team. It was wonderful. Going through somewhere like Garlow Cross I certainly recognised many faces. These really were my people. This time too, unlike three years previously, there was no nagging sense deep inside me that I didn't do myself justice. That was probably even more satisfying than winning it in '99. I had done myself justice.

We also avoided any flashpoints. There were no major bust ups this time, no nagging controversies and accusations of 'Dirty Meath.' Throughout our campaign we had defeated teams producing some quality football along the way. That too was satisfying. We had got the better of some hard, strong teams. We were true champions.

There was talk in the media of Meath now being a footballing dynasty. A team that had shown a physical and mental toughness needed to succeed.

Eventually all the hullabaloo, the celebrating, eased up, life slipped back to some normality. I returned to the land, to the life of farming, the familiar rhythms. There was a real warm feeling about what had just happened, how we had ended up champions and it wasn't finished yet. Towards the end of the year there was yet more recognition for what we had achieved.

A number of Meath players received nominations for All Star awards, including me. The invitation arrived to attend a dinner in Dublin where the award winners would be announced. I was delighted to get the call. I knew I had a chance. I was pleased with my form in most of the big games we played in '99. I had become accustomed to the demands of county football. At the awards dinner I was sitting beside Jarlath Burns, the Armagh footballer. Cork's Ciaran O'Sullivan was another player at the table. They were there with their wives and partners. The players who were nominated for the various positions were called out. Then the moment arrived when they team itself was named.

The winners of the All Stars are announced… 'Goalkeeper… Kevin O'Dwyer, Cork'… the winner in each position is named… 'At left half-back… it's Paddy Reynolds, Meath'. What a moment for me. What a moment in any player's career. My parents were there. I was following in my father's footsteps.

Same family, same club, same county. I don't care how many you get, it's a marvellous thing to be awarded an All Star.

The final All Star team included seven Meath players – Mark O'Reilly, Darren

Fay, Trevor Giles, John McDermott, Graham Geraghty, Ollie Murphy and little old me. It was another honour, the perfect way to mark a perfect year for us. *This is as good as it gets* I thought.

★★★

PAT

WE ALWAYS LIKED to freshen things up, to try and bring in new players but it was difficult to be doing that all the time. It wasn't easy to unearth the kind of players with the talent and the temperament to survive in the white heat of battle.

By the spring of 1991 the team was tired, on its last legs; there was a weariness in the air, but we drew Dublin in the first round and engaged with a long-drawn out arm wrestle with them – the famous Battle Royal as it has been called… the four-game saga. That seemed to energise us again.

The saga was great, wonderful to be involved in. The drama week after week. Cutting edge stuff. In each of the four games we should have been put way. They had us on the ropes; all they needed to do was to land the knockout punch, but they couldn't. We were like a boxer who had taken too many blows; we were sluggish at times yet still able to come up with sublime pieces of skill. Enough to keep us in the race. The whole country became captivated by the games. They were like All-Ireland finals. Each week we hung in there – and then we managed to summon up enough strength to land the big punch.

DURING THAT TIME, I brought a consignment of potatoes up to Northern Ireland, Tandragee. I was involved in bringing potatoes up to a factory in Ballymoney, in the heartland of Ian Paisley country. I had invested some money in the factory in Ballymoney which I suppose was a considerable risk in one sense at the time because the Troubles were still raging, but I never had any problems going up there. You might be stopped by the British Army but they were alright. The RUC would keep you longer, cause you more trouble.

Once going up to play a league game with Meath in the North in the early 70s when Dessie Ferguson was manager of the Meath team, the RUC stopped us. Made sure we got out and emptied everything out of the bus. Everything, searched everywhere. Eventually they let us on our way but it was very annoying.

I went up to Ballymena on a Monday after one of the Dublin matches in 1991. I drove the lorry myself. Just to generate a bit of banter I said to one of the lads up there, 'Did you see the match on Sunday?' He said something to me in reply, like we wouldn't look at that kind of football. He clearly didn't want to say he was looking at a gaelic football match.

Later, one of the other lads said, 'Don't mind him, he was mad to know who won, he was looking at the game too but he wouldn't want anybody to know he was. It was great stuff'. He told me there were many in the North enthralled and captivated by the Meath-Dublin saga – people on both sides of the divide in the North. That's how it had captured the imagination of so many.

To win the fourth game in that long-drawn out saga with Dublin was brilliant. A vital part of that win was the trip to Scotland the previous week. Seán Boylan was great at that. Knowing when the team needed a blowout, and they got that in Scotland that weekend. The following Saturday we played Dublin in the third replay and, of course, Kevin Foley scored his famous goal, with David Beggy popping up to fire over the winning point. Brilliant. It was like winning an All-Ireland.

The summer like none other unfolded and Meath kept winning. We struggled past Wicklow, beat Offaly, and Laois in the Leinster final. We kept making progress. Then we got the better of Roscommon in the All-Ireland semi-final. It was onto the All-Ireland final with Down. We shipped a heavy blow in the days leading up to the final when Colm O'Rourke became ill. He couldn't start the game; it was such a pity. Down took a grip on the game and we ended up losing. O'Rourke came on and he almost sparked a wonderful comeback. That was difficult to take.

It said an awful lot about the character of the players that they got to the 1991 final because the team was finished really before the championship had started. Players were feeling the effects of years of sustained effort. Injuries too were taking their toll. The team was winding down – and yet they nearly won the All-Ireland. Players had enough of it, they didn't want the extra training.

They weren't that young either, a lot of the players were in their thirties, and there were not enough young lads coming in. New blood was needed. The Dublin games had taken so much out of the players yet they persisted, kept going through the summer of '91, winning one game after another, pushing the boundaries all the time. We got back – we found our way back onto the path – and it was a pity we couldn't finish off the year with a victory.

There were a number of reasons why we lost the 1991 final. Other reasons. O'Rourke's illness was a huge blow and we didn't strengthen the panel enough in the year or two before '91. That came back to haunt us. Yet aside from all of that, I still blame myself for Meath losing the 1991 All-Ireland final and that's a big thing for anybody to admit.

I wanted a move in that game that just didn't work out. Brendan Reilly wasn't long on the team and I brought him back to corner-back. I wanted to make that move. I thought he would blot out the influence of James McCartan but, unfortunately, it didn't work out like that. It would have been better for us if we had brought Kevin Foley back to mark McCartan, who caused us a huge amount of problems that day. That was my call and I was very annoyed over it for ages after. Still rankles.

That's the joys of being a manager or selector. You make your decisions and hope they work out. If they don't, well, you have to face the consequences. Live with the fall-out, and that can be hard to stomach.

Being a selector of a county team is a demanding, tough job, it's about decisions, decisions. I had enjoyed the role but by the mid-90s I had enough. I had been there for eight years or so. Yes, I had enjoyed it for the most part but it wasn't easy, dealing with players, telling them they were dropped from the team or the panel. Ending their dreams of making it as an inter-county footballer. That's never easy.

There was a constant pressure on us to find new players who could freshen up the panel. Identify players who you felt could make it – and that's the crucial aspect in running a successful outfit. You have to keep it fresh all the time, bring in two or three players of the required quality each year and that's not easy – and that means two or three dropping out.

Sometimes they will take the decision themselves to leave but more often than not they have to be told they are no longer part of the set-up; no longer wanted. That's not easy; having to do that on a consistent basis. Demanding. These are people you know well, maybe for years. Good people, good men. It's not easy telling people they are not needed anymore, no matter what the context.

A selector has a big responsibility both to the team and the players he brings in, and for most of the time I was involved with Meath I enjoyed the involvement, the challenge, but by the early 90s the team was starting to break up.

SEÁN NEEDED TO bring in a new batch of players. We looked around and sought to identify young players who were emerging, who we felt might develop into county footballers… and among them was my son Paddy. I asked Seán was he thinking of bringing in young players like Paddy in the near future. He said he was and I said that was fine, that I would step off stage. I didn't want to compromise Paddy's position by staying on as a selector and have people say he was only on the panel because I was part of the management team.

I didn't want to put that kind of pressure on Paddy. I wanted to give him a chance to establish himself on the county stage.

The feats Meath had achieved under my time as a selector were, in many ways sweeter, more fulfilling than what I had achieved as a player but the time had come for me to walk away from that role also. I felt I had been part of a golden spell in Meath football, played my part, modest maybe, but it was great to be involved with that team of the 80s and early 90s. They were a great bunch of players.

It's only in subsequent years as Meath's fortunes have steadily declined that we now fully appreciate just how good the players of that era were. Meath, of course, went on to win the All-Ireland again in 1996 and '99 with my son Paddy involved and it was great to be part of that journey too, although it might only have been watching events unfold from the stand. The players from those years also showed great determination, courage and commitment in going all the way – although who would have thought that when they defeated Cork in the 1999 final that it would be Meath's last All-Ireland for over 20 years and, at the time of writing, we're still counting. Still waiting for the drought to end.

I never gave Paddy advice expect maybe drop your shoulder going for the ball, it's one way to protect yourself and give yourself a better chance of getting the ball. He had, I thought, a very good game in the 1999 All-Ireland final.

He was one of those players who excelled in dry conditions; he struggled in the winter time, wet ball, heavy conditions. Like me, he had pace and if he couldn't use that he was, I suppose like me also, not as effective as in dry conditions. We both were blessed with pace, that's one thing he inherited from me. Though, all of our children showed a love for the game and they each had an impressive measure of skill and ambition. All six of them played for Walterstown over the years, and Karl, Kit and Niamh also represented Meath at underage.

I firmly believe fathers can destroy their sons' confidence by shouting and roaring at them to do this, do that when they are young. I tried always to avoid that. It wasn't always easy but I did consciously want to give that a miss. I see an awful lot of it at under-age football especially and it's a disaster for the young player. Destroys their confidence. Leave him or her to it. Let them learn themselves or from other people, the coaches. Fathers shouting at sons achieves nothing.

Throughout the Celtic Tiger years, I was preoccupied in the farm, growing the business. Those years were times when banks sought to give away money and I nearly got caught up in the madness of it all. A certain bank would invite me to race meetings where I would be wined and dined along with other business people from various sectors. The day arrived when two people from the bank came out to meet me.

They wanted to talk about a great deal they had to offer. They could lend me millions to become involved in a building venture in England, a block of apartments. Millions with the prospect of earning a fabulous return. You could see how people would be tempted. Taken in. I resisted the urge to become involved in the project. I just felt it was a branch of business I didn't know anything about – and, seeing how others became entangled in business deals that went wrong – I'm glad I did sidestep that one.

I may have stopped being involved with Meath football in the 1990s but I still went to see the senior team play. It's terrible, alarming how Meath have fallen off the pace in football in recent times. At the time of writing, we haven't won Leinster since 2010… 12 years. Colm O'Rourke has taken over as manager and maybe he will lead us back to success. It would be great to see them win an All-Ireland, bring back the glory days.

I found it frustrating watching Meath and other gaelic football teams in recent years and how they played. Some county managers have players destroyed. The players appear programmed into playing in a certain way; they appear fearful of taking the initiative themselves. The minute a player gets the ball in his hands he is looking around wondering *What am I going to do?* He takes that split second to wait, instead of running for the open space and then making his mind up. They are always looking, *looking* when they need to get the ball in hand, get out of the ruck and then decide what they are going to do. There's nobody thinking for themselves, I don't understand it. They are not allowed. I have seen it in a number of county teams.

I THINK ALSO of the sad times.

That time in Singapore in 1968 when I was shocked to my core by seeing people in unimaginative poverty. I didn't think people could live like that.

I often think of my parents, Christy and Breda, and the fact that I didn't get a chance to say goodbye to either of them. They passed away in the 1990s and I was abroad when they both went to the other side. I knew my father wasn't well when I went to South Africa but I didn't know he was that ill; that it was that serious. He took a turn and died. It was terrible. Fr Jim Lynch was with us, Attracta's brother, and they couldn't find us to tell us the news. Fortunately enough, Fr Jim went to the convent and they told him they were looking for us. It was a terrible shock.

A few years later my mother passed away. She wasn't sick before we went but she was taken into hospital when Attracta and I were in New Zealand. We had just arrived, a day or two, when we got the news. Had to make plans to return. Another terrible shock. Never got a chance to say our goodbye to either of them. That was deep. As time moves on you think of so much from your past. My childhood, growing up on the farm among a big family. The great days I had with Meath as a player and selector. The great days in Croke Park when the old stadium seemed to tremble with the noise and emotion of the supporters and the summer sun shone brightly on us.

We were young, in our prime and God was in his heaven. The trips we had, the craic and the banter. The fun of it all. Great times. And great friends! Frank Cogan and I, for instance, soon forgot our rivalry as Meath and Cork footballers, and we have remained great friends down through the years; Frank and his wife Ann ended up meeting Attracta and myself on the plane on our honeymoon, and both newly married couples were also staying in the same hotel. Both of us are celebrating our 50th wedding anniversary this year.

Between the football and the farming, I've led a very full life and I still like to keep busy. Still driving on although I've gone down a gear or two in recent years. It was ingrained in me; to work, contribute in some way.

I now enjoy golf, trips to Portugal with a few friends. I tackle the course, and a have a drink afterwards. The golf is a sort of substitute for the football, I suppose. I'm competitive, always want to win, to be better.

It's part of my make-up, my DNA. It was always the same, in football and in farming. Be the best you can be. Try your best, be as honest as you can. No-one can fault you after that.

★★★

PADDY

WINNING ALL-IRELANDS BRING all sorts of rewards. There are the tangible awards, the medals, recognition among your own people for what has been achieved. The famous Celtic Cross, an indication that you had been part of a wonderful journey, to be put aside for the grandchildren.

There are other benefits. You become better known and it does open doors in the business world. When you meet someone for the first time it can be a topic of conversation, an icebreaker. It certainly helped. Still does.

As gaelic footballers we didn't get paid of course but we were richly rewarded in other ways – and one of the paybacks for winning All-Irelands and getting All Star awards are the trips abroad. They were always fun-filled, sunny trips away to exotic locations.

After we won the 1996 All Ireland we were brought to the Canaries. Wonderful craic, endless laughs and, of course, a few drinks! Mocky Regan our physio had a little bar in a boathouse near our hotel. 'Mocky's Boathouse' we named the place. We'd go down there early enough in the day, start off the festivities. The party would get underway and continue on. Party central. My father would be on those trips, he would enjoy them just as much as we did. Golden times. Halcyon days. Up to 80 people or more would be on those trips, wives, girlfriends.

There was a trip to Boston, to play an exhibition game over there. There was a trip to South Africa with Meath. Big country, beautiful country, breathtaking scenery. We travelled widely but no matter where we went there was always the craic, the laughs, although there were some hairy moments too.

This day in South Africa a few of us went down to a beach near our hotel where there was a sign… **SHARKS**. A few of us were standing on a nearby hill looking down and there below us, some distance away, is my brother Christopher, who was also on the Meath panel, and Charles McCarthy, another Walterstown player. There they were out in the water, up to their knees, and a little further off we could see the blades of the sharks circling in the water. We had to shout at the lads to get out. Quickly.

There was a serious side to those trips too. Seán Boylan would want us to see another side of the country we were visiting, another side of life. On one trip he took us off this day on a bus to one of the townships, outside Cape Town. We visited schools, brought jerseys and footballs. The people were friendly, inviting, but the poverty was shocking, a real eye-opener. Makes you think about the ways of the world. Seán would want us to see the other side of life on those trips, that it wasn't all about partying. There was another reality.

I went to Dubai twice, once with Meath, once with the All Stars. A wonderful land. Desert country, wonderful landscape, unbelievable opulence too but poverty also, although we stayed in the holiday resorts mostly. A land of unforgettable sunsets and lavish scenery that seemed to go on for ever.

On those trips to Dubai there were plenty of colourful characters but none quite as colourful as Páidí Ó Sé. What a man. Someone you could always have a chat with if you met him in a hotel lobby or elevator, beside the pool or at the bar. He was always on for a laugh, the craic. Character. If that description applied to anyone it was to him. He knew how the game worked. How the world worked. He had won the Sam Maguire as a player many times, as a manager too. He had travelled to Dubai on an All Star trip not too long after he had been to the Far East with the Kerry team.

He knew how to have a good time which is a great trait too; that ability to enjoy life. When the time came to play, to train hard there was nobody better than Páidí. Equally when the time came to wind down, enjoy yourself, he could do that also. There were others around who became embroiled in the general sense of fun that prevailed on those trips.

Talking to people like Páidí, to other players, top quality players, was an opportunity to hear their stories, the battles they overcame, their attitude to training and playing. I knew I could learn a lot from them and I did – but underpinning everything was the fun and the banter.

But no matter where we went on Meath trips or with the All Stars, there always arrived that time when we had to pack up and head back home again. It was time to resume our lives – work, families, mortgages, but at least we had our memories when, for a few weeks at least, we lived like kings in some of the most exotic places on earth.

Our lives back home were waiting. Our real lives. The farming year kept rolling along, crops to be planted or harvested – and of course there was the football. Always the football.

WE HAD A super 1999, and there was no reason to doubt we couldn't have another good year in 2000. We had ended the old millennium as champions, why couldn't we stay champions. Why not? We had the same group of players, we had the same desire for success didn't we? There was every reason for us to be optimistic. Hopeful.

Events, however, were to overtake us, conspire against us. We were to become bogged down in a quagmire, like a tractor that becomes bogged down in a wet, churned up field.

There was an unusual start to 2000. We qualified for the NFL semi-final. We were fixed to play Kerry down in Thurles. We were originally going to go down on a bus, nothing unusual about that, but then somehow Seán Boylan got a fleet of limousines to bring us down. Maybe somebody offered to bring us in that mode of transport. However it happened, it *happened*. There we were on the morning of the game getting into a limousine, a stretch limousine no less, and being ferried off down to the game.

Before we started out, we had chauffeurs putting our gear into the cars for us, the whole works. The only thing we lacked was a glass of champagne! We just laughed at the good of it all. About four or five or us would fit in each car and there were about five cars available to take us down to the south west.

Seán's idea was we would be too cramped going down in a bus for too long. It was then about a three-hour journey down to Tipperary back then. That's the reason he gave us. I feel he wanted to reinforce to us that we were one of the best teams around, that this was the way champions travelled and we were, after all, All-Ireland champions. He wanted to reinforce the kind of confidence that had helped us win the Sam Maguire the previous September. That we would travel with a bit of swagger and let them know we were coming. That we were arriving in town.

Seán was great at doing that. Doing things differently from time to time. It helped to sustain a certain freshness in the squad. He did it before the 1999 All-Ireland final when we went to Holyhead and this was another example.

That freshness, confidence, call it what you will was certainly evident in the way we defeated Kerry that day – at least the way we finished the game. We trailed by something like 10 points at one stage. Looked like we were going to get a hammering. We keep playing and got two goals back from Ollie Murphy and Barry Callaghan. He added a few points and we end up winning. It was one of Meath's great comebacks. What a game. What a victory. What a day.

We looked poised to land our first NFL title since 1994 – but then reality strikes in the final. Harsh reality. We struggle to beat our opponents Derry. We ship a real body-blow when Graham Geraghty is sent off. We draw with them before they get the better of us in a replay in Clones. The fact that the final is drawn out disrupts our training schedule. We are undercooked, not quite right when we face Offaly in the Leinster Championship. Weary, heavy-legged. They are better than us on the day.

Colm Quinn had the game of his life. He shot over a raft of points. We weren't able to get any traction. We just couldn't get a proper foothold, the momentum we needed. We can't spark one of our comebacks either. We were champions going into the championship in 2000; the kings of the castle. That meant teams tried that little bit harder when they played us. It's the fate of all champions, of course. The reigning champions are there to be brought low, hauled back down to earth – and that's exactly what happened to us as the new millennium got underway.

We had shown we were the better team when we defeated Offaly in 1999, yet when we faced them again in 2000 we were the inferior side. We were the vanquished side. It was a bitter blow. Bewildering. Talk about landing back to earth with a bang. It was painful and a reminder you couldn't take anything for granted. It was a hard lesson for us. Not that we took Offaly for granted, we didn't, but we weren't fully ready for them, either. If we were, we would have won.

The bitter reality was that we lost. We relinquished our crown in a tame manner. That hurt as we made our way home. The hurt could linger for a week or two, then you just have to move on. Pick through the wreckage. Try to learn from it.

By that autumn we were already turning our thoughts to the 2001 campaign. Could we get back to the top of the mountain?

XVIII

2001
In the Cold
Kerry
Mocking The Kingdom
Doomed
Galway
The End

PADDY

THE DAY AFTER the All-Ireland football final and it's not a good day for us. Defeated, and well beaten too by a Padraic Joyce inspired Galway side that rocked and rolled and toyed with us, especially in the second-half.

Galway had played so well in that second-half, and deserved to win. No doubt. I was not able to do a thing about it either. Frustration, annoyance, regret, disappointment submerged me. We had gone into the final as red-hot favourites. That was our downfall. On the big day, All-Ireland final day, the whole thing falls apart for us.

I had played in two previous All-Ireland senior finals and won both of them. Now we got a taste of what it was like to lose one – and it wasn't nice. It wasn't one bit nice. There are no consolations. At least it felt like that in the hours and days after the game. The game from hell.

Losing the All-Ireland final was a lousy, stomach-wrenching way to end a journey that had promised so many riches. We had made a faltering enough start. We had struggled in the league right enough; the 2000/2001 campaign held little joy for us and pushed on into the championship. We trained hard as usual, put the miles in the legs, went through the pain barrier. Suffered, knowing there could be rich rewards further down the line.

We had lost our way in the 2000 championship before we really got going, but we were highly-motivated, driven, to regain our status in 2001, our status as genuine All-Ireland contenders – and in seeking to do that we rediscovered our hunger too. There was a low-wattage start to our championship campaign when we beat Westmeath. It was a bit of a struggle for us but we tapped into our fitness, our resolve and experience, and got over the line.

There was an incident in that game I will always remember and it was the difference between winning the game and losing it – or at least that's what I was told later by no less a person than Seán Boylan. The sides were level coming towards the end of the game. We were clinging on. We were the strong favourites, but we were struggling. They had a kickout.

The Westmeath half-back was in front of me and their goalkeeper had kicked out the ball a few times and this half-back had grabbed it. I felt this was part of their plan. It was working well for them, they were on a roll. They tried it again from another kickout. I decided to gamble. Sure enough, the goalkeeper put the ball out to the half-back. This time I'm ready. I go for it, hell for leather. I sneaked in front of the Westmeath player it was aimed for, took it away from him. I soloed up-field, got fouled in front of the posts and Giles put it over the bar. In an instant we turned defence into attack. Instead of finding us on the backfoot we were on the attack.

That was a score that we desperately needed at the time because the game wasn't working out as we would have hoped. It was a moment I was pleased with, it gave me a great sense of fulfilment. It was a catalyst that sparked us into life. From then on, we started to play football. Pushed on to win.

For half-backs, those moments can be deeply gratifying because you have the satisfaction of knowing you did your job. It might not have been noticed by many, nobody outside the group might even comment on it but you know yourself you've done good. That incident also was a perfect example how a gamble paid off. My foray up field bore fruit. It didn't always happen as well as that of course. It worked well then. Boylan said it to me afterwards. 'That was a vital moment!'

Westmeath had never beaten Meath in a championship game but for chunks of that afternoon it looked like Luke Dempsey's well-prepared side might make history. They missed good chances, Ollie Murphy got a late goal and we were safe. We didn't play particularly well but we had won. We would get better. I always felt optimistic that we could get better as the year went on.

WE HAD REASONS to be optimistic. There was certainly no reason to feel undermined by doubts as the summer of 2001 unfolded. We were starting to motor well. I felt fit. I felt strong. At the peak of my career. Flying. I was making the right calls. I felt like I did in 1999 and that had turned out pretty well for us, hadn't it? Training was going well. Those warm, sunny days, championship days held no fear. They were the days I lived for.

After Westmeath, it was Kildare. Back in Croker. A big crowd. The place was buzzing. We started well, then in a couple of madcap moments it all went a bit crazy. At least for me. Seasons can hinge on a moment. Careers can hinge on a moment. I had one of those moments against Kildare that had a profound effect on my summer; on my career. I got sent off.

I didn't get sent off very often – but I did twice that year and the second time was to cost me. Big time. I was dismissed in a National League game earlier in the year against Mayo. David Brady was saying some stuff to me. I reacted, gave him a slap. I shouldn't have done it. Of course, I shouldn't. I knew that very soon after I did do it, but, in a flash, the dreaded red mist descended. 'Off you go!' said the referee.

Then in Croke Park in the championship in the summer, it happened again. Deja vu all over again. We had beaten Westmeath. We were motoring. Then BANG. Next time out against Kildare, before a heaving crowd, real championship stuff; the kind of days I grew to love. Then the wheels fall off, at least as far as I'm concerned. I have a vivid picture in my mind of what happened that day, possibly because of the significance of the series of events that followed.

We weren't playing well, things weren't working out for us, everything was a chore. It felt like we were trying to run in a sea of treacle. Bogged down. *We're f**king stuck here*, I remember thinking to myself as another move breaks down. Kildare would have quickly sussed out we weren't flowing as well as we can that afternoon. That perception would have given them encouragement. It would have provided them with a lift.

Ken Doyle was marking Ollie Murphy in the corner between the Hill and the Cusack. He was a good player, a good marker was Ken, and he was keeping the shackles on Murphy, who was then the most lethal forward in the country. At the peak of his career, a lethal finisher who had dug us out of tight corners before with his ability to conjure up goals out of nothing.

If we do nothing else but stop Doyle having an influence and get Murphy going, create a chance or two for him, we can get motoring, I think. So that's what I focus on, to free Ollie so that he can do what he does best. I take that task on. Nobody tells me to it, I just decided I should. For the good of the cause.

Part of Seán's management was to empower us; to make decisions on our own; deal with situations as they evolved at any given time. He didn't confine players. 'Oh, you have to do this. You can't do that.' You had a sense of freedom playing for him. He trusted you and your instincts and what you should or shouldn't do as you went about solving problems as they evolved during the course of a game… which they did second by second, minute by minute. It worked well, very well – most of the time.

So, I take on this project, this assignment to try and free up Ollie. Create a yard or two of space for him to do his work. That partly means distracting Ken Doyle who wasn't giving Ollie a look in. Ollie had been flying in training and the thinking among some of the players before the game was that unless he got opportunities to score, we would struggle.

I get on this ball. I deliver a pass to Murphy. Not only that, I follow through to nail Doyle with an elbow. Distract him. I miss. Instead, he gets me with an elbow. He knew what I was thinking. He only did to me what I was going to do to him. All's fair in love and war. BANG. I take the brunt of the blow. Without thought of any consequences, I turn back and hit him a box. BANG.

I had sought to do something for the cause, for the team. Make life easier for us by taking Doyle out of the equation so that Murphy could play away. That's the kind of mentality we had. You tried to do anything you could for the team; for the greater good.

It wasn't about yourself.

I probably thought I would get away with hitting Doyle. I don't. The referee sees me striking him. Everyone in Croke Park seems to see it. Kildare fans go berserk. The referee rushes over to me. I know I'm in trouble.

'You're off!' he says.

It has all happened in an instant. *F**k. I'm out of here.* There are only minutes on the clock. The game continues, Meath survive a man short, manage to win the game – but it's not cut and dry as far as I'm concerned. There are consequences. A nasty fall-out.

THERE WAS A definite connection between a hand injury I picked up before the game and the red card I received. I knew I wasn't at my best, I felt under pressure. I was doing okay in the game but I wasn't thinking straight. I was full of antibiotics, I was concerned about the hand. Minding it, subconsciously. I knew I wasn't one hundred percent but I was trying to offer what I could, and in the process I did too much. I went too far. I tried to ensure Ollie was in a position to score, to get the space he needed to do his work but it backfired. Badly.

I know I'm in the soup. I know I'm facing suspension but you always hope against hope that they will look favourably on you. Give you another chance. I'm still miffed and not a little shocked when I do get my punishment from the GAA's disciplinary committee. Because I was sent off earlier in the year, they throw the book at me.

I get two months.

Automatic.

It effectively means the end of the championship for me. The end of my summer. Disaster.

The more the weeks go on, the more disgusted I am with myself as much as anyone else. It's only afterwards the real frustration sets in. As the summer unfolds Meath keep on winning – without me. I'm pleased in one sense but deeply frustrated as well. The hand injury heals. I'm as fit as I have ever been, at the top of my game but I'm out of the loop. I'm at my prime as a footballer yet I can't do anything. I have to watch from the sidelines. Helpless and frustrated. It's enough to put years on me.

I continue to train with the team. Continue to do everything I would be doing if I was playing – except run onto the pitch at the start of games. I miss the build-up to games, the anticipation, that little world I and the other players live in before a game where a sense of anticipation mingles with a certain nervousness.

I even miss the wrestle with the doubts that players go through before games, the edginess. That's all part of it too. I miss not having to get into the zone so that I am mentally prepared for whatever awaits. I miss everything about playing in big games before a raucous, rocking Croke Park, some fans baying for your blood, others urging you on. I miss the one-to-one confrontation with the man I'm assigned to mark in these games. I miss the battle of wits involved, the sweet taste of victory if the cards fall our way. I miss it all.

Missing games like the Leinster final against Dublin. Painful. We beat the Dubs, capitalise on their mistakes. We meet Westmeath again, this time in the All-Ireland quarter-final. I watch it from the sideline. We trail by nine points at one stage. Then we fight back, show some of the old spirit. We have to rely once more on the goal-poaching instincts of Ollie Murphy to get us a draw. We win the replay, 2-10 to 0-11. Not a classic display but we play better and, most importantly win. That's bad news for someone trying to get back into the team. Seán never changes a winning team – but I live in hope, however forlorn that hope is.

Then after training on the Thursday night before the All-Ireland semi-final against Kerry, I see Seán walking over to me. Because my suspension was up literally hours before the game I'm back in the frame, but when I see him approach me, I know. I just know I'm not in the team. I know his form. I know how he disliked changing a winning team but when you're on the outside looking for a way to get back in, one part of you, a little voice somewhere inside your head, is going… *Yeah, maybe he will change his habit and go with you. You've trained hard, you're fit, you're ready, maybe he will put me back in there.*

So he walks over and starts chatting. 'We're not going to include you in the starting team for Sunday Paddy!' he says. 'We're sticking with the same players we finished with the last day.'

'Fair enough,' I say. 'I knew you wouldn't change, I wasn't expecting you to do anything different,' There's an acceptance, but also a certain bitterness. Now it's confirmed I wouldn't be playing. An All-Ireland semi-final, a big production on the big stage, and I'm reduced to watching it from the bench. A bit part player. F**k.

It's not long before the voice starts up again. I start thinking that maybe I will be brought on. Maybe I can be sprung off the bench and make a difference. Help us win a tight game. Maybe. Maybe. When you are on the outside you convince yourself all sorts of scenarios can evolve that will allow you to get back in and make a difference.

THE SEMI-FINAL DOESN'T turn out to be anything like any of us could have imagined. Kerry don't show up. Whatever is going on they are unable to raise a gallop. We win pulling up. We win by 15 points and when we are 10 points up and so superior it's not true, I turn around to Colm Coyle, my old buddy who by 2001 had changed his role from that of player to that of selector.

'Colm, do you not think it's time to put on a few players to get us ready for the next game, the final!' I say, 'I think it's an ideal time to give players a run.' Of course, I'm including myself in that and the game has turned into a cakewalk, a stroll for us. This is a chance to get some game for the final – time back in the legs. I'm itching to get going, to contribute in some way.

They do bring a few subs on, including me, but there's only a few minutes remaining. The game is over. Long over by then. By that stage the Meath supporters had started to cheer with extra gusto as all our scores went over the bar. Every time we'd deliver a pass there would be a cheer; sardonic, mocking. It was rubbing it in to Kerry. It was a disaster.

Some people might trace the demise of Meath football back to that afternoon and you would have to think there is some merit in that. It showed a certain arrogance, a certain expectation that we could now beat a team like Kerry yet afford also to jeer them as well. The players didn't want to humiliate them in any way because we knew next time out it could be us on the receiving end of a right old hammering ourselves. We win by a landslide, 2-14 to 0-5. We should be elated but the victory somehow has a hollowness about it.

The hype starts as the countdown to the All-Ireland final against Galway gets underway. One evening in particular stands out for me. We're training in Dunsany and it's mayhem. It feels like there's thousands of people there, it's like the circus has come to town.

Gardai are called to help with sorting the traffic out. It seems like the whole county has gone mad. It's like we are champions already. I know people showed up in huge numbers in Dalgan Park when the team trained there back in the 80s. I was there myself, an eager youngster retrieving the footballs for the players when they went behind the posts, delighted to be part of it all, but this is different. It's a lot more intense, everybody is convinced the title is ours. Nothing was going to stop Meath now, was the general sense. 'You'll never beat Meath', people were saying.

That can seep into a player's consciousness, distract him or her from the task in hand; affect his or her focus. One of the worst things that can happen to a team is that they win a semi-final by a big margin.

I hadn't been playing so I was one step removed from the team; the inner sanctum. It's very, very different when you are one of the substitutes instead of a regular in the team. Massive. You're not fully engaged. You're an outsider.

So, it's like a carnival at training. Players are distracted all the time. There's no bite to training, lads are just going through the motions. There's no sense that we need to drive on from here. There's a party feeling; that sense we have already won the Sam Maguire and now we're getting ready for a post-final exhibition game. That kind of aura around the place is like a virus. Seán tried to keep the players focused, to remind them the final hadn't been won yet. *Nothing* had been won yet. He was fighting a losing battle. He was one man standing against a tsunami of expectation and optimism. He had no chance.

I knew we were on the wrong track. My father asks me, 'What way are you going?' He would always ask me before big games how things were shaping up. 'Not good.' I said.

'People think we've won it already… it's not good.'

OFTEN DOWN THE years Seán would bring us up to Bellinter for meals after training and we'd be sitting out on the steps afterwards, perhaps a beautiful summer's evening, and he'd talk to us about whatever game we were going to play at the weekend. Often, you'd get a sense from meetings that there was a vibe among the players, a bite, an eagerness to get going and prove ourselves. You'd get a real sense of what's going to happen. How we would fare out.

Sometimes you'd feel that edge, that nervousness among the players ahead of a game. That was good. You knew we were ready for the battle – and there was a reassurance in that. Leading up to the 2001 All-Ireland final it was different.

In the days before the game the players were nervous, yes, edgy too, but there was a certain lethargic feeling also, overhanging the team like a dark cloud. A lack of urgency, a terrible lethargy – and in the end it dragged us down. So, on that Saturday, the night before the final, I knew we were in trouble. The same edge just wasn't there in the same way as previous games. The kind of edge you need going into a big game.

The players were down on themselves. Subdued. They were burdened down by the weight of expectation, they weren't buzzed up, looking forward to the game with the kind of eagerness you would have expected. All the hype, that sense we had already done the business, already won the Sam Maguire, put an extra pressure on us. I felt it myself, I knew it. I said to myself this is not a good feeling. The mood is not right, the feeling is not right. There is just something missing.

I WAS LIKE a bull on the sideline watching the game as it unfolded. I had sensed, like others had, the mood in the camp and I knew we were in trouble beforehand. There's an old saying in American sport that teams are beaten in the locker room. We were like that. We were like that in 2001. Not that we were terrible, at least not in the opening half. The teams were level at half-time. We were motoring very well and we were still in it despite my misgivings.

Then gradually it all started to unravel. Among the early things to go wrong for us was that Ollie Murphy got injured, hurt his finger. The man whose goals had helped us so much on our journey was in trouble. Little bushfires started to break out elsewhere. Bushfires we couldn't put out. There was 44 minutes played when I'm sent on for Ollie. I go into the half-forwards. I certainly wasn't noted as a scorer but I wasn't going to turn down a chance to make some kind of contribution in an All-Ireland final.

I was nominally at least a wing forward but in situations like that you went on and assessed the situation and did what you felt was the right thing to do for the team, the cause. Again, it was about taking responsibility for your own display rather than strictly following a set of instructions. You had to meet the challenge as you saw fit. Evaluate the situation and do what you felt is right, using the experience I had. So, I drifted back behind midfield and tried to gather the ball and move forward with it as best I could. I didn't play as an orthodox wing forward, I was more like a sweeping half-forward.

I just found the game very, very difficult. It was so hard to get a grip on things. It was like trying to catch the wind. I had never come on in a game like that where we were losing our way. I hadn't found myself very often coming off the subs bench and going into the helter-skelter of a game, the tempo like a whirlwind. I found it difficult and it didn't help that Galway were gradually, but firmly, so much better than us.

A player coming on to replace someone else is a specific skill only suited to those with a certain temperament and experience in the role. One minute you're sitting on the bench looking at the game from a distance; next you are in the thick of the action. There's a big transition there.

Some players can deal with that, process that uncertainty naturally. Emerge from the bench and immediately get to the pitch of the game straightaway. Do their bit. Mattie McCabe was brilliant at doing that for Meath, coming on and making a difference; Jody Devine too. Not everyone can do that. There's a mentality, a temperament needed to be really effective in coming off the bench and going on to make an impact, perhaps changing the course of a game. To be a super sub requires certain qualities.

DARREN FAY, ONE of the best full-backs in the country then, stopped marking Padraic Joyce after about 15 minutes. Joyce had come out for the second-half and won a few balls and fired over a couple of points. To counteract his influence Fay takes the decision to swap with Mark O'Reilly, who is now marking Joyce. It's a move that unbalances the defence.

As the second-half unfolds we start to lose our way as Joyce takes over. He helps himself to a goal. He fires over a few points. Suddenly, the game is fast slipping away from us. We lose 0-17 to 0-8.

I still argue with Coyler over this – all these years later it still eats me up thinking about it. When we were in total control against Kerry in the semi-final that was the time to fire on a raft of subs take the heat out of the whole thing. That's not just hindsight, that's what I felt at the time. Take the heat out of the whole thing and extinguish the flames of expectation that I knew would start to consume us as soon as the semi-final ended. Beating Kerry by 15 points put us in an impossible position.

The margin of our win created unrealistic expectations; put us in a lofty position where we couldn't go any higher. The only way was down after that. That put an unbelievable burden on the players. A burden that cost us in the end. Dearly.

A management team needs to shake things up when something like that happens, when you win a semi-final by a cricket score. You can't just go back to the training as if normal service is resumed. Beating a team like Kerry by so much put us on a pedestal but we needed to be brought back down to earth. That could have been done by maybe dropping somebody for the final. A regular. It would be a massive call, a harsh call in one respect, but it would put everyone back on their toes. Make people sit up. We needed to get some kind of shock to shake us out of that space where we and the fans felt we had the job done.

Seán was so loyal to the players who did the business for him, he was never going to change the team. It was a massive strength, but a weakness also. He was such a loyal manager. He was loyal to me in 1996, believed in me – but loyalty can sometimes rebound on you too.

Of course, as a player you think a manager should be loyal to you and drop someone else. That's the way a player's mentality works. As long as it is someone else. That's the funny side of things. Players might want to see changes but they don't want to be given the door or left languishing on the bench themselves. It's human nature I suppose.

ONE OF THE most difficult jobs a manager has in football is to construct a new team from the wreckage of an old one. It can also take time for the trust to develop between the players who are already there for a few years, the seasoned campaigners, and the newcomers. It's a delicate balance.

The players who have been there for years wonder if the new recruits are up to the task; will they be able for the rigours of life in the trenches? Have they got the hunger, the ability? The newcomers might wonder if the older players still have got what it takes to thrive at the highest level. There is an element of understanding required that has to evolve and develop.

As the process of putting a new team together got underway, we were vulnerable at times as new players sought to make an impact – it led to a period of turbulence. There were also clear signs of slippage. We were defeated by Dublin in the Leinster semi-final in 2002, the first time our old rivals had defeated us in Leinster since 1995. We went into the qualifiers where we were drawn against Louth.

It was to prove something of a last hurrah for Meath. It is certainly a game that has become recognised as one of the great contests in Seán Boylan's latter years as manager. Understandable too. Just look at how it worked out.

It's a summer's evening in Navan. A beautiful warm summer's evening. We're playing our neighbours. Páirc Tailteann is packed. There's a cracking atmosphere. There's always an extra little edge to a game when we play Louth, especially in a do-or-die championship game. Neighbours and all that. Maybe it goes back down the years; back to the 40s when they played a three-game saga that became the stuff of legend.

Anyway, they rock up to Páirc Tailteann. To add some glamour and excitement to the occasion, Graham Geraghty arrives for the match in a helicopter. He was at a wedding in Wexford earlier in the day and it's organised to take him back up the country. We need him but for most of the game we trailed. It looks like we are going to lose. With three minutes of normal time to go we were four points behind. Then the comeback started. Richie Kealy grabbed a goal on the 70th minute. Then Graham produces a little magic, scores a goal that rescues us from defeat. We break Louth hearts. We win 3-8 to 2-9. The Meath supporters go mad. What a comeback.

There were 20,000 shoe-horned into Páirc Tailteann that evening. It was a wonderful occasion for Meath football. One of the great revivals, but I don't recall much of it. I remember poor Paddy Carr, who played for Walterstown and was the Louth manager. He was distraught on the line. There's a famous photograph of him holding his head in his hands. Distraught. Understandable too. They had the game won then we conjured up two late, *late* goals out of thin air. I recall the goals, some other details too, but so much of the match I don't recall. It's the same way with other games I played in.

I was always completely focused on the game. I knew if I didn't concentrate and concentrate hard, I would be lost. I made sure I didn't drift. That was crucial for me. I wasn't the biggest player around, I wasn't the most talented, but I stayed focused on what I needed to do. I was never going to be caught out because I didn't concentrate or focus on the job at hand.

Sometimes after a game you would wonder what happened during this or that incident – it was only when you looked at it on TV afterwards you would realise what really transpired. When I was there on the pitch it often didn't register.

THAT VICTORY OVER Louth, the way we came back was to turn out to be a significant moment in the story of Meath football at the time. It was one of the last of the great comebacks of the Boylan era. It was arguably the last real example of how the kind of self-belief he instilled in the team could be utilised to inspire the most unlikeliest of revivals. I was a part of some of those famous comebacks and it was strange because a game could be unfolding and we were falling further and further behind, but you wouldn't panic and you wouldn't sense anybody else panicking either in the team. No sense that the situation had slipped out of our control. It was about doing your job. Keep doing your job because you knew your fortunes could change. It was a wonderful quality we had in the team.

Now, all these years later, I might look at a game and see a team I might want to win fall behind with three or four minutes to go. I would start panicking for them. I would wonder, *How did we stay so calm in these situations when we were playing?* I guess I always believed, really *believed*, something would change to help our cause. I knew we had done the work in training, we had prepared properly. That was in the back of my mind. We had the strength in our legs and that gave us strength of mind. We had the resources available to us to get us out of a tight situation. It was a matter of keep working, keep believing. We had also done our work with our sports psychologist Brian Smyth. He would have encouraged us not to lose faith – and invariably that approach worked. That game against Louth was a perfect example of that.

There was another central reason for the belief. You had serious faith in the players around you. Faith in their ability, in what they could do. Faith in their character. Players like Trevor Giles, Graham Geraghty, Darren Fay, Mark O'Reilly, Barry Callaghan. All over the team there were players I knew I could trust. Implicitly.

Colm Coyle had a saying. When he would be discussing a player, he would say, 'Would you bring him into the trenches with you?' If someone wasn't going to get into the trenches, stand there with you shoulder to shoulder, you don't need him, that was his philosophy and it was so true. If you don't trust someone to go into the trenches with you, then forget it.

That comeback against Louth was something else. Special. A throwback to the great days. Memorable, but it didn't always happen like that when we fell behind. We defeated Laois in the next round of the qualifiers. Encouraging, but we still weren't functioning as well as we needed to be. We then qualified to play Donegal. We fell behind in that game too only this time we couldn't muster a comeback. We were unable to find an extra gear. We were tired perhaps, worn out. The hunger was still there but there was something else missing against Donegal.

That extra little zip and zest you need sometimes. Players were being introduced into the team but I wasn't sure if some of them were ready. They needed more time to develop as players. They were fine players but just needed that extra year or two, but that time isn't always available when a new team is under construction. Bringing in new, inexperienced players into a team is a delicate, difficult process. You have to judge if they are ready or not. Some are. Some aren't. It's difficult to get it right. More often than not, what you want coming into a game is someone with experience, someone who can get control of a game, earn respect. Someone who can make their presence felt. Someone who can inspire and change the course of a game.

We had less and less of those players.

The defeat to Donegal was a dispiriting end to a season that held so much promise. In 2002 we had some great moments such as that win over Louth but ultimately it was a frustrating end to the campaign; the following year was no less frustrating.

THE SIGNS OF a team struggling to find traction was there in 2003 in our opening Leinster Championship clash with Westmeath. They were the better team for much of the game. Should have beaten us. Dessie Dolan missed a sitter in front of the posts near the end of the game, when the teams were level? We ended up drawing, helped by a classy Graham Geraghty goal. What a player. He was the man for us, year after year. So talented he just kept playing no matter how the team was faring out. He is the best player to have played for Meath over the last 30 or 40 years, at least.

Graham scored many vital goals for Meath, including that one against Westmeath in 2003. We pushed on to win the replay in Portloaise. Blessed. Next time out we lost in the Leinster semi-final to Kildare. Just couldn't muster the level of performance we needed, a sign we were losing our place in the scheme of things. Falling behind. Slipping. We embarked on the precarious journey through the qualifiers, again. We defeated Colm Coyle's Monaghan along the way. There was a bit of banter before and after that game. Plenty of craic with Coyler but we weren't laughing next time out when we lost to Fermanagh in Brewster Park. To some it might have constituted a shock but from inside the camp it was easy to see we were struggling to find the momentum of old.

The empire was crumbling.

There were reasons for our decline, sure. One of those reasons was the absence of John McDermott, a player who brought so much quality to the team – and not just in a footballing context. He had retired, and returned, before finally leaving the stage in 2001 and he left a vacuum that was difficult to fill. Impossible.

While we could manage the occasional flourish, like the late finish against Louth we were sure to suffer the absence of a player with his leadership qualities in our ranks. He was a serious leader on the field and in the dressing-room. Not that he ever said a whole lot; in fact, he never spoke much. Didn't have to.

Instead, his leadership qualities were manifested in the way he played the game. The way he would drop back to catch a ball. When a ball came descending from the sky into a crowded goalmouth you knew, more times than not, he was going to catch it. He made it his business to catch it. In ways like that he led by example.

Others might have taken more of the limelight but he was a true leader, quietly going about his business. He was like a Paul O'Connell of Irish rugby, leading, showing the way although he wouldn't be shouting at you saying you should be doing this, doing that. He earned serious respect from the other players by showing example. He was the kind of player every successful team needs and the more players like him they have the more successful they will be.

We felt the loss of players like that, and in 2003 we were starting to struggle. Suddenly, there just weren't enough leaders.

That sense of the ground shifting, of the old order being put under scrutiny was evident during one team meeting in Dalgan Park. There were a lot of forthright things said at these meetings. Things were said by players about other players. What they thought they were doing wrong or whatever. How we should put things right. You would be better to leave your sensitivity outside the door before you came into meetings like that. One night, Seán became the target. Two or three complained about our training; that we weren't going in the right direction, at least in their view.

The game was changing, our training needed to change. They felt we needed to change our tactics. These same players were after enjoying a lot of success under Seán Boylan yet now they were saying he wasn't modern enough. It was hard for me to listen to all this – and it wouldn't have happened if John McDermott had been around. He wouldn't have allowed that to happen. Those players who criticised Boylan would not have talked out of turn if McDermott was in the dressing-room, I'm certain of that.

He commanded that much respect.

When players start to undermine a manager, that manager is in serious trouble, especially if a majority of the players start to feel the same way. I'm not saying that a majority did with Meath, but some did. After a few bad seasons Boylan's credibility was suddenly being questioned.

I WAS CAPTAIN at the time and I said it to the players, not to let that undermining process continue. Looking back now, maybe I should have had more authority over the players, say it louder and clearer than I did. Be more forceful about it. Tell them in no uncertain terms that we have to trust the manager as well as each other. Tell the players they have to be totally behind the manager. Otherwise, we were going nowhere.

When a manager is undermined in any way, when his methods are questioned by older players, the younger players don't have the same respect for him that they should have. Then the whole project is undermined, that's what happens. I was sorry to see that happen with Seán Boylan; sorry to see a great manager be undermined.

Maybe people took Seán for granted at that stage but it was the beginning of the end for him as Meath manager. Once a manager's methods are questioned, it is the end. That was one of the things that turned me off playing for Meath. His approach to management had proved so successful yet he was undermined in a way that wasn't very respectful. Of course, we had the bad years, poor harvests, but there was always next year when things would be better. We could always improve. That was the ethos in the camp.

I HAD BEEN there since 1996 as a player, but after 2004 I decided to walk away from it all. I was approaching the 30 mark, I had won two All-Irelands, an All Star. A major rebuilding job was required but we needed more leaders to do the work that was necessary. Show the way, like great leaders such as John McDermott and Tommy Dowd had shown the route to success in previous years.

That loss to Fermanagh in 2003 in Brewster Park was hurtful. They had some very good players but we should have beaten them. The moment that made my mind up, that it was time to leave the county scene, came after we were defeated by Fermanagh, AGAIN, in 2004, this time in Clones. Here was history repeating itself and it was like a kick in the stomach.

Trust is a huge thing in any team. It's like any relationship. Trust is the cement that keeps everything together. Trust that your colleagues, those who are in the trenches with you will give it everything. Trust that they will dig deep when they need to most. When that is undermined in any way, then there's trouble ahead. When things are not going well that's when you need people to step up and dig you out of a hole. Such characters are not always easy to find.

I let it be known to certain people after the loss to Fermanagh in Clones I was going, leaving the camp. Coyler and others asked me to go back for one more year, not to raise the white flag just yet. To have another go; there was no telling what could happen, just as was the case in 1996 when we went beyond all expectations, achieved more than most believed we could. I was somewhat sceptical history would repeat itself but I relented. I went back for one more trip on the not so merry-go-round.

There was by now a familiar, numbing sameness about the summers for Meath. Put up a decent fight in the Leinster Championship, lose to Dublin, Kildare or somebody… set out on the precarious route that is the qualifiers.

Win a game or two. Then lose and get knocked out.

LIKE A REEL of a film repeating itself, it happens again in 2005. We're beaten by Dublin yet again in Leinster, this time in a belter of a match, a real humdinger before a crowd of over 65,000 at Croker. It's like old times. I come on as a substitute. That's my role now. The game flashes past but there's no late surge by us. We lose.

Then we move on to the qualifiers and get beaten by Cavan on a bright summer's day in Clones, but for Meath, for me, it was the bleakest of days. *Enough. I'm done here* I told myself in the dressing-room. Not long afterwards, Seán Boylan announces he is stepping down as manager. He had enough too. So had I. There was certainly no going back this time.

It's funny how it all worked out for me when I ended my career as a county footballer in 2005. How I stepped away from football without the least regret. Once I took the step away, I didn't miss it. Not one bit. Didn't missing the training – or even the big games. Nothing about it really, apart from the laughs with the lads, the banter. Maybe that perhaps.

So, football was no longer part of the deal, but there were plenty of other things to keep me busy. The same year I got married to Marie Louise. Since then, Marie Louise and myself have been blessed with three children. There's Nicole, who plays camogie, a game she enjoys. She is very interested in horse riding and is starting out in football. She's tenacious. She loves her sport and gives her full commitment. It's the same with our sons Darragh and Casey, who both play football. Casey is very conscientious also when it comes to his sport. Plays rugby, soccer and football, always in the right position at the right time, an intelligent player. Darragh too loves his sport, rugby, hurling, football. He's blessed with pace. His motto is to get the ball and go forward with it. Wonder where he got that from! He's tenacious too. It's just wonderful to see them all pursuing some sporting activity because youngsters can learn so much that way. About life. About themselves.

After I got married, I pulled the pin on both my county and club careers – and for about five years I didn't even go to a game. I didn't attend a county or club game. Not once. I had enough.

I had been at it since I was 16, playing for Meath teams at various levels. A huge chunk of each year would be taken up with football. Every Tuesday and Thursday evening, and weekends as well, would be taken up with football. Football, football… *football*. Your whole life is put on hold for 15, 16 years and there comes a stage where you just don't have the hunger for it anymore. You just decide… *I have enough of this*.

My friends often would be out for a night, a Saturday night, and I'd get a call. 'Why don't you join us, just for one?' And in the background you could hear the party was in full swing; the craic mighty. It took considerable resolve to say no thanks I've training in the morning at 11 o'clock. You wouldn't go out because you knew if you didn't give it all in training you weren't giving 'the project' everything you could. I knew if I copped out in training, when it came to the game that nagging thought would be there at the back of my mind, *You didn't do all the training the way you should have.* Your colleagues had trusted you, the manager had trusted you, so you didn't want to let them down by betraying that trust. That was a big thing, at least for me and I know others looked at it in exactly the same way.

The only way to have your mind clear as you went into battle was to know that you had given everything in terms of preparing for the big day in Croke Park, Portlaoise, Clones, wherever. The grounds might change but the same demands, pressures were the same – and you had to be ready to deal with those pressures. You had to be at ease with yourself that you had given yourself every chance before you stepped onto the battlefield.

All the lads on the Meath teams of say 1996 and '99 were the same. Darren Fay was the same, Mark O'Reilly, Barry Callaghan, Ollie Murphy, all of them. It was one of the cornerstones of our success, the fact that all those involved were prepared to make the sacrifices – and we did make the sacrifices and won All-Irelands. You need other things as well to be successful, such as luck, but you have to have the foundations in place. That trust, that desire to be a winner. Strong.

Once I stopped playing people asked me to get involved in various teams as a coach, selector, manager, but I told them no. I told them I was sick of football, I didn't want to see a game even. Sick of it. Some might have been surprised, shocked even with that response but that is what I honestly felt. I had enough of it. I didn't want to be involved in any way for some years afterwards, as a player, coach, official, any role and that's very common among players, at least for a few years after they take out the six-inch nail and hang up their boots.

It's only in recent years that it has begun to change for me as my own children have started to grow up. I helped out Barry Callaghan when he was manager of the Meath under-21s for a time a few years ago. That, I suppose, was another indication that I had refound some of the appetite for the game.

I WAS PREOCCUPIED with the farming. There was always something going on and like everything else, there were changes we had to keep up with. Our own enterprise for instance changed over the years. We have diversified more. It's better to spread yourself rather than be confined to one sector. Helps to deal with the fluctuations in the whole business.

The connection between business and sport is very close. Focus and belief can bring you a long way. You have to believe in what you are doing, what you are producing, your product, and be focused on doing it properly and as well as you can. To be better at producing the product than anybody else; to strive towards doing that. Very simple really. If you get complacent in your work, you're gone. It's the same in football. Allow yourself to get complacent and that's when the troubles start.

When I reflect on my club career, I realise just how much time I spent with Meath. A lot of time. I was never really locked into the club for a sustained spell. We had Paddy Carr who managed Louth and Donegal over us at one stage, Frank O'Sullivan too and we played Trim in a big championship game in Dunsany. We were five or six points up but Trim came back and beat us. We had a seriously good team at the time but just couldn't push on and win a senior county title.

Walterstown were good but we just couldn't translate enough chances into scores. We got into quarter-finals and semi-finals, but just couldn't push on. We had great battles with Dunshaughlin, who were a wonderful team at the time... Trim, Cortown, O'Mahonys. Hard, physical games, the kind I loved but we didn't win enough of them sadly.

We had a lot of changes... players, managers, and fluctuating times. We just couldn't land the big prize – the Keegan Cup. Still, I can look back on my career with a deep sense of satisfaction. And some amazing memories! Like the day I played on a Walterstown under-21 team with my four brothers and three cousins (Niall, Raymond and Peter) against Kells, who had another cousin, Paul Murphy, lining out for them.

Sure, I could have won more with Meath but I was part of two All-Ireland triumphs. I tasted the big time, experienced some great days. Shared wonderful moments with colleagues.

There is no price on those memories.

As I stood in the tunnel and waited to step out onto the green sward of Croke Park before the 2022 All-Ireland final to be introduced to the crowd with the rest of the Meath players from 1996, momentarily, flashes came back into my mind of those days... the glory days, when we were young, and fit.

And God was in his Heaven.

PADDY REYNOLDS
1996 AND '99 ALL-IRELAND WINNER
1999 ALL STAR

*Paddy Reynolds in full flight, making one of his
trademark surges out of defence for Meath.*

The Meath and Mayo players begin one of the most infamous rows in the history of Croke Park (top). Paddy in action in the 1996 All-Ireland final replay, and (left) captain Tommy Dowd lifts the Sam Maguire Cup high in the air.

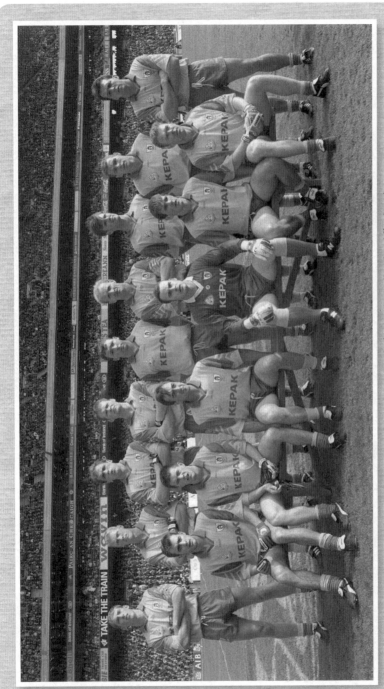

The Meath team which defeated Mayo in the 1996 All-Ireland final replay.

Paddy on the ball in the 1999 All-Ireland final victory over Cork (top), and celebrating with Trevor Giles and John McDermott after the game. Paddy (below) lifts the Sam Maguire Cup.

The Meath team which defeated Cork in the 1999 All-Ireland final.

A bloodied Paddy sees red in the Leinster Championship against Kildare in Croke Park in 2001 (top), and his last outing in Croke Park (below) against The Dubs in the 2005 Leinster Championship.

Paddy and Marie-Louise, and their family Nicole, Darragh and Casey.

Pat and Attracta's grandchildren: Back (left to right) – Nicole, Darragh, Lauren, Casey, Harry, Rose, June, Jamie, Conor, David, Hugo, Robyn and Sam.

Pat and Paddy, and their All Star awards from 1967 and 1999.

*Pat congratulates his grand-daughter Nicole (centre) and Casey
(left) and Darragh continue the tradition of the Reynolds family
doing themselves proud in the famous Black.*